NíObE

SHE is LifE

With a world divided,
who do you turn to?

Niobe
She is Life

WRITERS
Sebastian A. Jones
Amandla Stenberg

ARTIST
Ashley A. Woods

LAYOUT ARTIST
Darrell May

LETTERER AND DESIGNER
A Larger World Studios

EDITOR
Joshua Cozine

ASSOCIATES
Ken Locsmandi
Mark Hammond
Terrance Bouldin-Johnson

CHIEF CREATIVE OFFICER
Darrell May

EDITOR-IN-CHIEF
Joshua Cozine

PUBLISHER
Sebastian A. Jones

BASED IN THE WORLD OF ASUNDA CREATED BY SEBASTIAN A. JONES

SECOND PRINTING. PRINTED IN SOUTH KOREA. ISBN 978-1-939834-27-0

Chapter 1

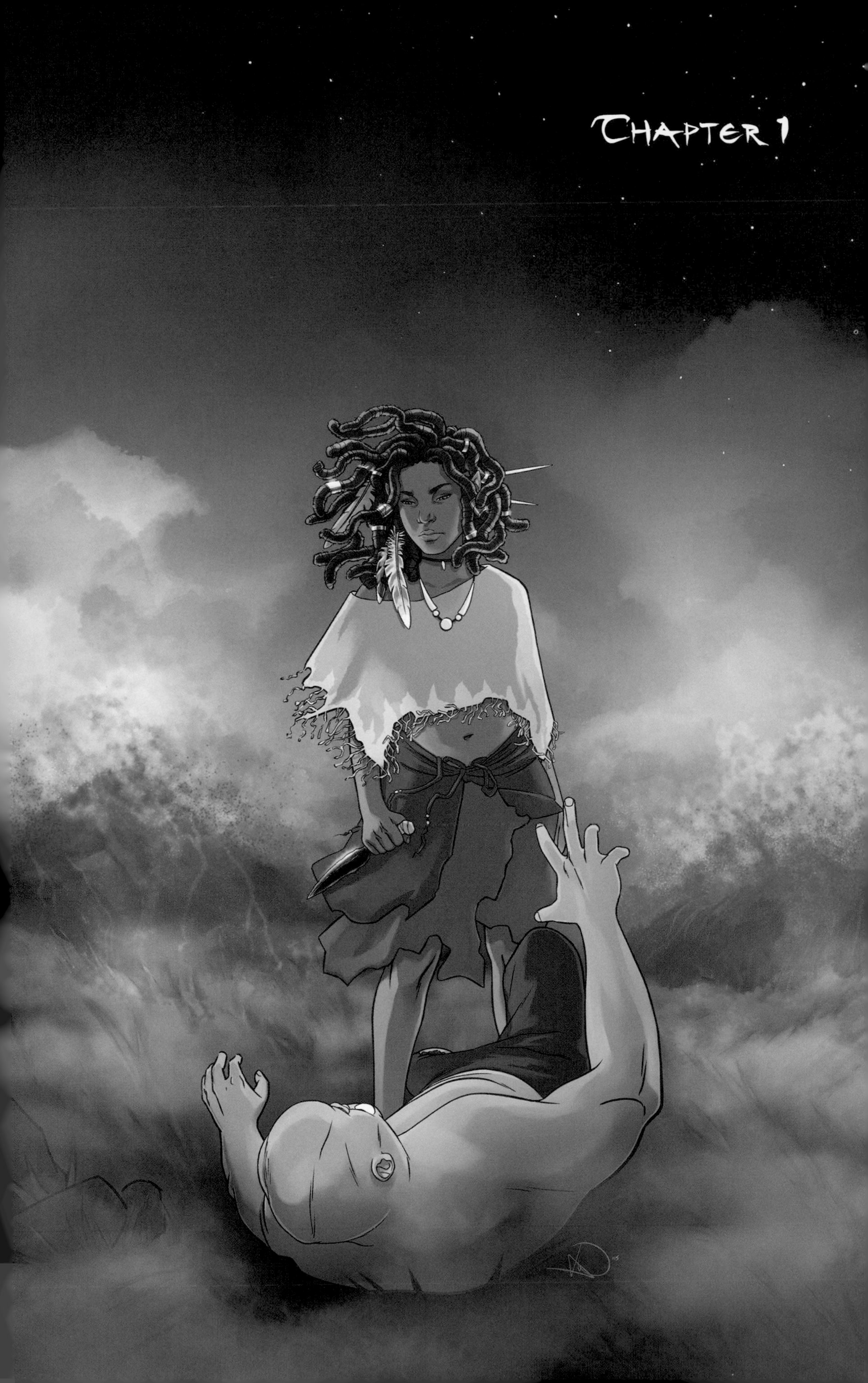

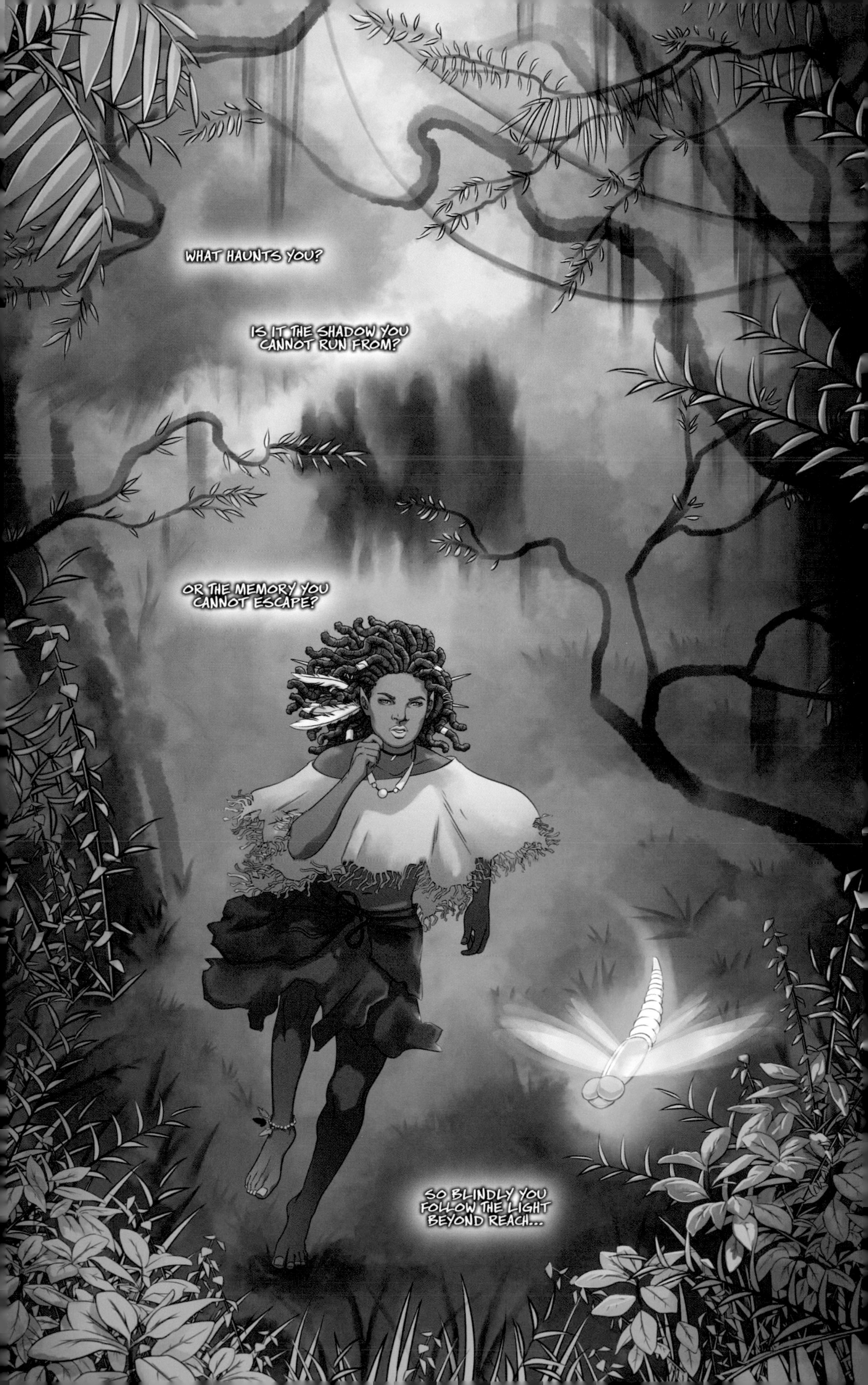
WHAT HAUNTS YOU?
IS IT THE SHADOW YOU CANNOT RUN FROM?
OR THE MEMORY YOU CANNOT ESCAPE?
SO BLINDLY YOU FOLLOW THE LIGHT BEYOND REACH...

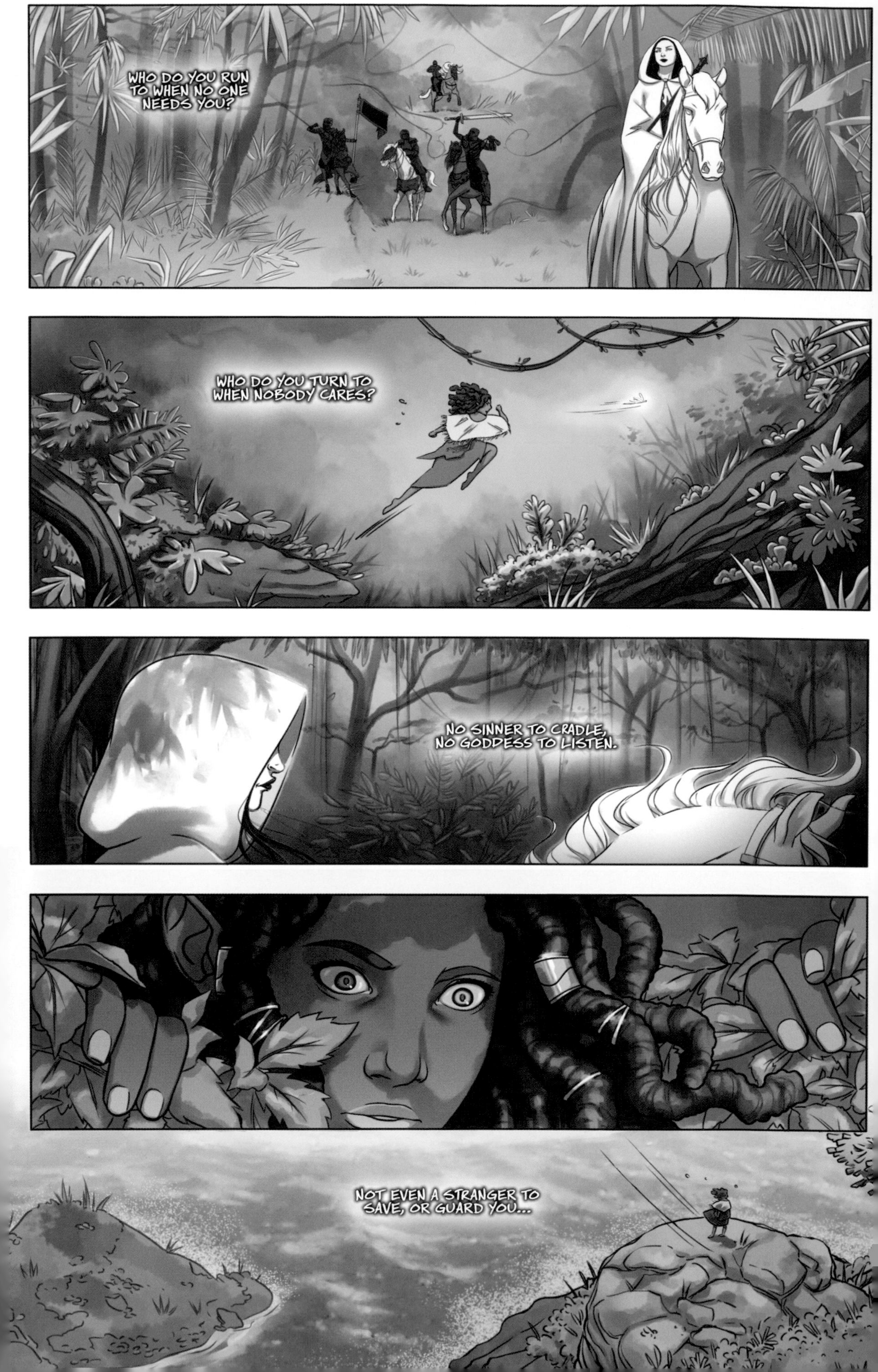
WHO DO YOU RUN TO WHEN NO ONE NEEDS YOU?
WHO DO YOU TURN TO WHEN NOBODY CARES?
NO SINNER TO CRADLE, NO GODDESS TO LISTEN.
NOT EVEN A STRANGER TO SAVE, OR GUARD YOU...

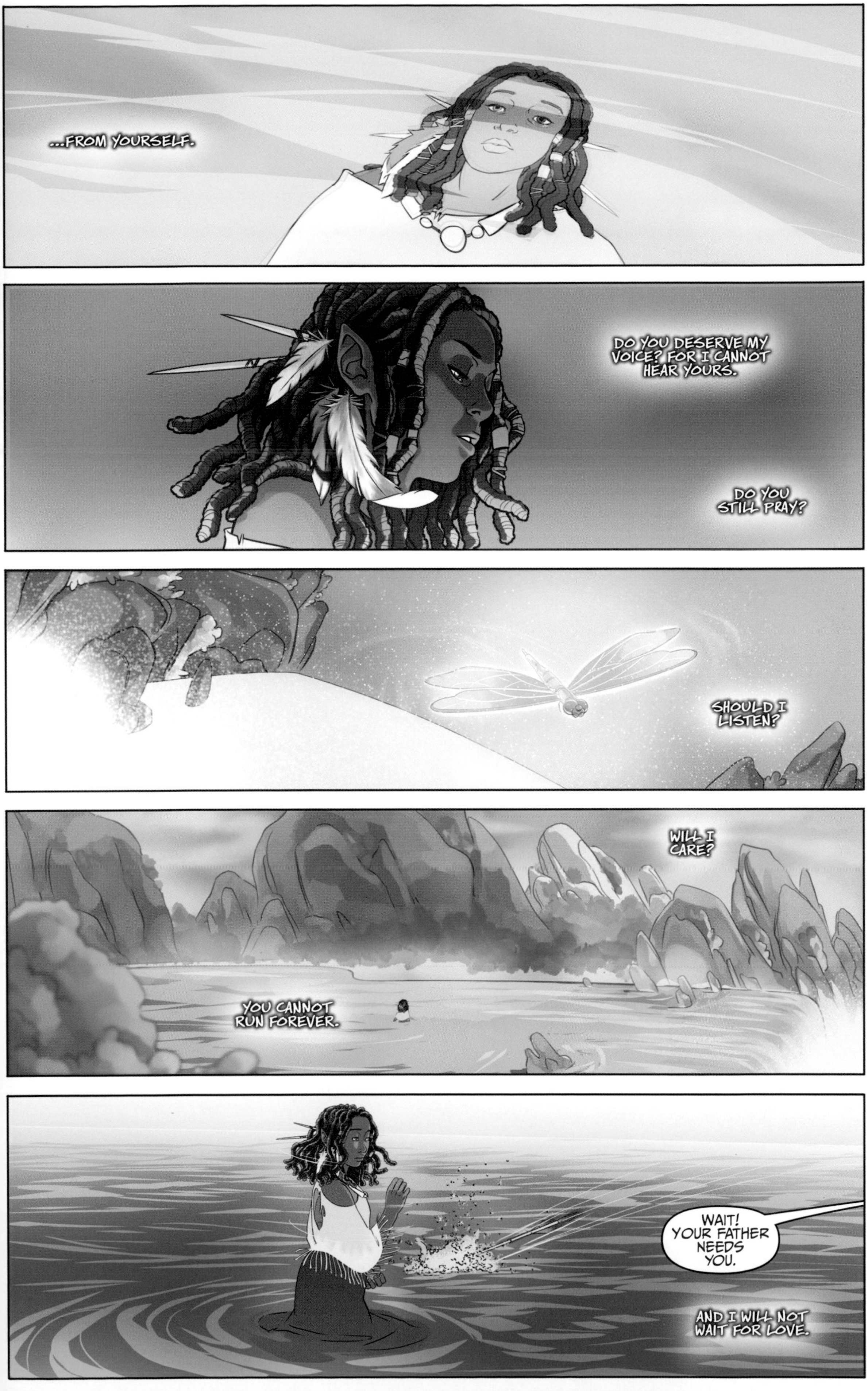
...FROM YOURSELF.
DO YOU DESERVE MY VOICE? FOR I CANNOT HEAR YOURS.
DO YOU STILL PRAY?
SHOULD I LISTEN?
WILL I CARE?
YOU CANNOT RUN FOREVER.
WAIT! YOUR FATHER NEEDS YOU.
AND I WILL NOT WAIT FOR LOVE.

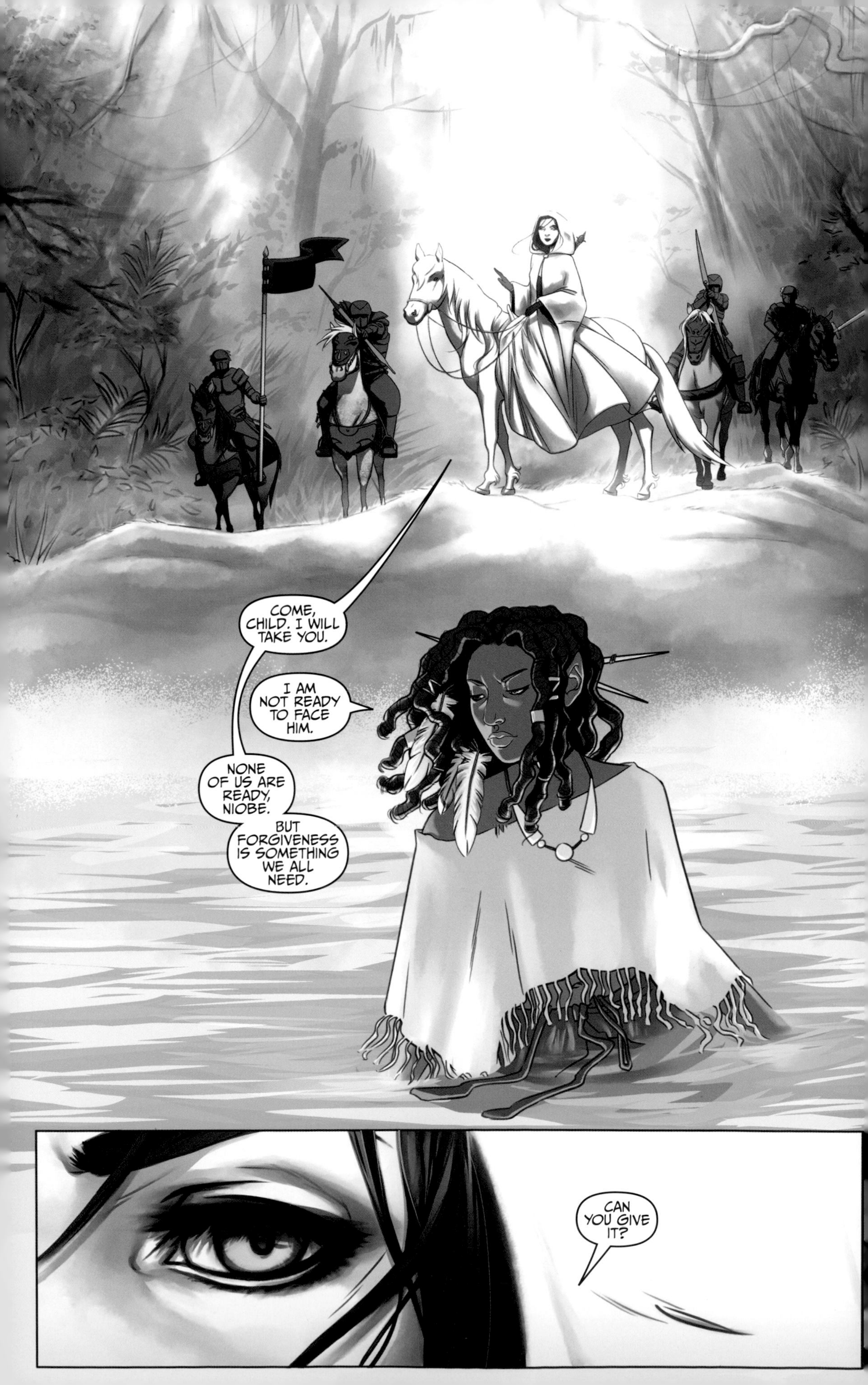
COME, CHILD. I WILL TAKE YOU.
I AM NOT READY TO FACE HIM.
NONE OF US ARE READY, NIOBE.
BUT FORGIVENESS IS SOMETHING WE ALL NEED.
CAN YOU GIVE IT?

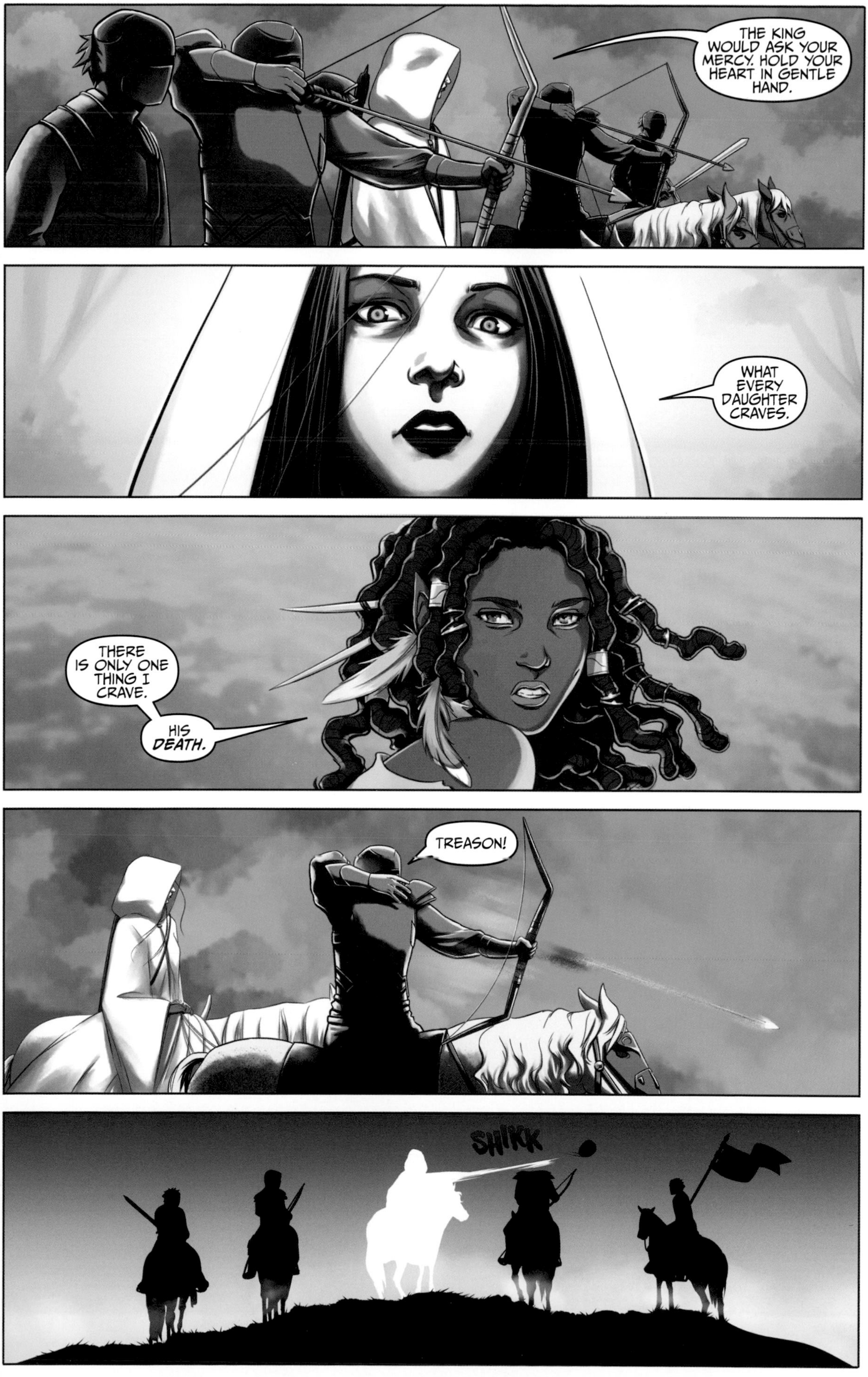
THE KING WOULD ASK YOUR MERCY. HOLD YOUR HEART IN GENTLE HAND.
WHAT EVERY DAUGHTER CRAVES.
THERE IS ONLY ONE THING I CRAVE.
HIS *DEATH.*
TREASON!
SHIKK

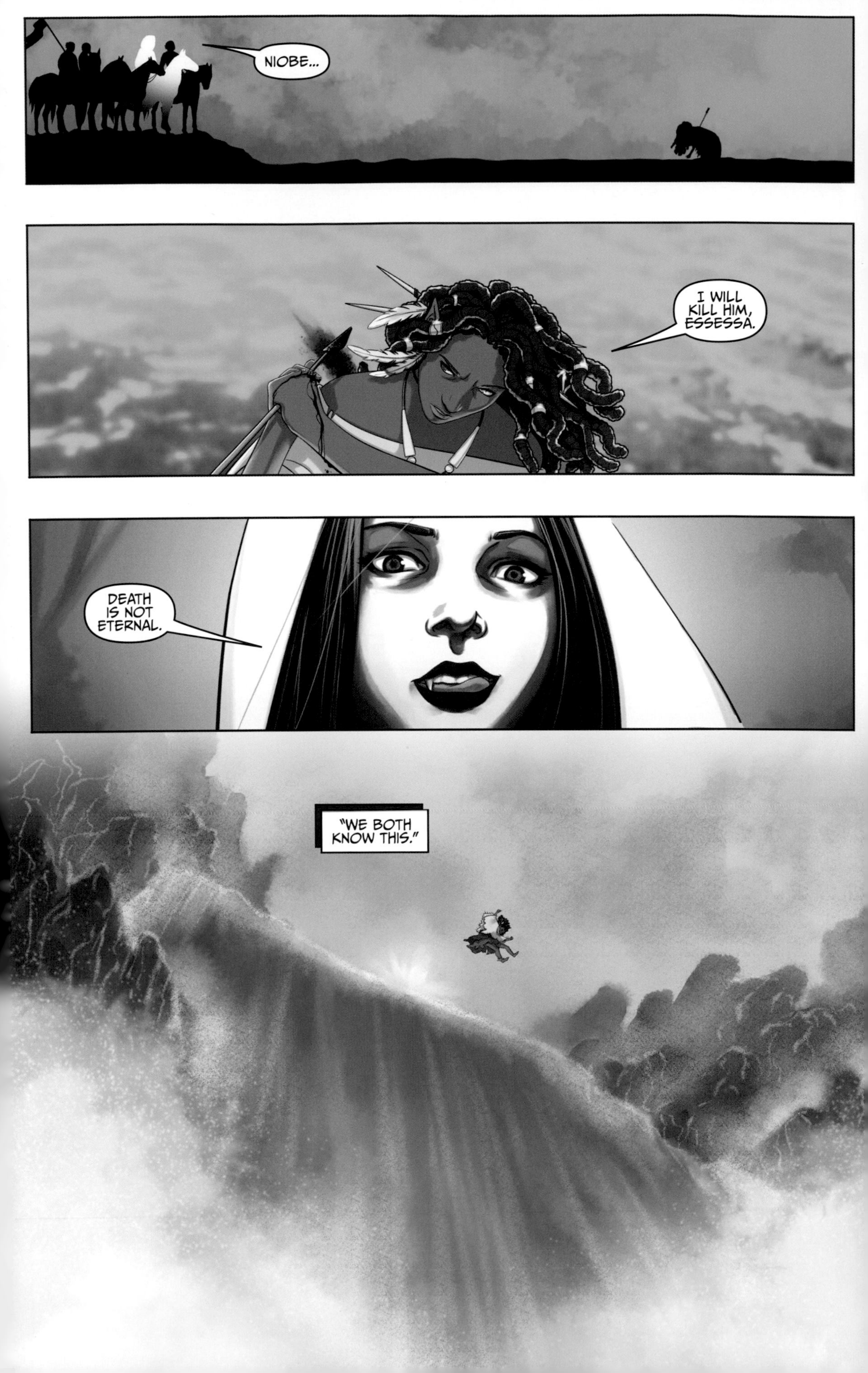
NIOBE...
I WILL KILL HIM, ESSESSA.
DEATH IS NOT ETERNAL.
"WE BOTH KNOW THIS."

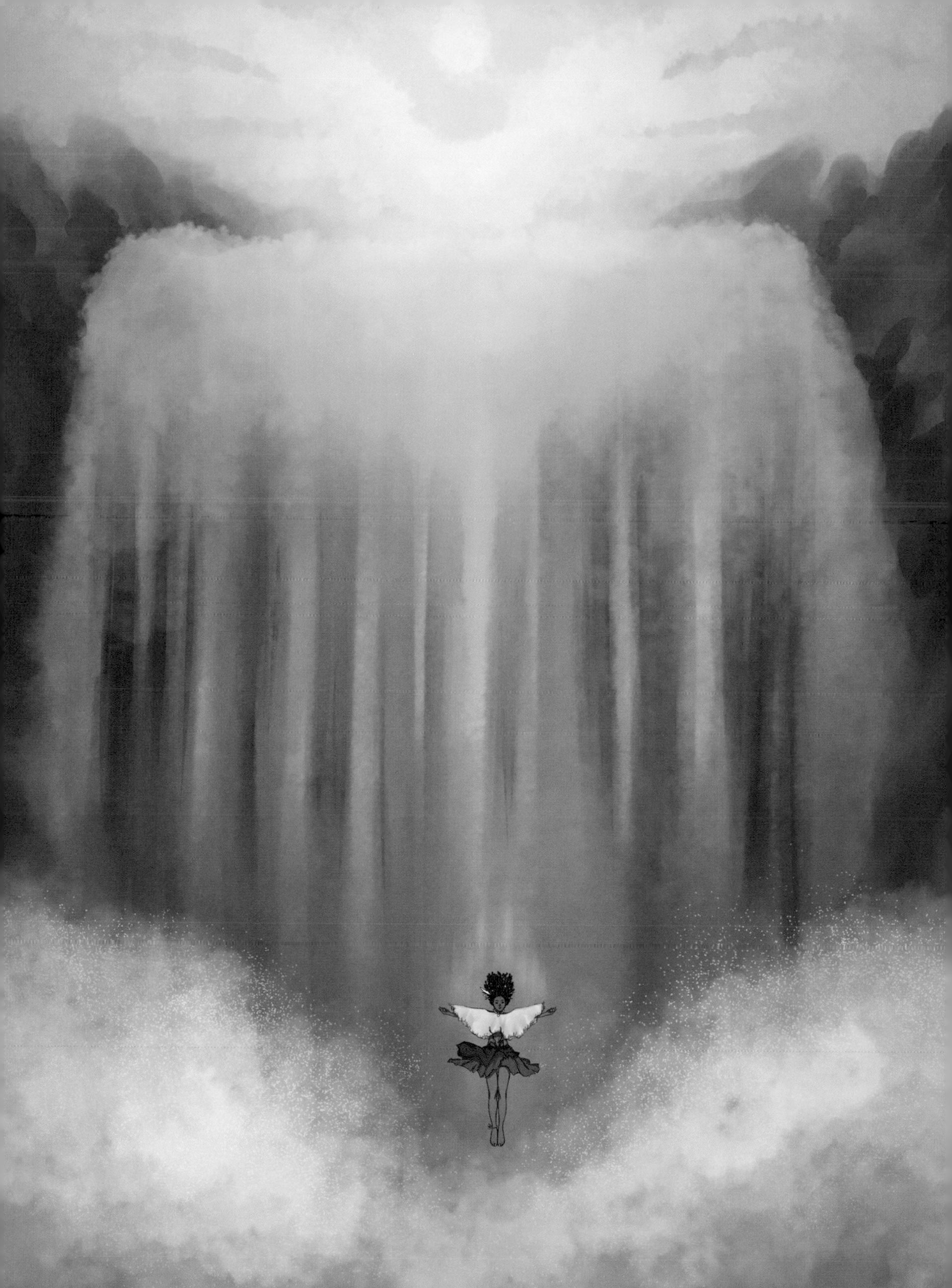

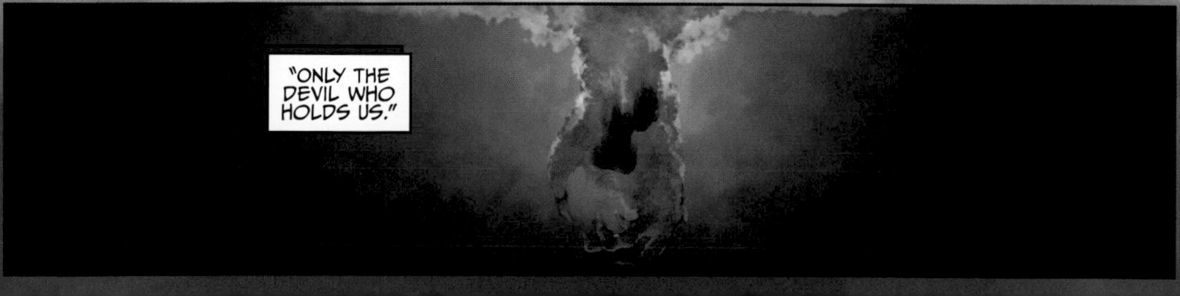
"ONLY THE DEVIL WHO HOLDS US."

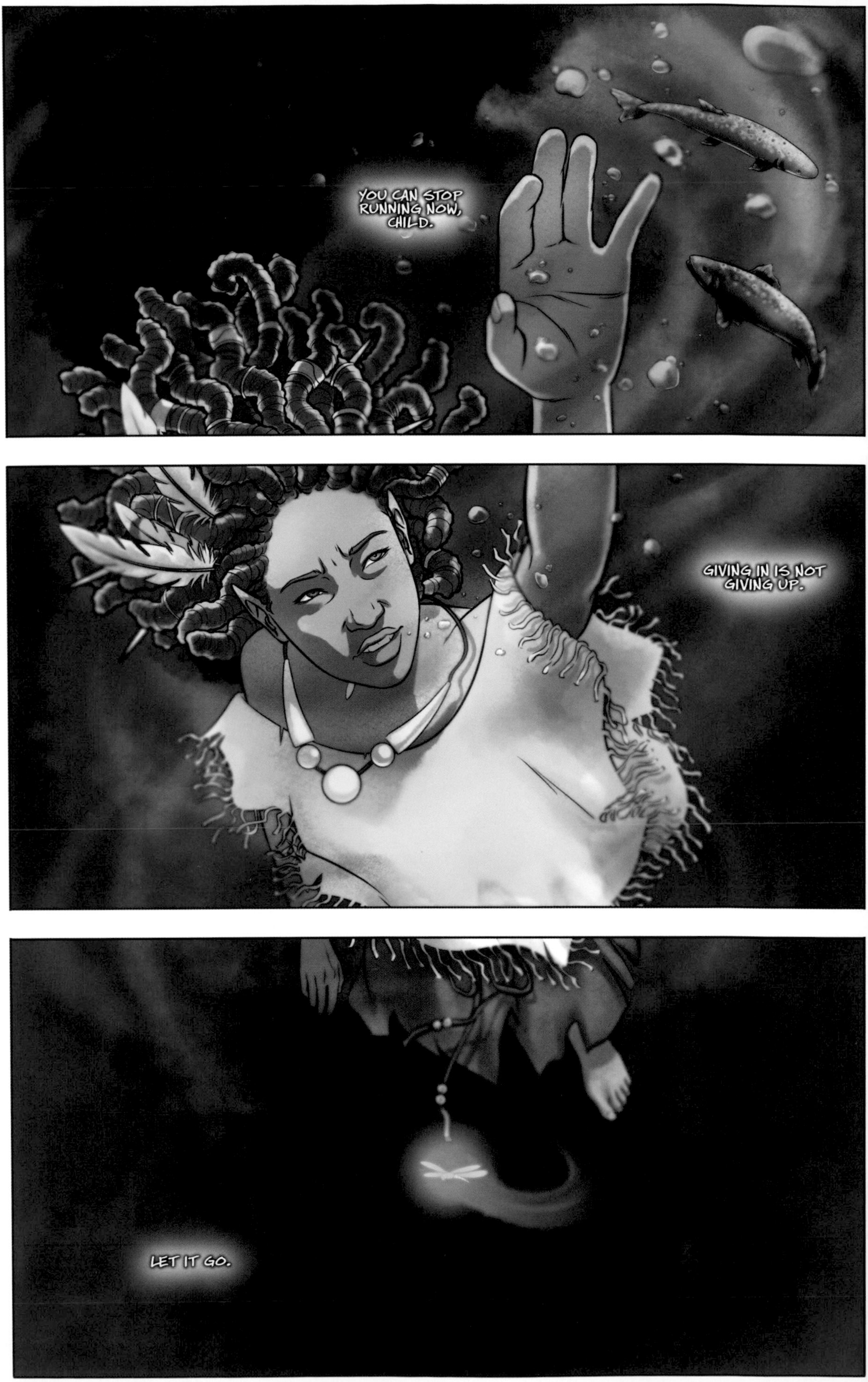
YOU CAN STOP RUNNING NOW, CHILD.
GIVING IN IS NOT GIVING UP.
LET IT GO.

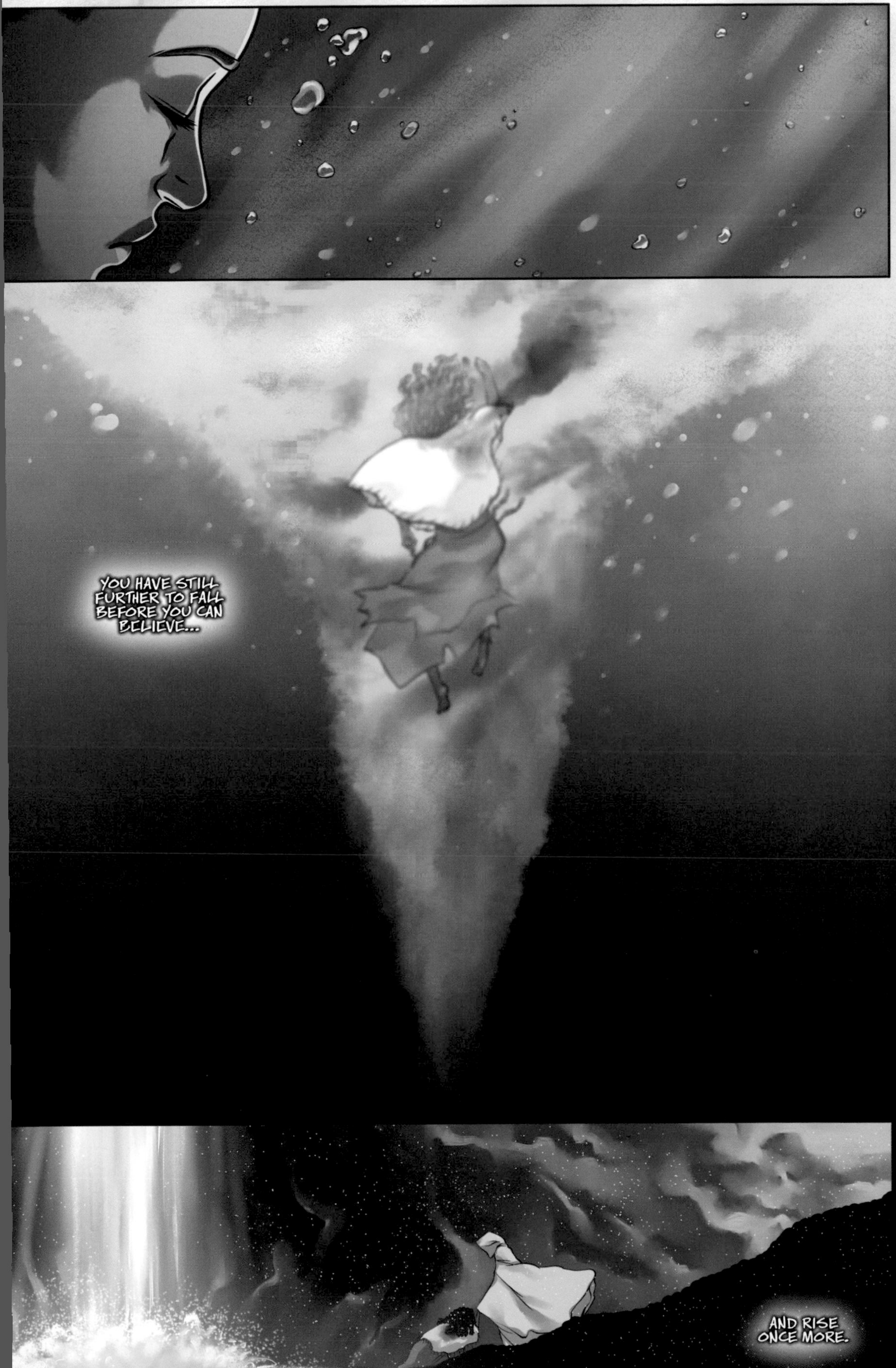
YOU HAVE STILL FURTHER TO FALL BEFORE YOU CAN BELIEVE...
AND RISE ONCE MORE.

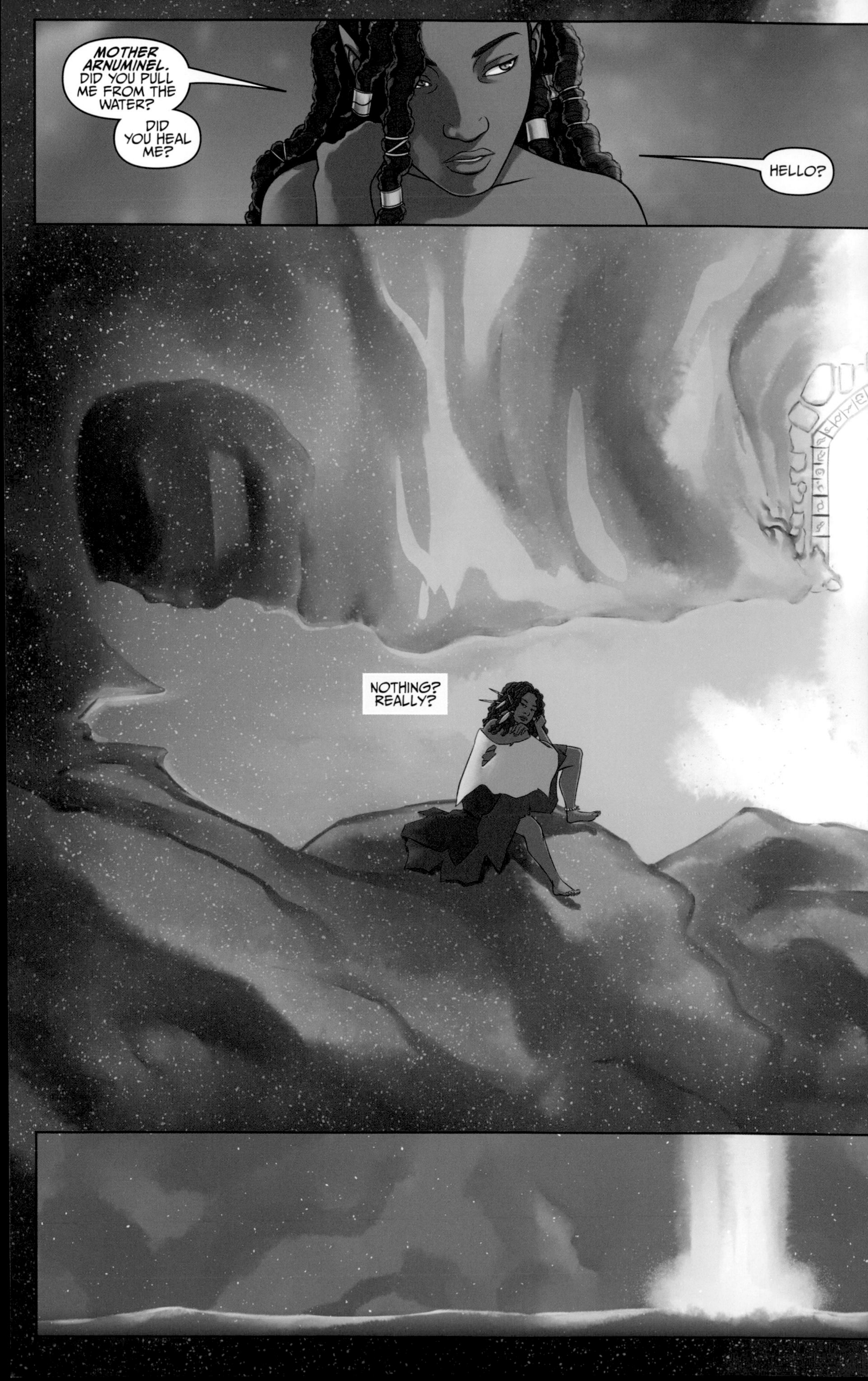
MOTHER ARNUMINEL. DID YOU PULL ME FROM THE WATER?
DID YOU HEAL ME?
HELLO?
NOTHING? REALLY?

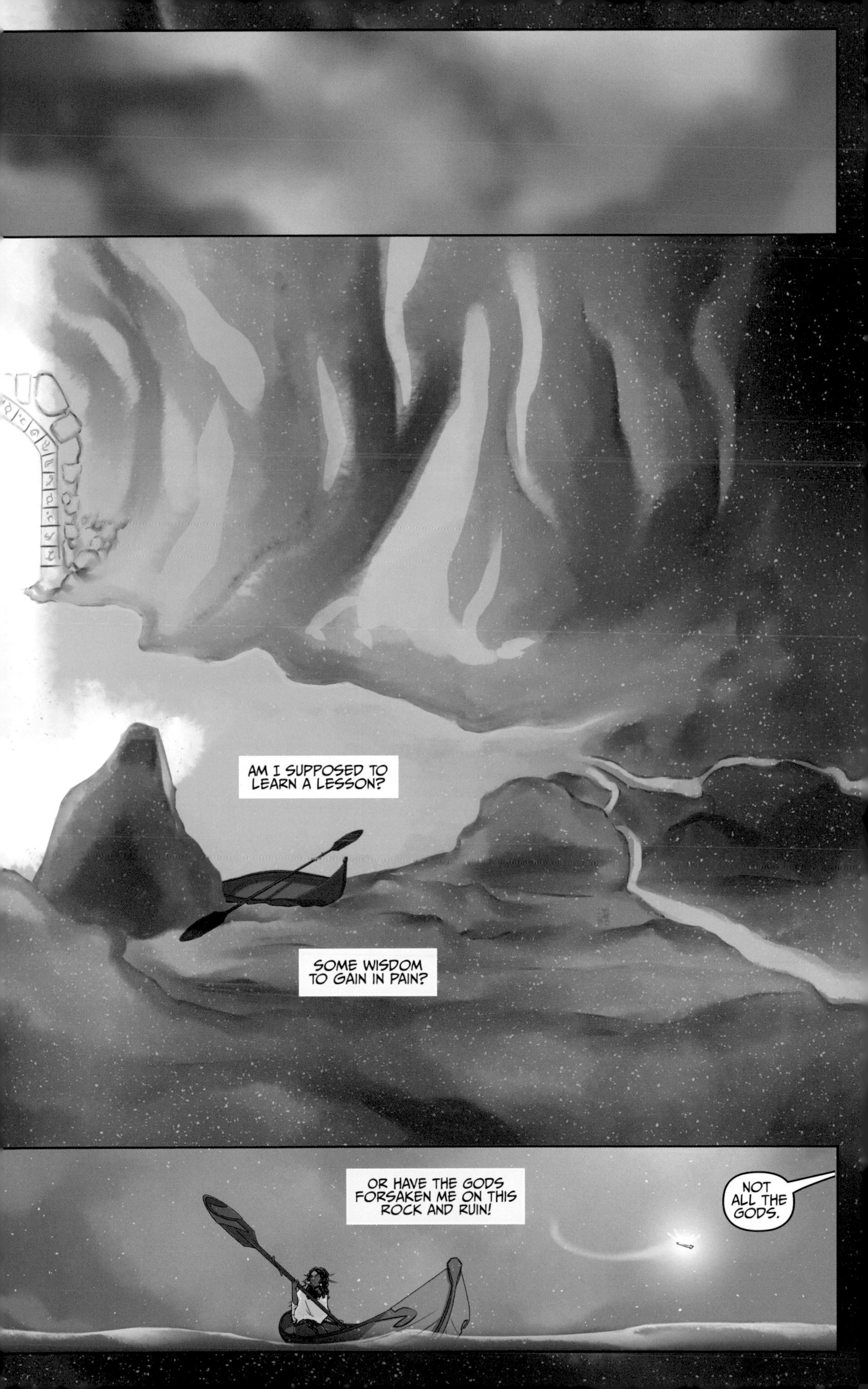
AM I SUPPOSED TO LEARN A LESSON?
SOME WISDOM TO GAIN IN PAIN?
OR HAVE THE GODS FORSAKEN ME ON THIS ROCK AND RUIN!
NOT ALL THE GODS.

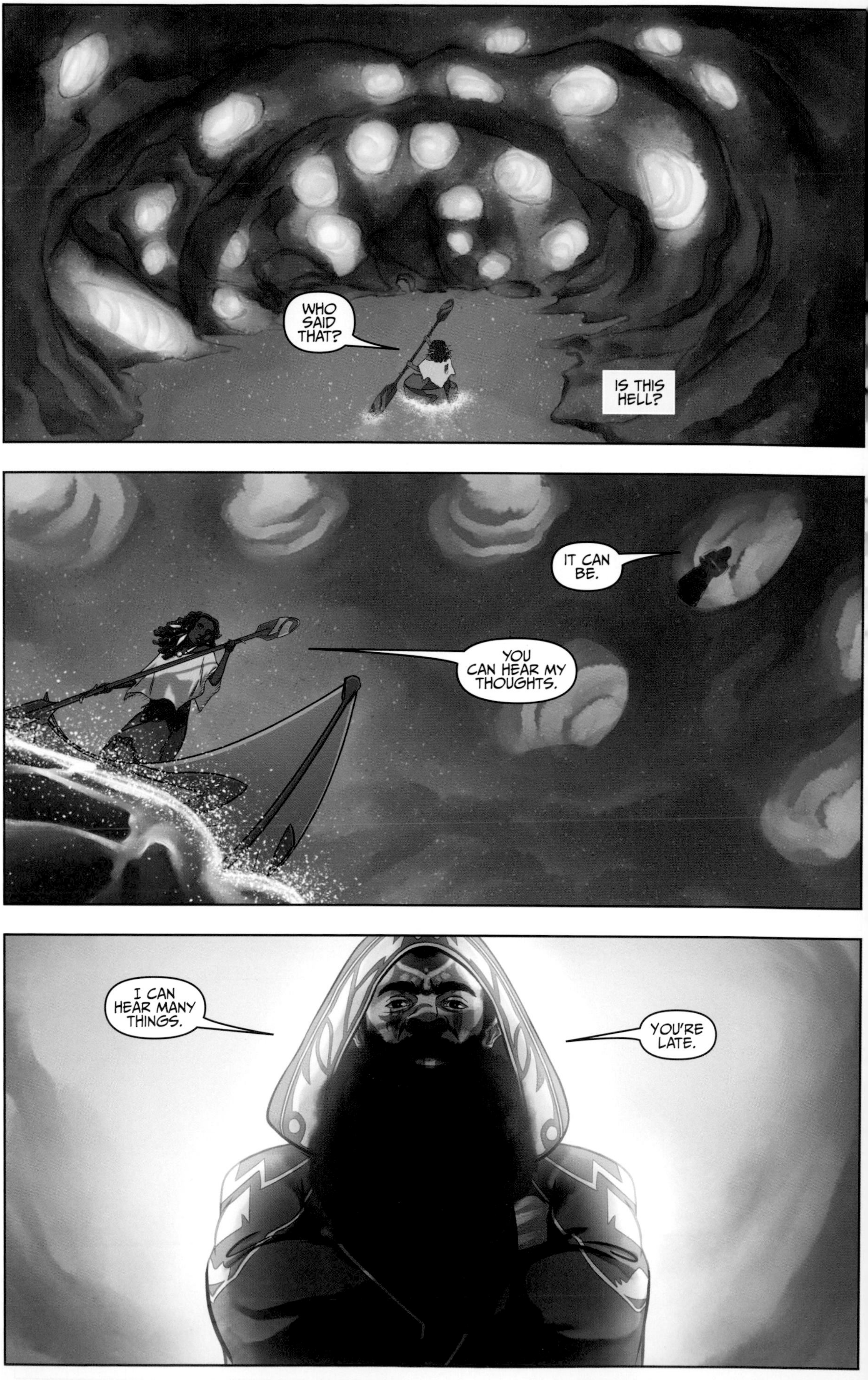
WHO SAID THAT?
IS THIS HELL?
IT CAN BE.
YOU CAN HEAR MY THOUGHTS.
I CAN HEAR MANY THINGS.
YOU'RE LATE.

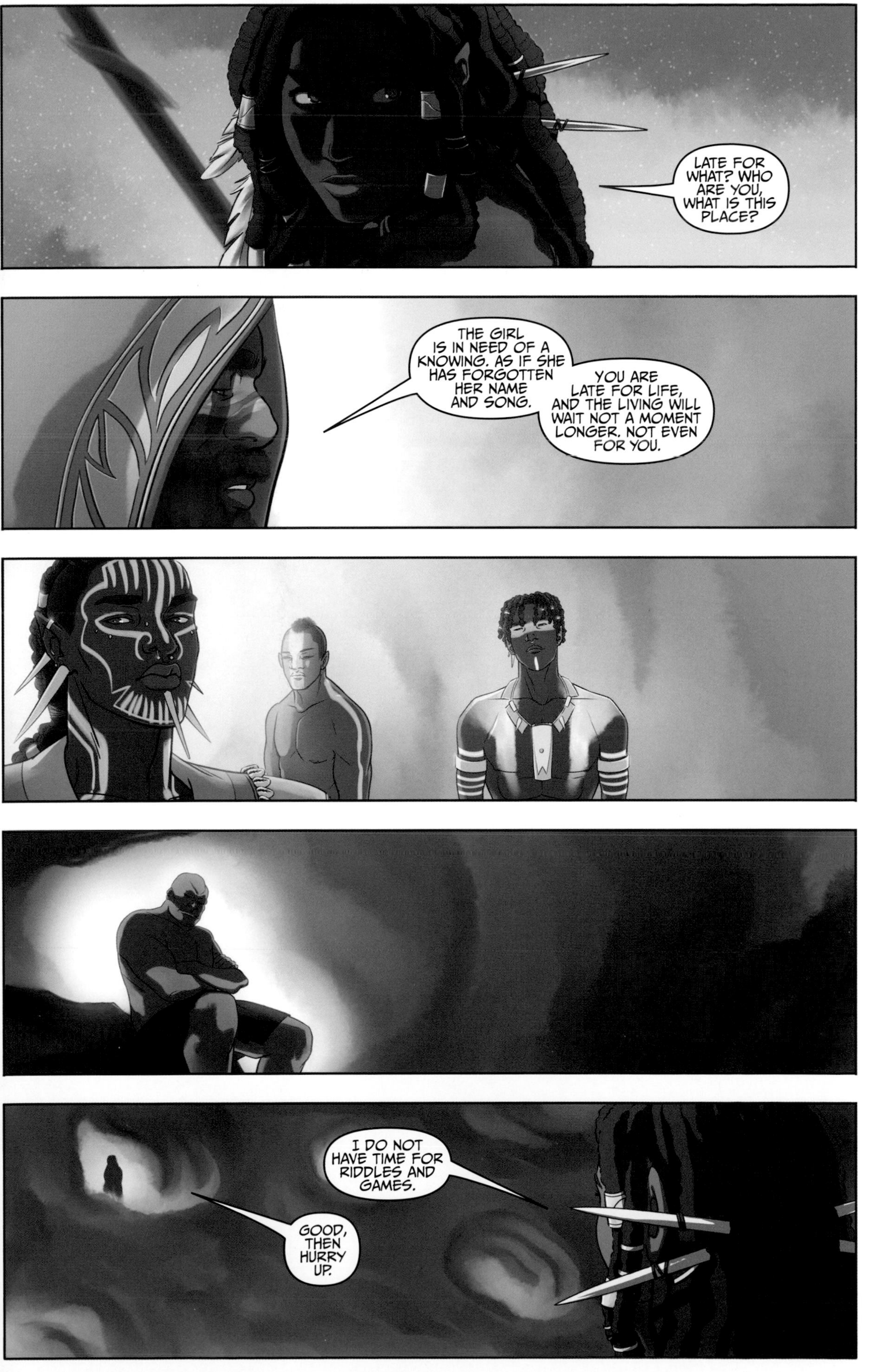
LATE FOR WHAT? WHO ARE YOU, WHAT IS THIS PLACE?
THE GIRL IS IN NEED OF A KNOWING. AS IF SHE HAS FORGOTTEN HER NAME AND SONG.
YOU ARE LATE FOR LIFE, AND THE LIVING WILL WAIT NOT A MOMENT LONGER. NOT EVEN FOR YOU.
I DO NOT HAVE TIME FOR RIDDLES AND GAMES.
GOOD, THEN HURRY UP.

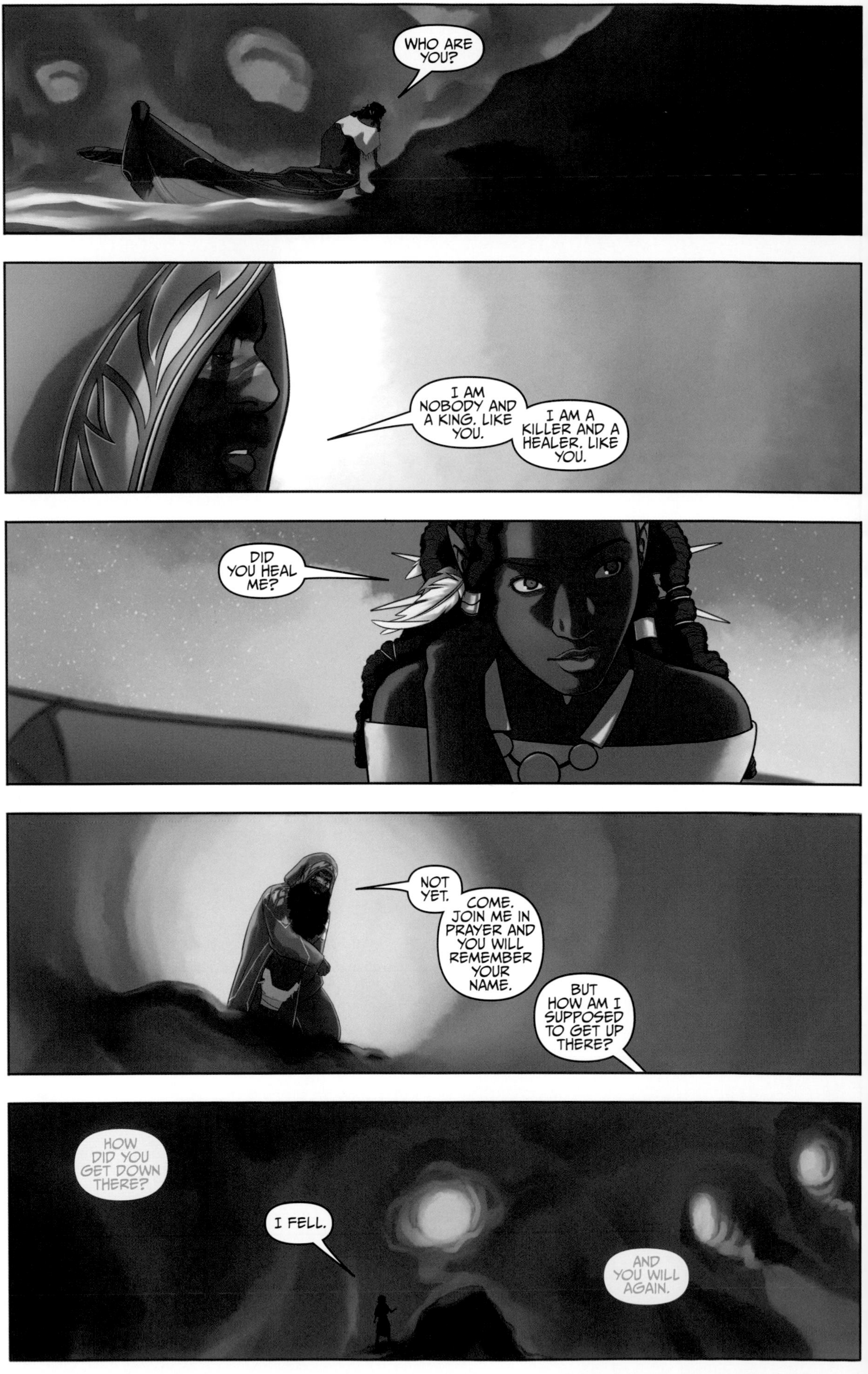
WHO ARE YOU?
I AM NOBODY AND A KING. LIKE YOU.
I AM A KILLER AND A HEALER. LIKE YOU.
DID YOU HEAL ME?
NOT YET.
COME. JOIN ME IN PRAYER AND YOU WILL REMEMBER YOUR NAME.
BUT HOW AM I SUPPOSED TO GET UP THERE?
HOW DID YOU GET DOWN THERE?
I FELL.
AND YOU WILL AGAIN.

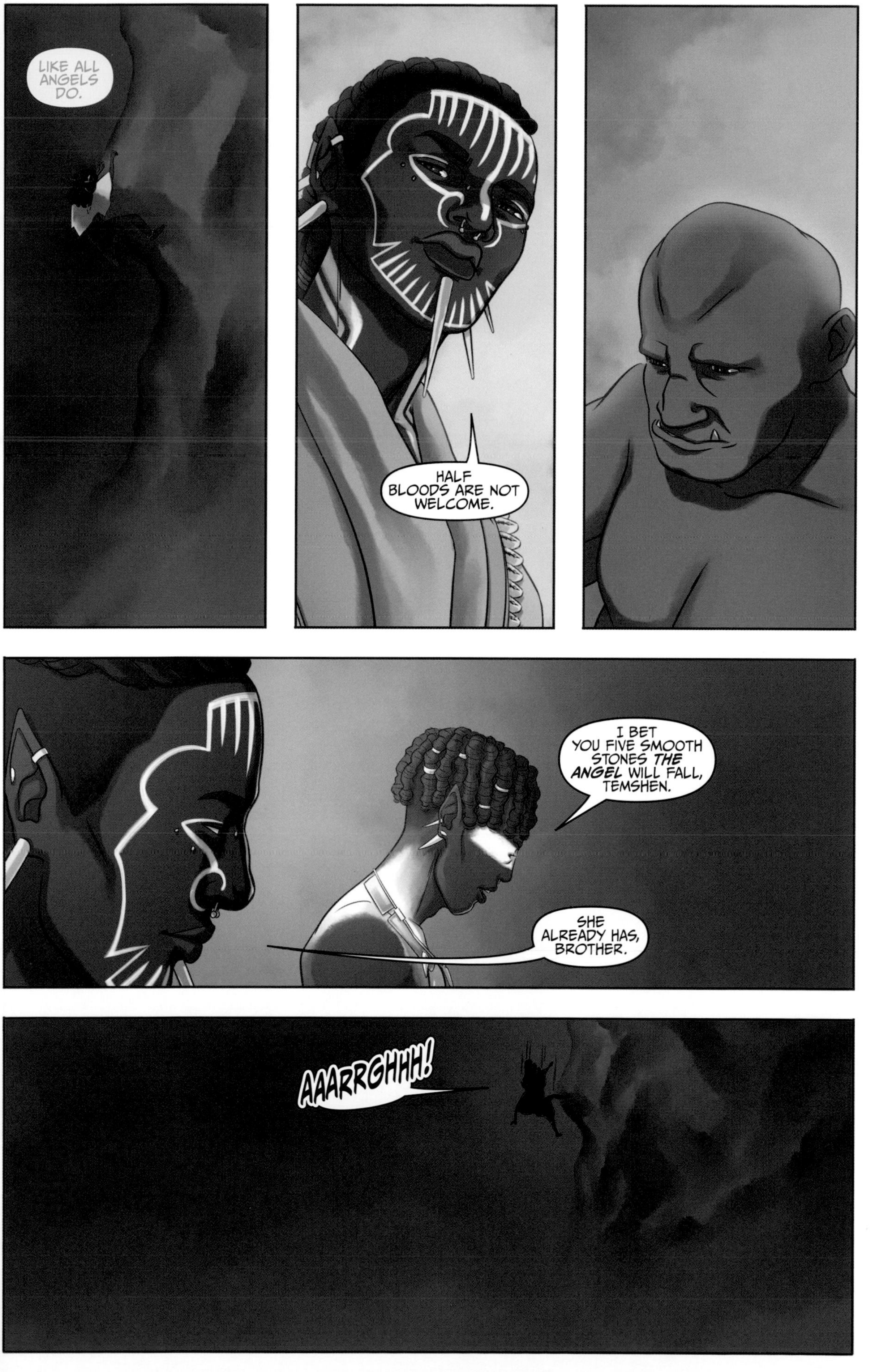

LIKE ALL ANGELS DO.
HALF BLOODS ARE NOT WELCOME.
I BET YOU FIVE SMOOTH STONES *THE ANGEL* WILL FALL, TEMSHEN.
SHE ALREADY HAS, BROTHER.
AAARRGHHH!

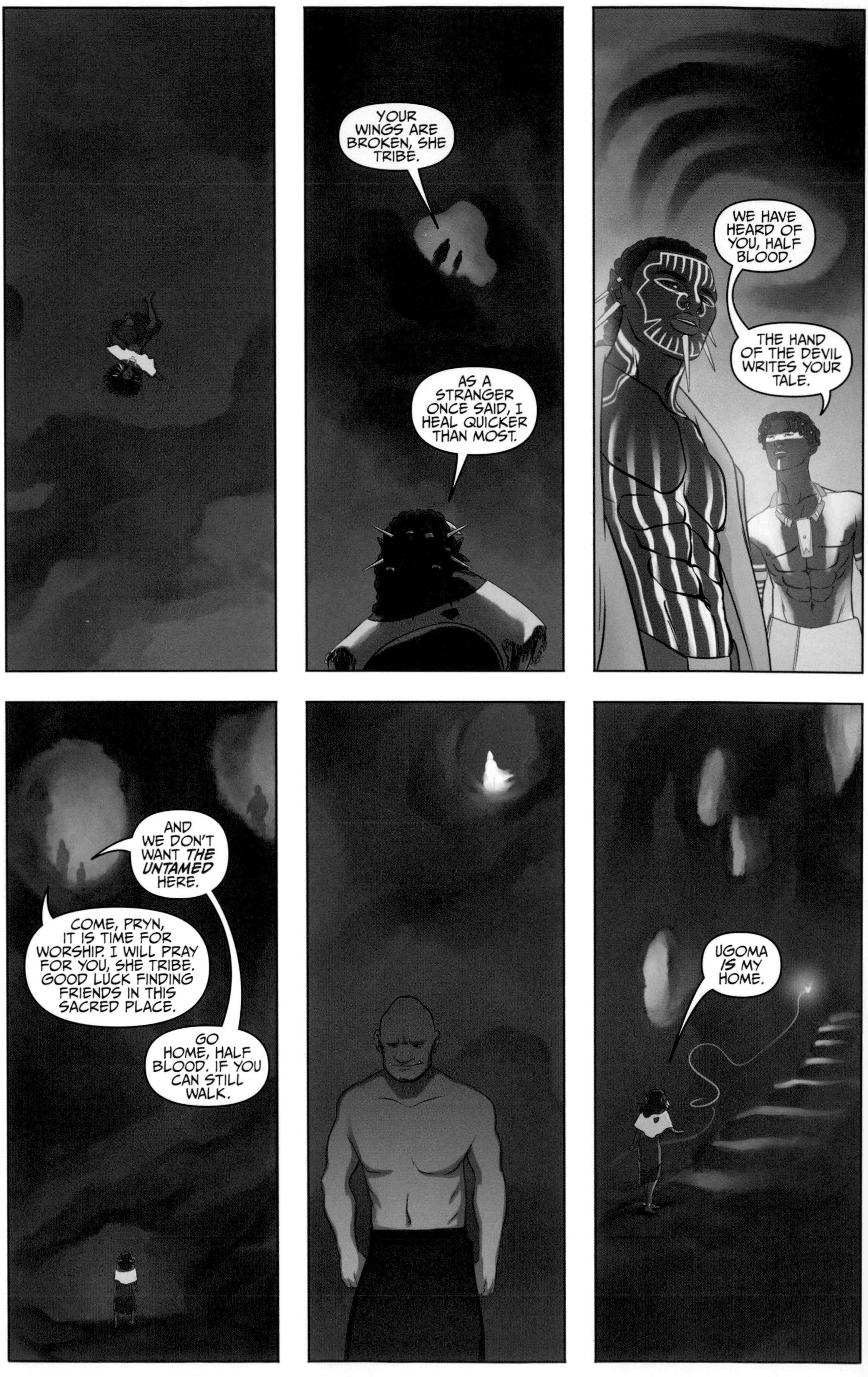
YOUR WINGS ARE BROKEN, SHE TRIBE.
AS A STRANGER ONCE SAID, I HEAL QUICKER THAN MOST.
WE HAVE HEARD OF YOU, HALF BLOOD.
THE HAND OF THE DEVIL WRITES YOUR TALE.
AND WE DON'T WANT *THE UNTAMED* HERE.
COME, PRYN, IT IS TIME FOR WORSHIP. I WILL PRAY FOR YOU, SHE TRIBE. GOOD LUCK FINDING FRIENDS IN THIS SACRED PLACE.
GO HOME, HALF BLOOD. IF YOU CAN STILL WALK.
UGOMA *IS* MY HOME.

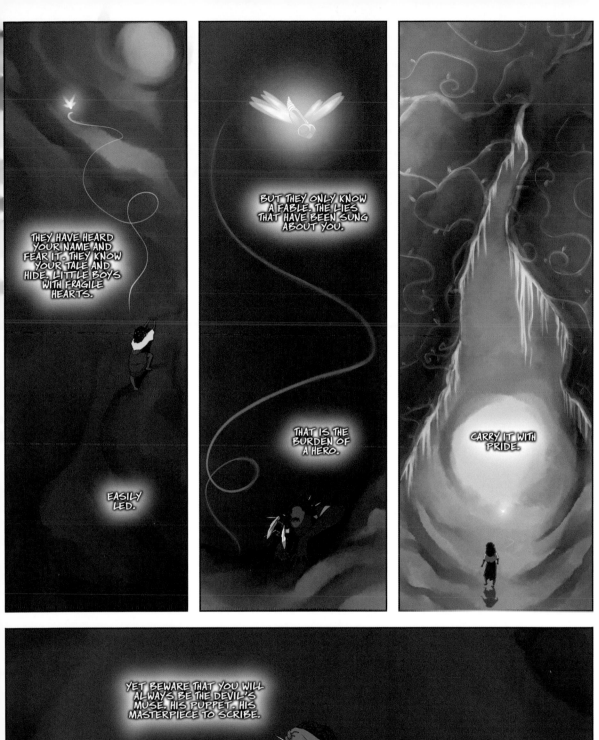

THEY HAVE HEARD YOUR NAME AND FEAR IT. THEY KNOW YOUR TALE AND HIDE. LITTLE BOYS WITH FRAGILE HEARTS.

EASILY LED.

BUT THEY ONLY KNOW A FABLE. THE LIES THAT HAVE BEEN SUNG ABOUT YOU.

THAT IS THE BURDEN OF A HERO.

CARRY IT WITH PRIDE.

YET BEWARE THAT YOU WILL ALWAYS BE THE DEVIL'S MUSE. HIS PUPPET. HIS MASTERPIECE TO SCRIBE.

ARE YOU WICKED?

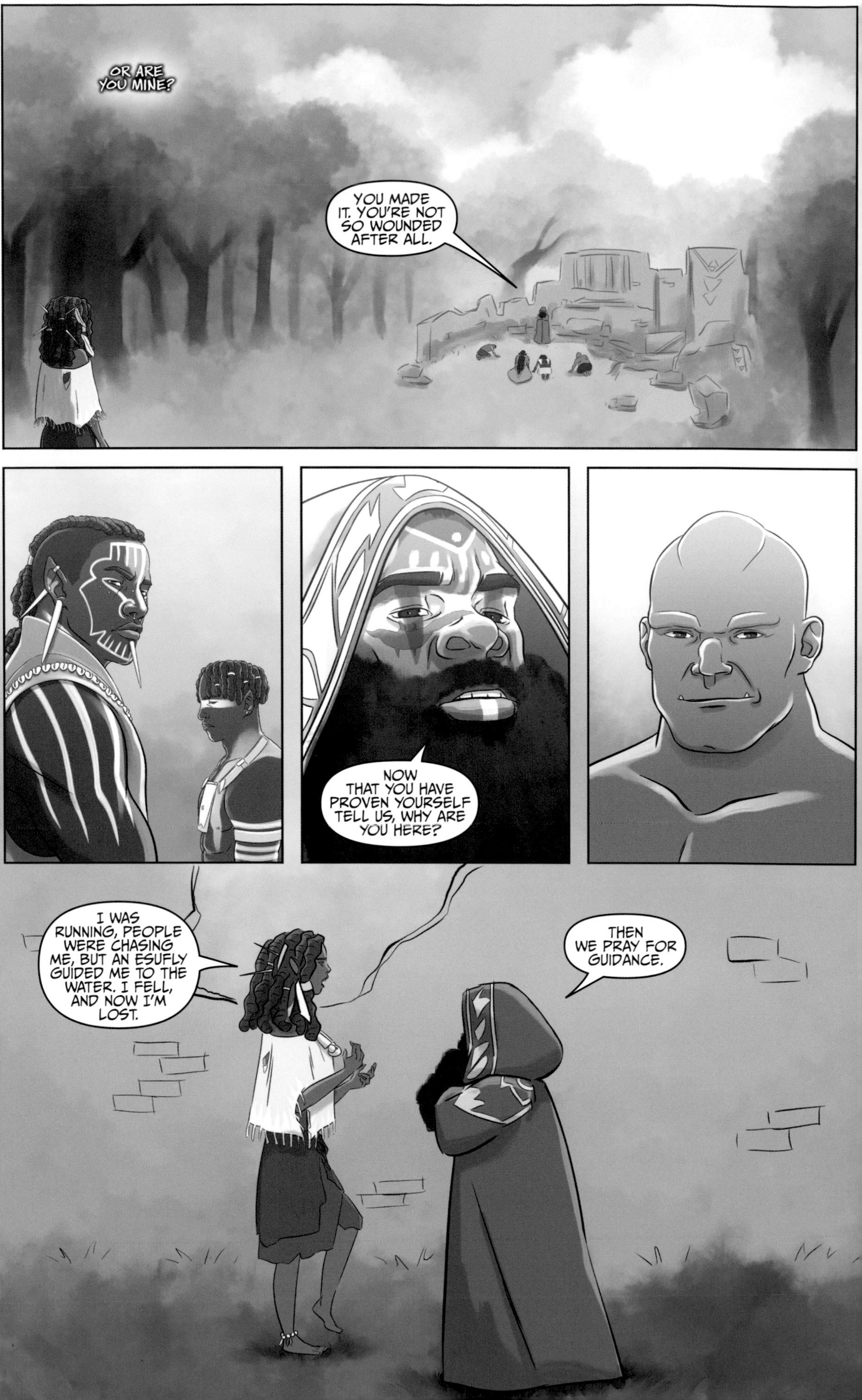
OR ARE YOU MINE?
YOU MADE IT. YOU'RE NOT SO WOUNDED AFTER ALL.
NOW THAT YOU HAVE PROVEN YOURSELF TELL US, WHY ARE YOU HERE?
I WAS RUNNING, PEOPLE WERE CHASING ME, BUT AN ESUFLY GUIDED ME TO THE WATER. I FELL, AND NOW I'M LOST.
THEN WE PRAY FOR GUIDANCE.

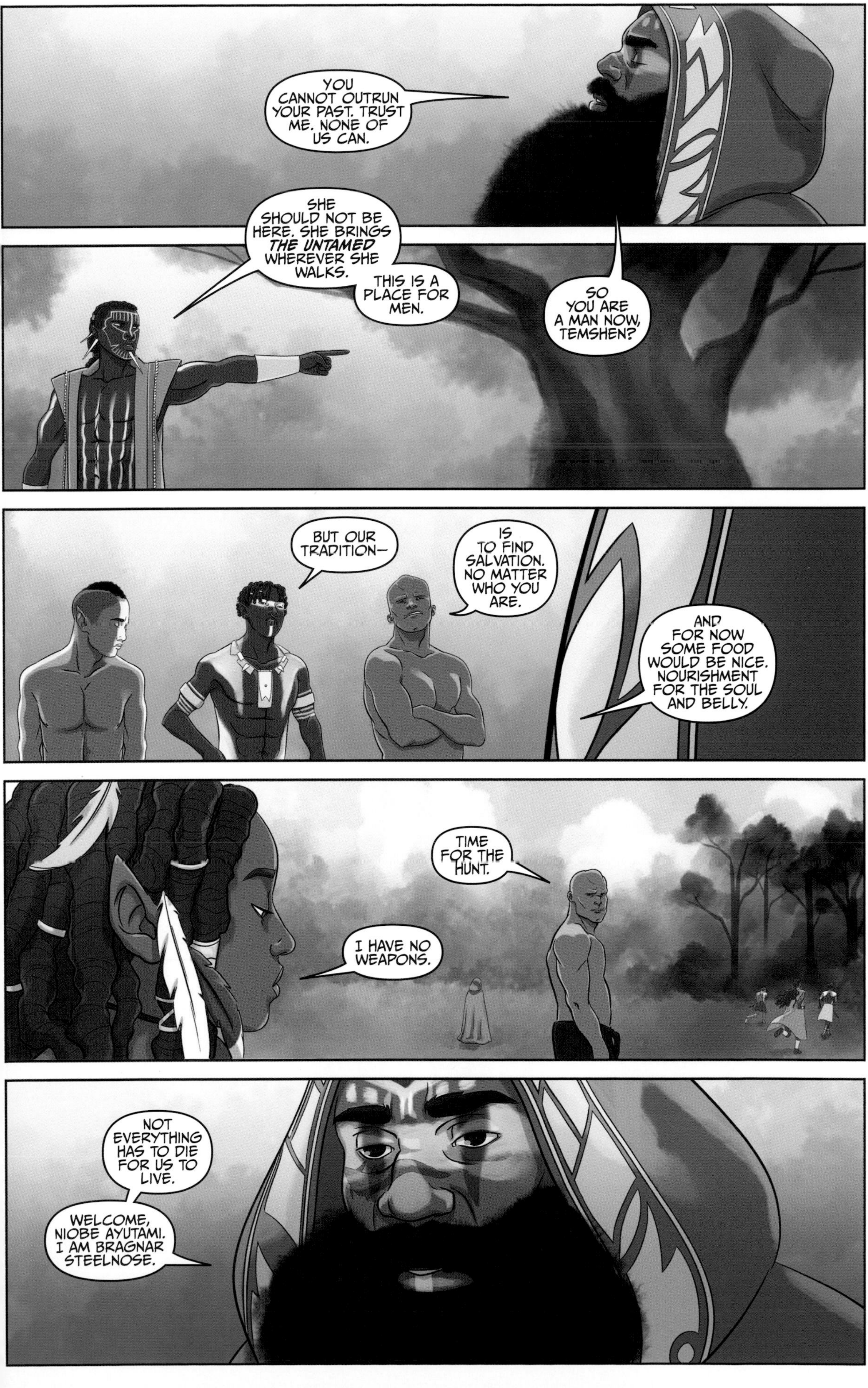
YOU CANNOT OUTRUN YOUR PAST. TRUST ME. NONE OF US CAN.
SHE SHOULD NOT BE HERE. SHE BRINGS ***THE UNTAMED*** WHEREVER SHE WALKS.
THIS IS A PLACE FOR MEN.
SO YOU ARE A MAN NOW, TEMSHEN?
BUT OUR TRADITION—
IS TO FIND SALVATION. NO MATTER WHO YOU ARE.
AND FOR NOW SOME FOOD WOULD BE NICE. NOURISHMENT FOR THE SOUL AND BELLY.
TIME FOR THE HUNT.
I HAVE NO WEAPONS.
NOT EVERYTHING HAS TO DIE FOR US TO LIVE.
WELCOME, NIOBE AYUTAMI. I AM BRAGNAR STEELNOSE.

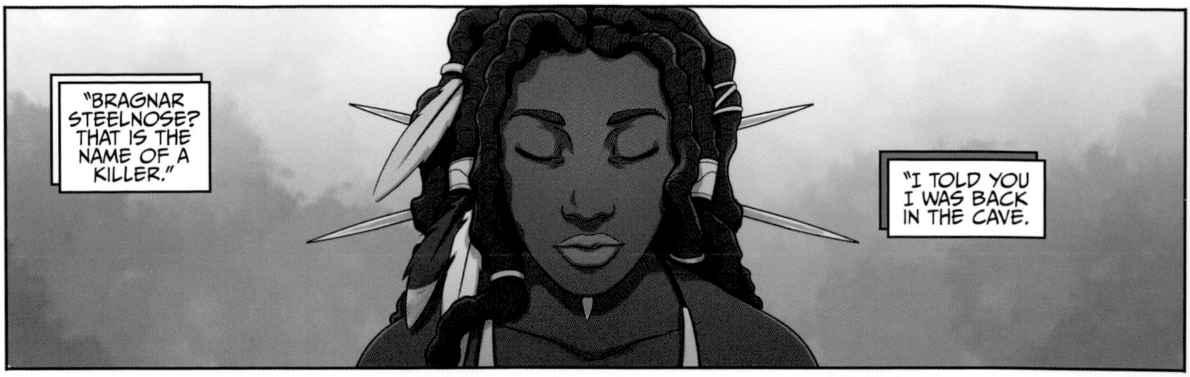
"BRAGNAR STEELNOSE? THAT IS THE NAME OF A KILLER."
"I TOLD YOU I WAS BACK IN THE CAVE.

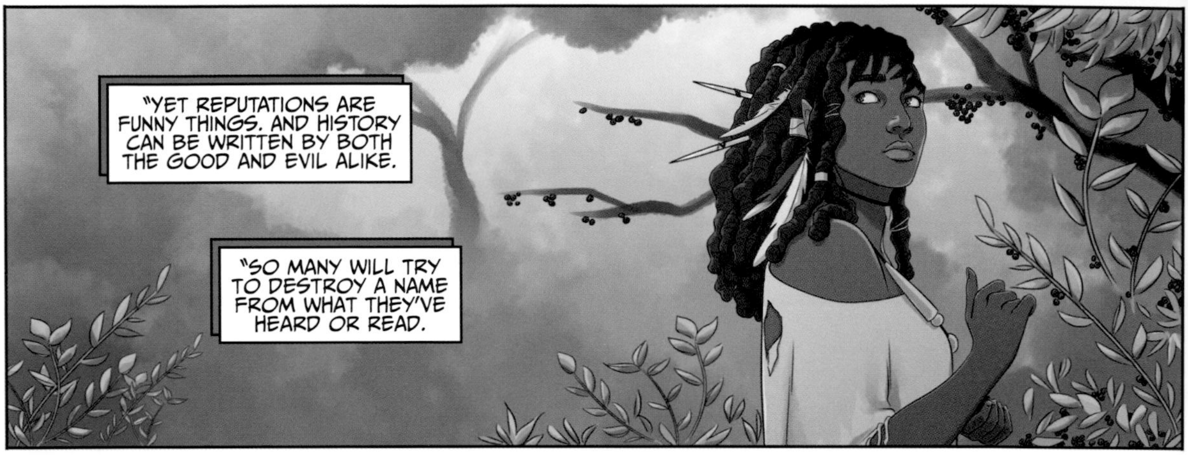
"YET REPUTATIONS ARE FUNNY THINGS. AND HISTORY CAN BE WRITTEN BY BOTH THE GOOD AND EVIL ALIKE.
"SO MANY WILL TRY TO DESTROY A NAME FROM WHAT THEY'VE HEARD OR READ.

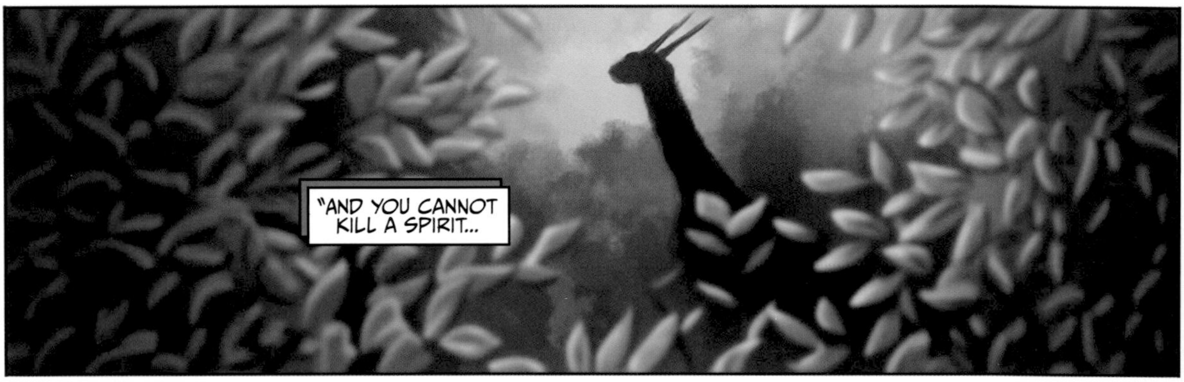
"AND YOU CANNOT KILL A SPIRIT...

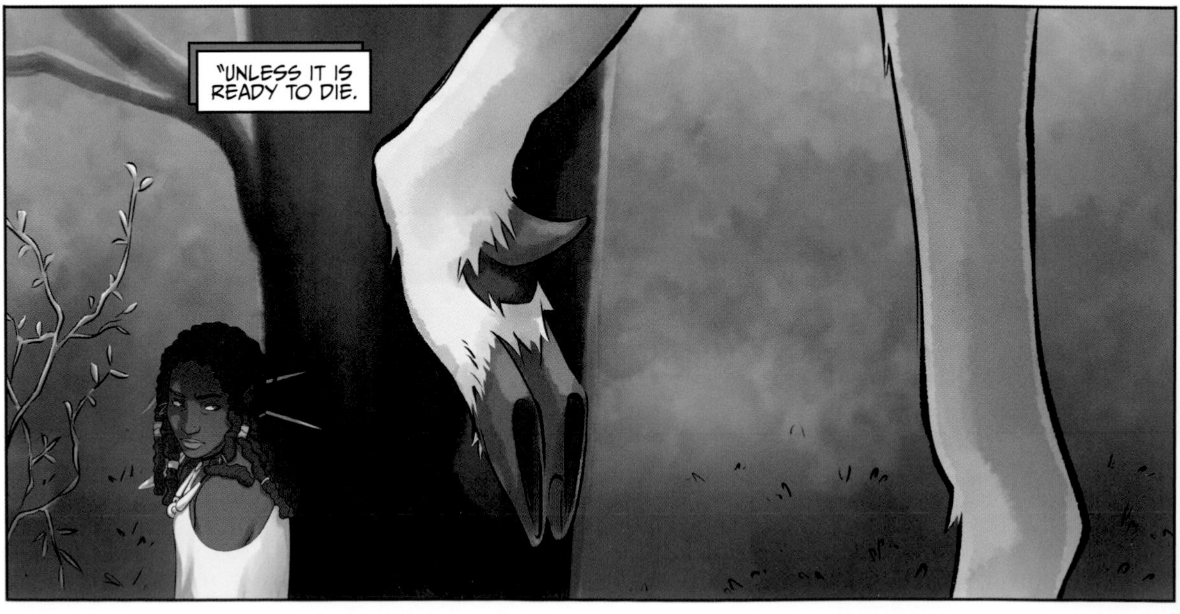
"UNLESS IT IS READY TO DIE.

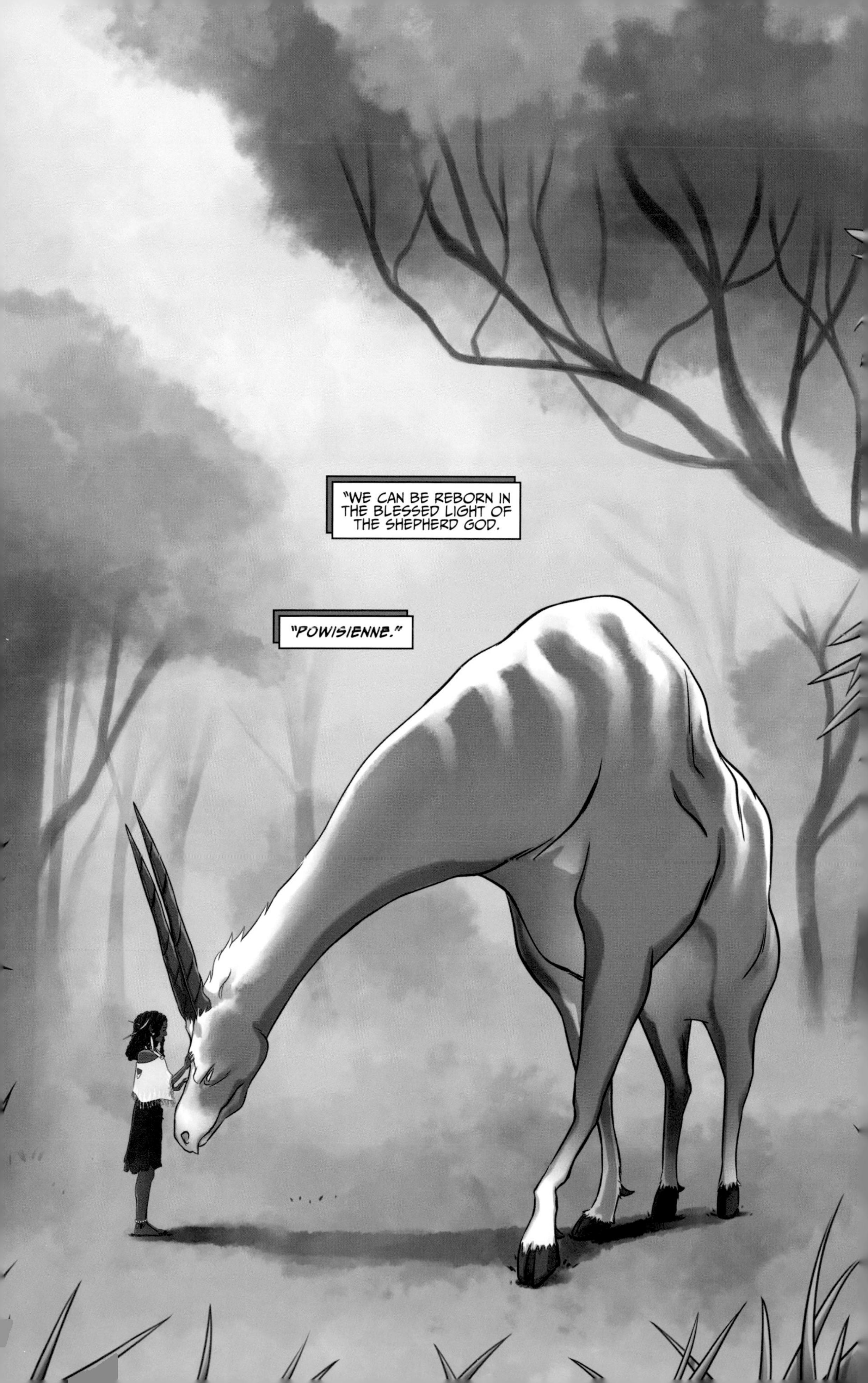
"WE CAN BE REBORN IN THE BLESSED LIGHT OF THE SHEPHERD GOD.
"POWISIENNE."

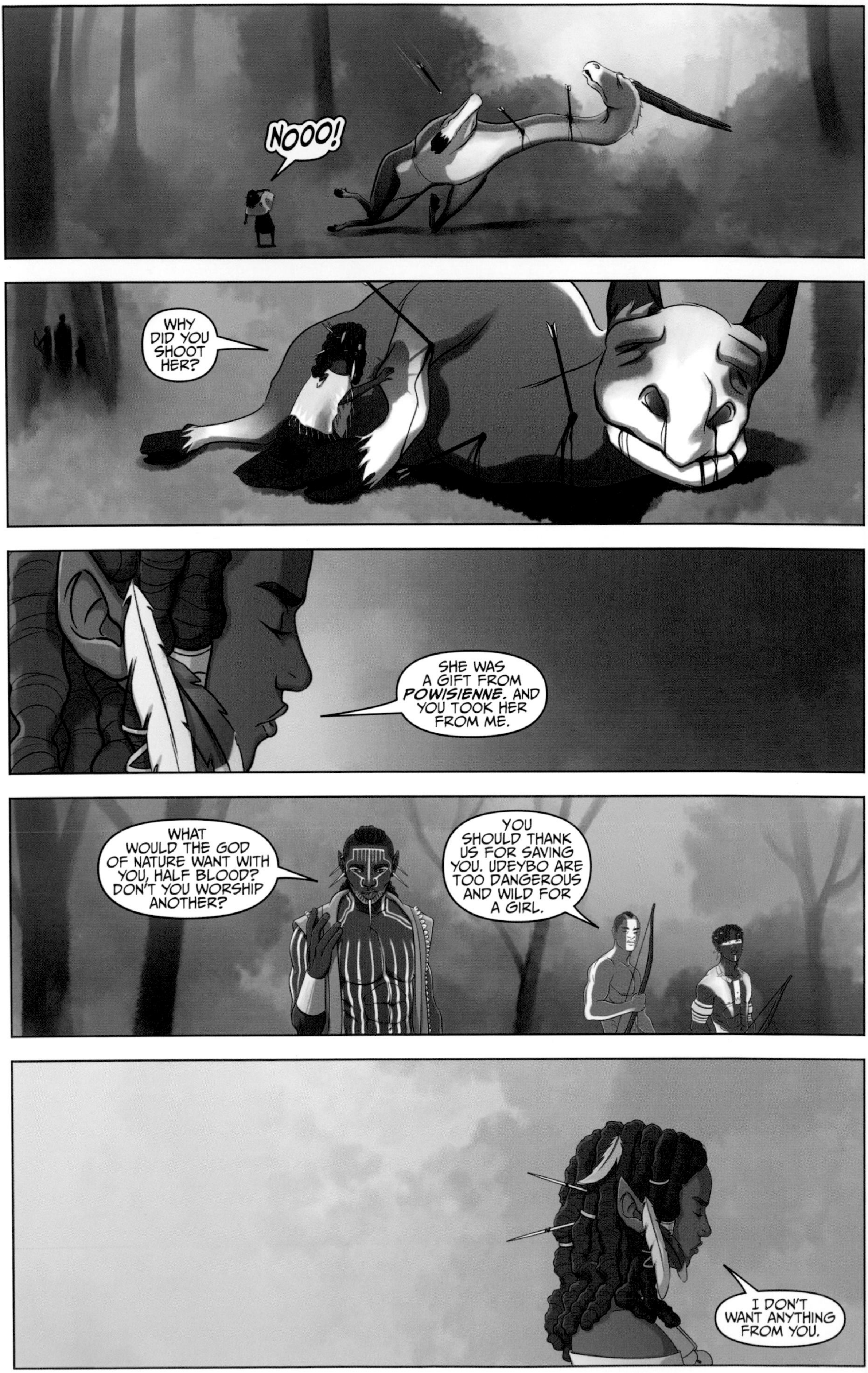
NOOO!
WHY DID YOU SHOOT HER?
SHE WAS A GIFT FROM POWISIENNE. AND YOU TOOK HER FROM ME.
WHAT WOULD THE GOD OF NATURE WANT WITH YOU, HALF BLOOD? DON'T YOU WORSHIP ANOTHER?
YOU SHOULD THANK US FOR SAVING YOU. UDEYBO ARE TOO DANGEROUS AND WILD FOR A GIRL.
I DON'T WANT ANYTHING FROM YOU.

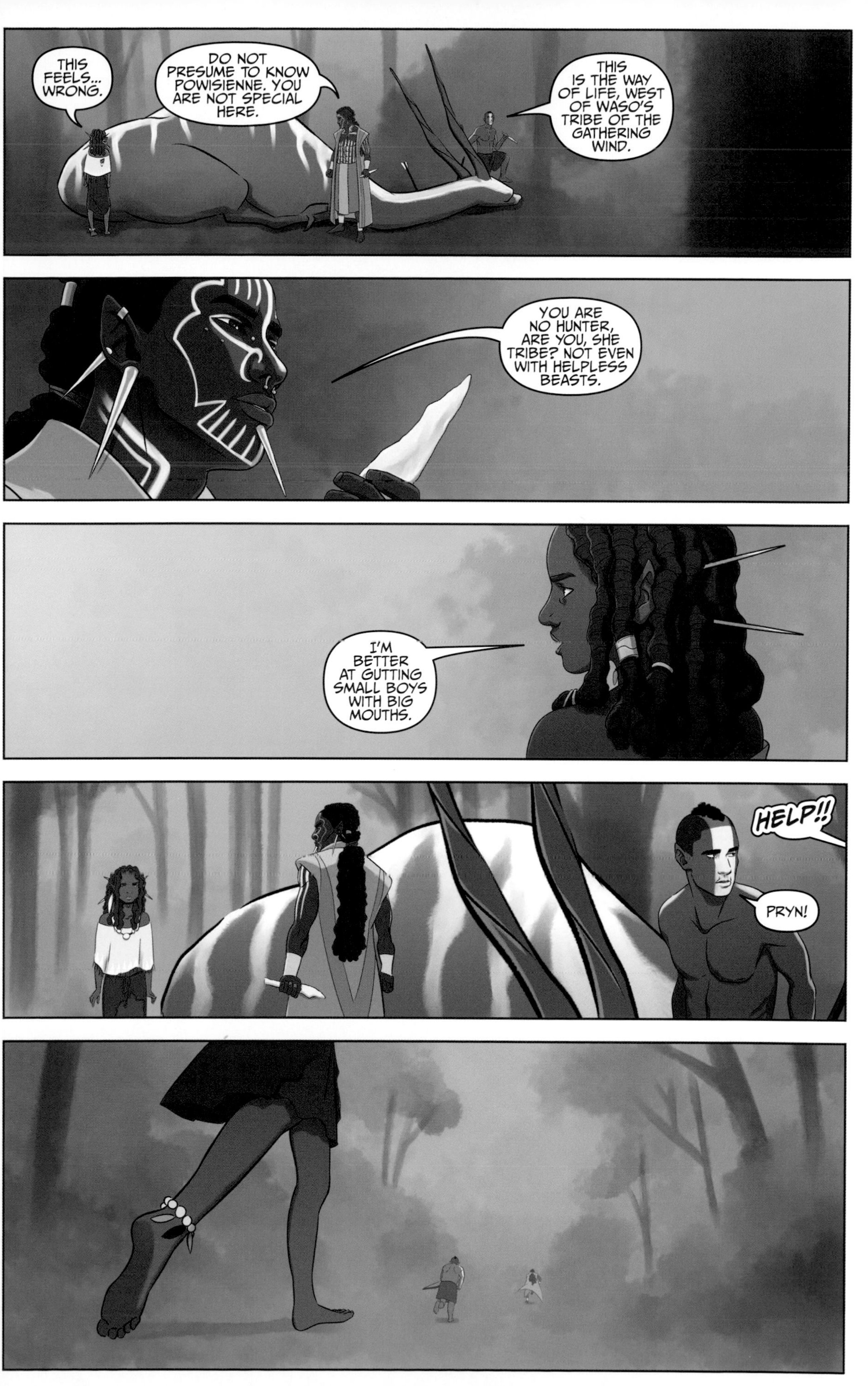
THIS FEELS... WRONG.
DO NOT PRESUME TO KNOW POWISIENNE. YOU ARE NOT SPECIAL HERE.
THIS IS THE WAY OF LIFE, WEST OF WASO'S TRIBE OF THE GATHERING WIND.
YOU ARE NO HUNTER, ARE YOU, SHE TRIBE? NOT EVEN WITH HELPLESS BEASTS.
I'M BETTER AT GUTTING SMALL BOYS WITH BIG MOUTHS.
HELP!!
PRYN!

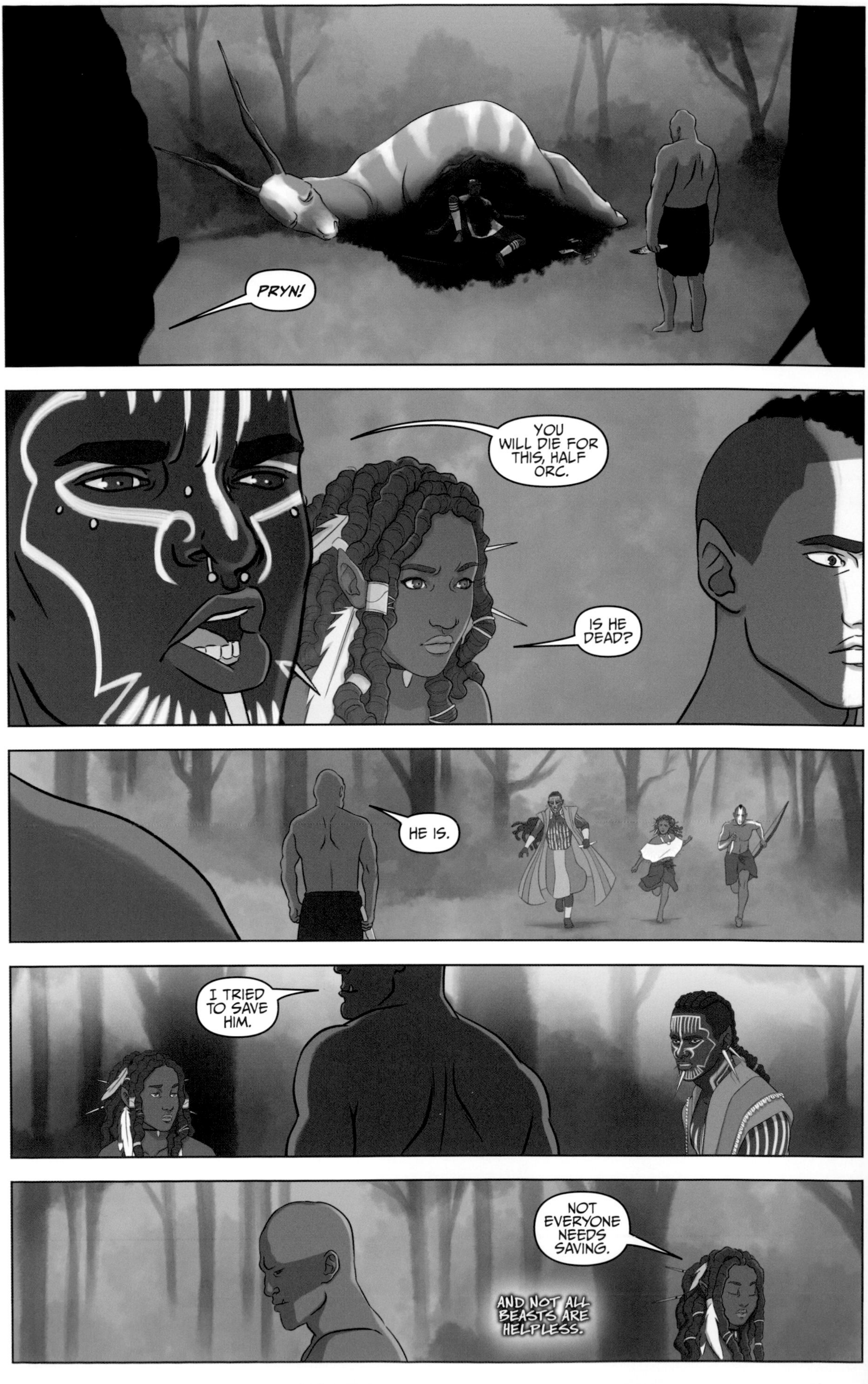
PRYN!
YOU WILL DIE FOR THIS, HALF ORC.
IS HE DEAD?
HE IS.
I TRIED TO SAVE HIM.
NOT EVERYONE NEEDS SAVING.
AND NOT ALL BEASTS ARE HELPLESS.

Hello Stranger,

She came from the cold wasteland of The Errekath with a single purpose... to hunt down a child and return her to the king she was sworn to serve. Andrek VII was not a good king, she knew, but it had been an age since she was a good knight. At one time, she had been perhaps the greatest in the southern or western realms, known for both honor and skills with a blade.

But she had given her soul to The Untamed so she could live an immortal life with her beloved Hanariel. Before her turning, she was a mortal but he was elven kind, Isinniel, those born of Powisienne. The devil had given her what she wanted, but in return she was cursed with a much deeper longing than love... a craving, an insatiable thirst to drink the souls of men.

The white warrior, Essessa, the Vorkas vampire of legend, will one day face the child of tomorrow, Niobe Ayutami, born of two worlds.

And the fate of a world will be decided.

CHAPTER 2

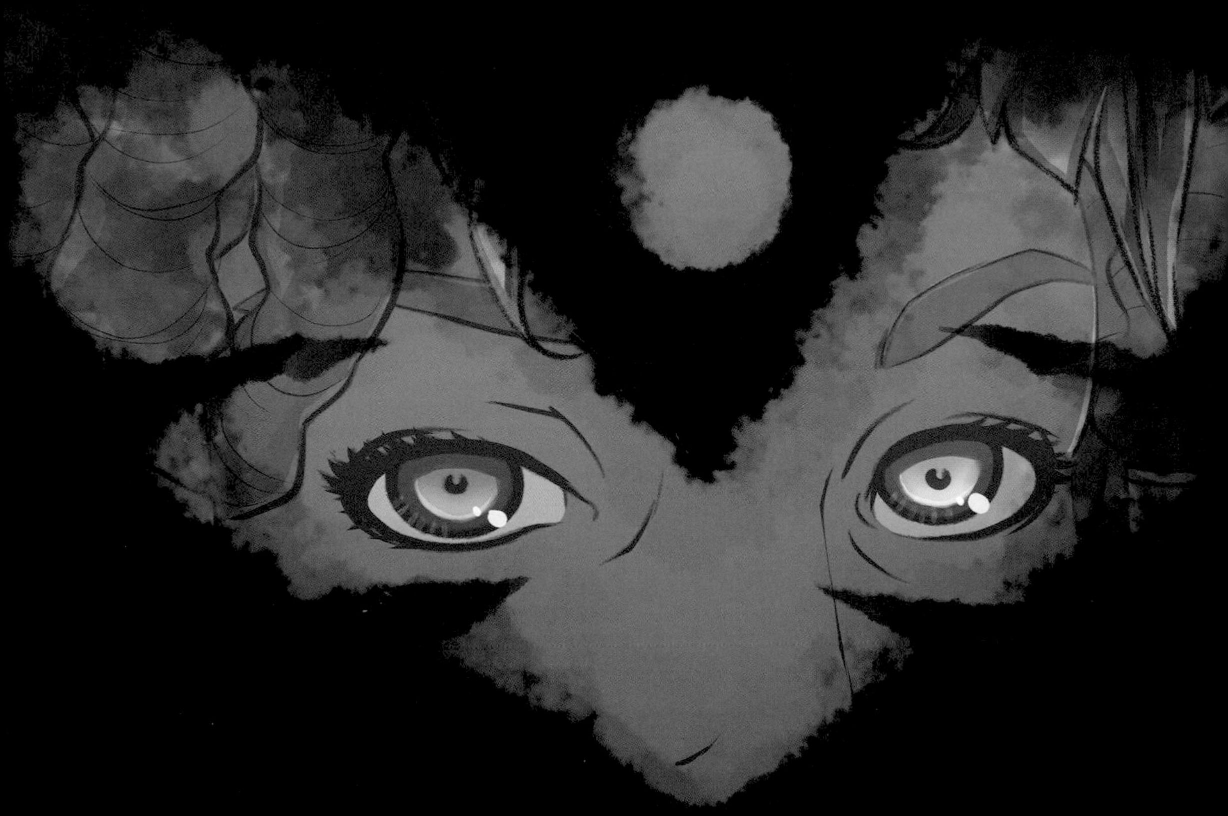

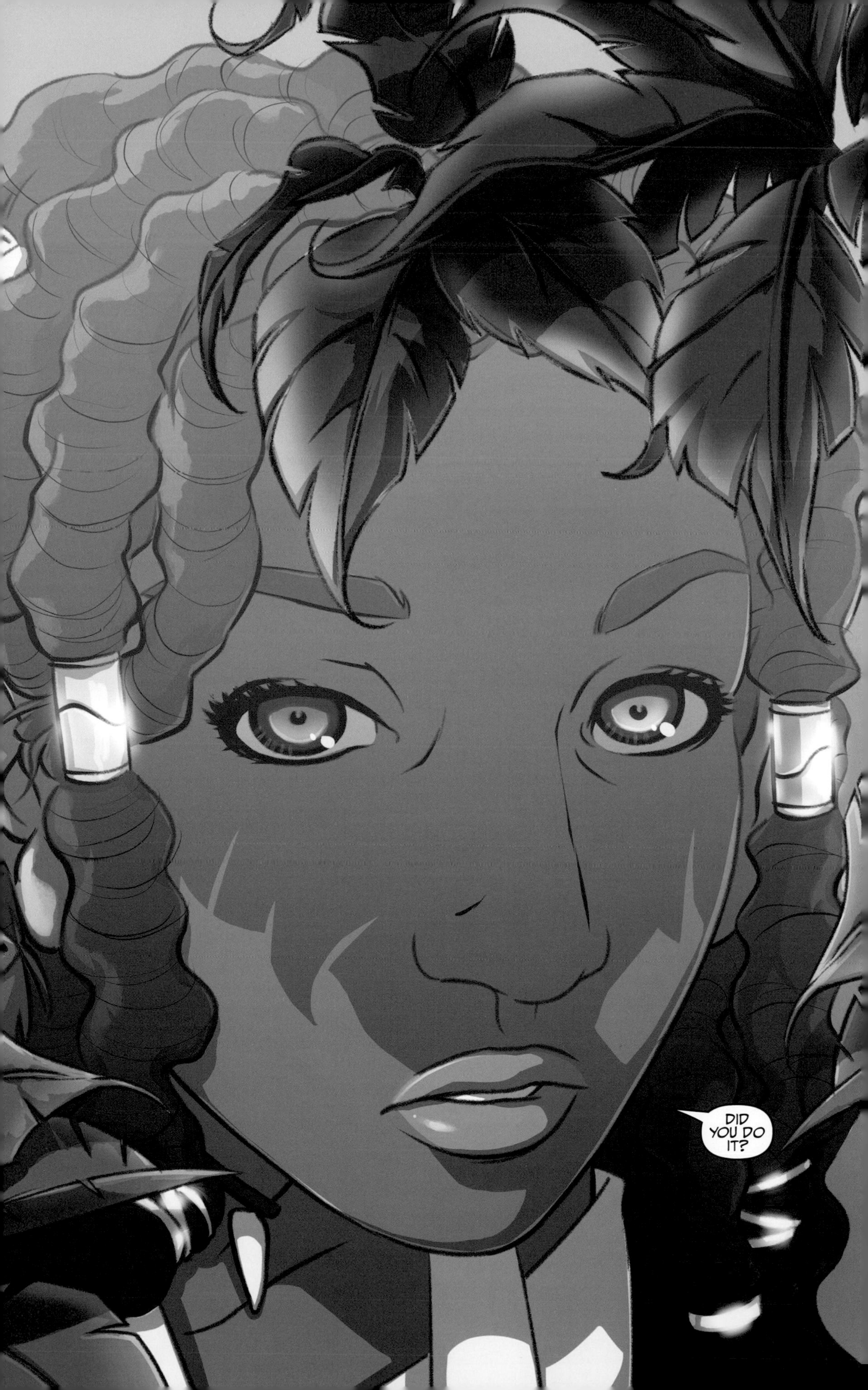
DID YOU DO IT?

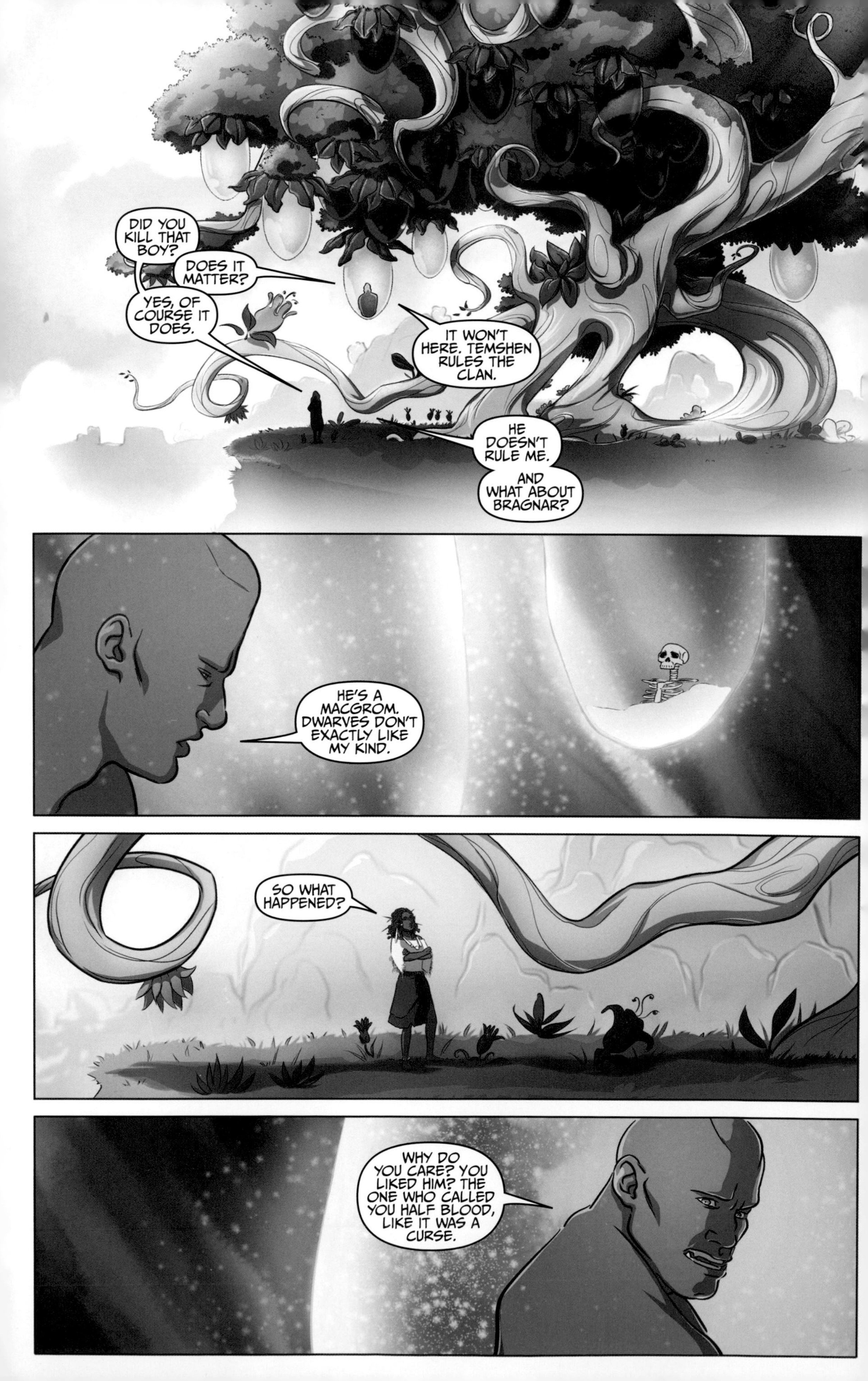
DID YOU KILL THAT BOY?
DOES IT MATTER?
YES, OF COURSE IT DOES.
IT WON'T HERE. TEMSHEN RULES THE CLAN.
HE DOESN'T RULE ME.
AND WHAT ABOUT BRAGNAR?
HE'S A MACGROM. DWARVES DON'T EXACTLY LIKE MY KIND.
SO WHAT HAPPENED?
WHY DO YOU CARE? YOU LIKED HIM? THE ONE WHO CALLED YOU HALF BLOOD, LIKE IT WAS A CURSE.

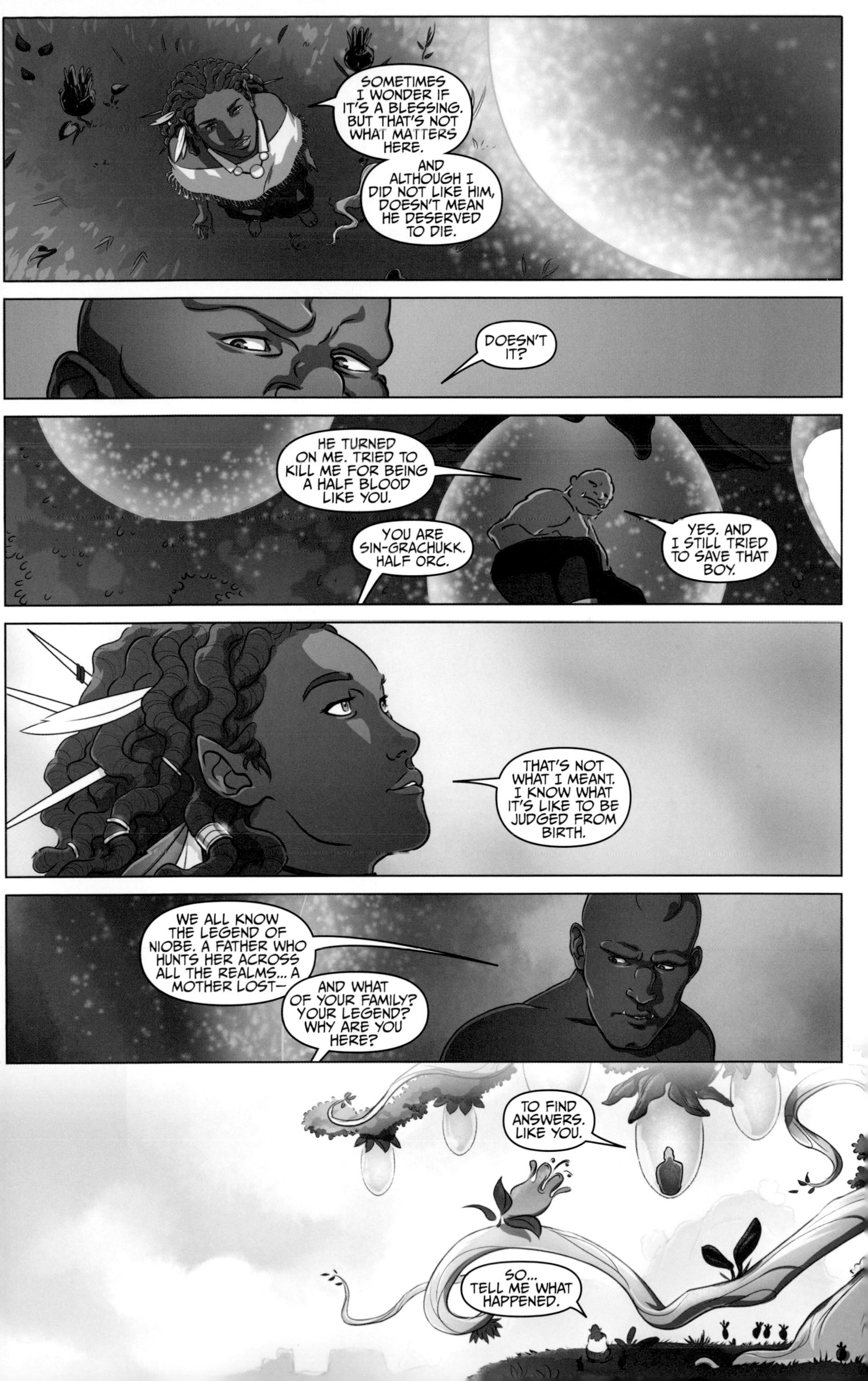
SOMETIMES I WONDER IF IT'S A BLESSING. BUT THAT'S NOT WHAT MATTERS HERE.
AND ALTHOUGH I DID NOT LIKE HIM, DOESN'T MEAN HE DESERVED TO DIE.
DOESN'T IT?
HE TURNED ON ME. TRIED TO KILL ME FOR BEING A HALF BLOOD LIKE YOU.
YOU ARE SIN-GRACHUKK. HALF ORC.
YES. AND I STILL TRIED TO SAVE THAT BOY.
THAT'S NOT WHAT I MEANT. I KNOW WHAT IT'S LIKE TO BE JUDGED FROM BIRTH.
WE ALL KNOW THE LEGEND OF NIOBE. A FATHER WHO HUNTS HER ACROSS ALL THE REALMS... A MOTHER LOST—
AND WHAT OF YOUR FAMILY? YOUR LEGEND? WHY ARE YOU HERE?
TO FIND ANSWERS. LIKE YOU.
SO... TELL ME WHAT HAPPENED.

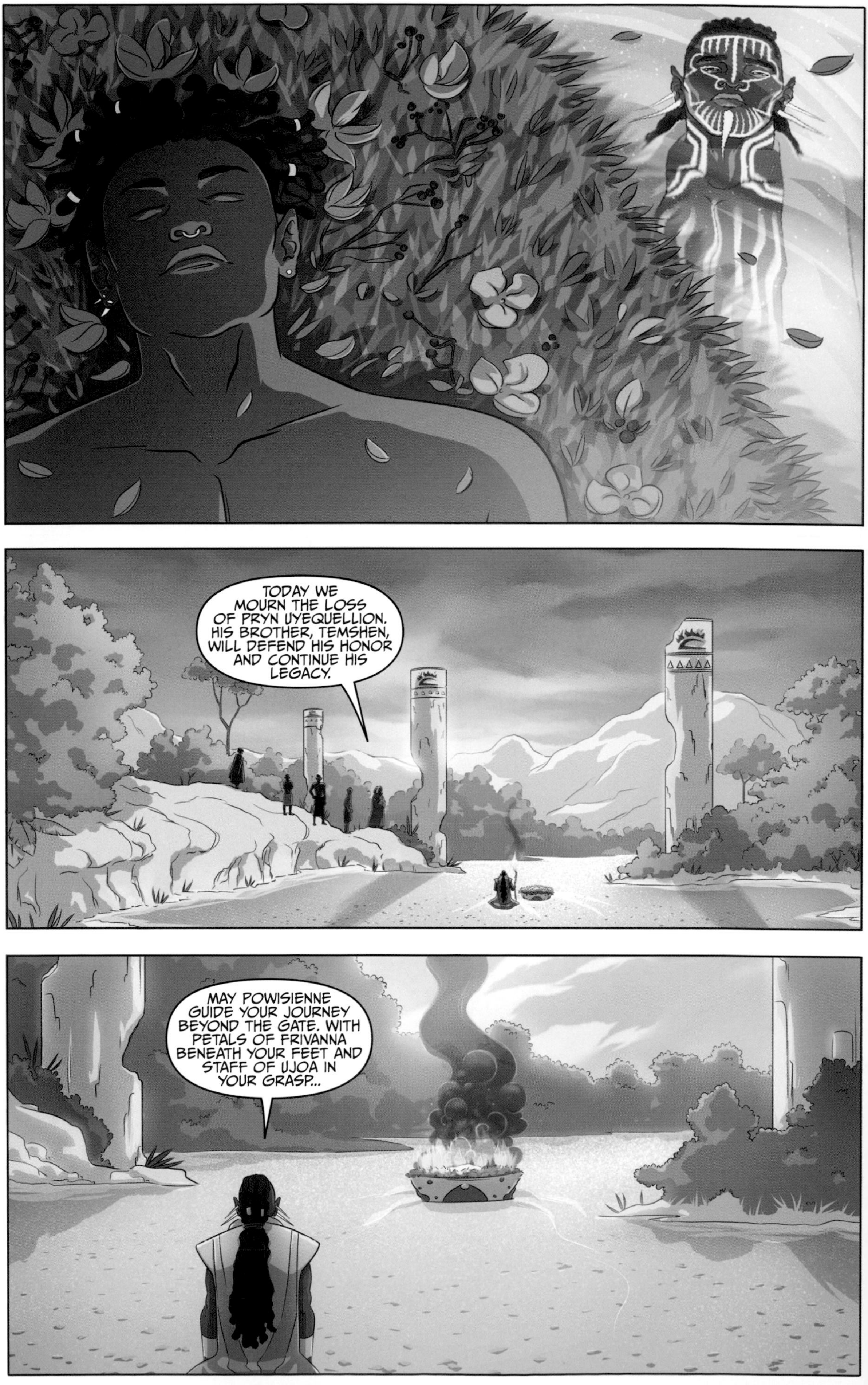
TODAY WE MOURN THE LOSS OF PRYN UYEQUELLION. HIS BROTHER, TEMSHEN, WILL DEFEND HIS HONOR AND CONTINUE HIS LEGACY.
MAY POWISIENNE GUIDE YOUR JOURNEY BEYOND THE GATE. WITH PETALS OF FRIVANNA BENEATH YOUR FEET AND STAFF OF UJOA IN YOUR GRASP...

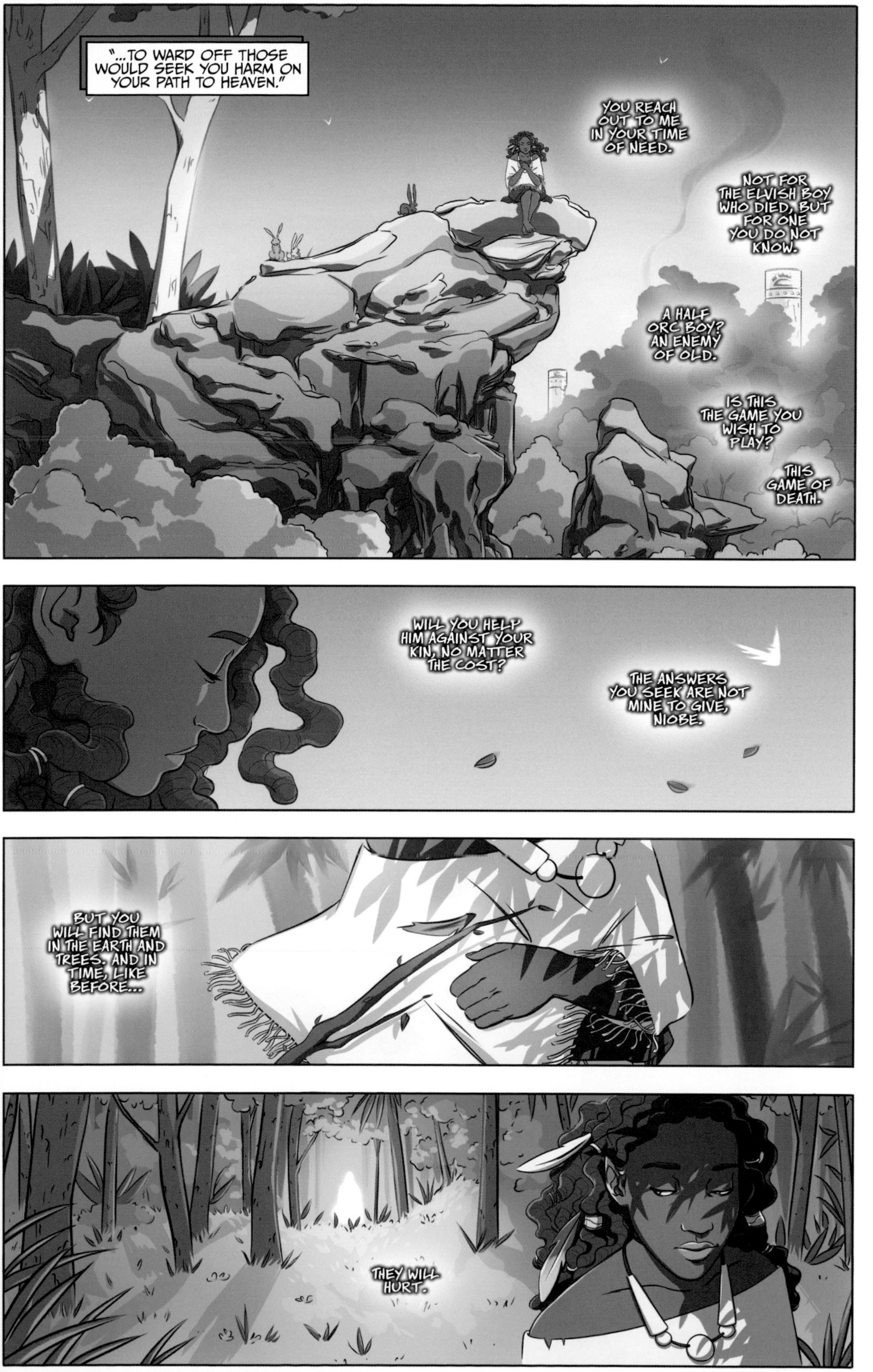
"...TO WARD OFF THOSE WOULD SEEK YOU HARM ON YOUR PATH TO HEAVEN."
YOU REACH OUT TO ME IN YOUR TIME OF NEED.
NOT FOR THE ELVISH BOY WHO DIED, BUT FOR ONE YOU DO NOT KNOW.
A HALF ORC BOY? AN ENEMY OF OLD.
IS THIS THE GAME YOU WISH TO PLAY?
THIS GAME OF DEATH.
WILL YOU HELP HIM AGAINST YOUR KIN, NO MATTER THE COST?
THE ANSWERS YOU SEEK ARE NOT MINE TO GIVE, NIOBE.
BUT YOU WILL FIND THEM IN THE EARTH AND TREES. AND IN TIME, LIKE BEFORE...
THEY WILL HURT.

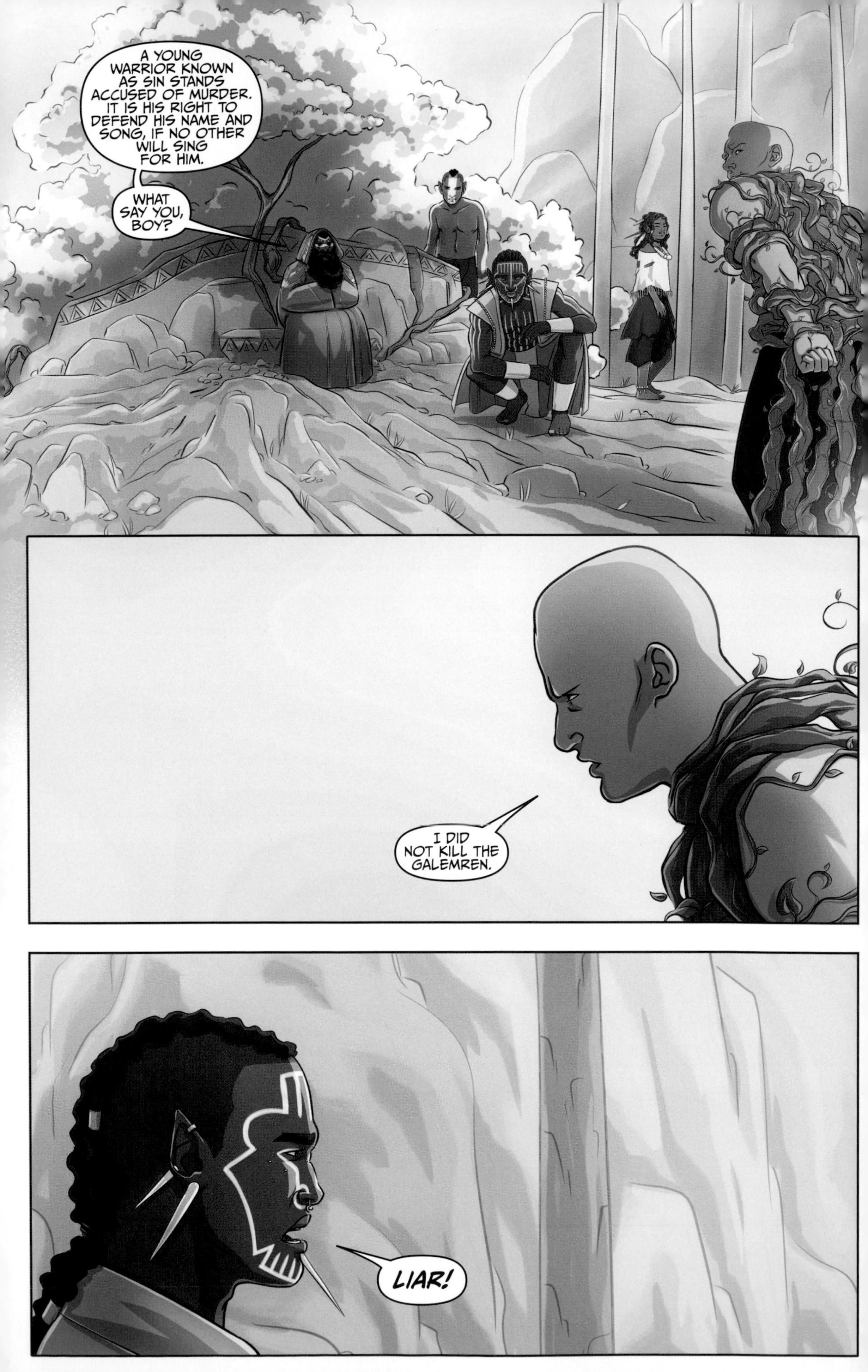
A YOUNG WARRIOR KNOWN AS SIN STANDS ACCUSED OF MURDER. IT IS HIS RIGHT TO DEFEND HIS NAME AND SONG, IF NO OTHER WILL SING FOR HIM.
WHAT SAY YOU, BOY?
I DID NOT KILL THE GALEMREN.
LIAR!

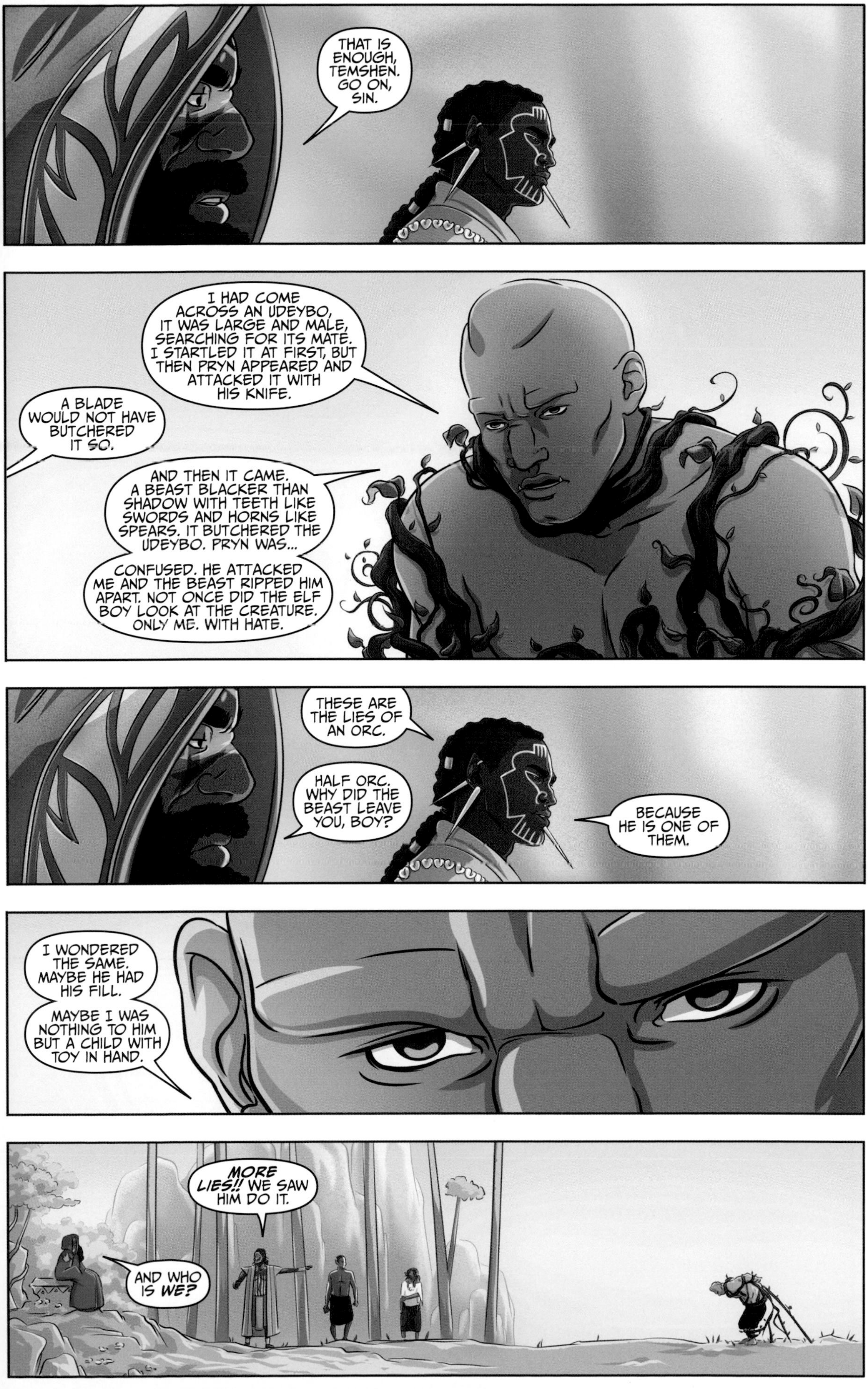
THAT IS ENOUGH, TEMSHEN. GO ON, SIN.
I HAD COME ACROSS AN UDEYBO, IT WAS LARGE AND MALE, SEARCHING FOR ITS MATE. I STARTLED IT AT FIRST, BUT THEN PRYN APPEARED AND ATTACKED IT WITH HIS KNIFE.
A BLADE WOULD NOT HAVE BUTCHERED IT SO.
AND THEN IT CAME. A BEAST BLACKER THAN SHADOW WITH TEETH LIKE SWORDS AND HORNS LIKE SPEARS. IT BUTCHERED THE UDEYBO. PRYN WAS...
CONFUSED. HE ATTACKED ME AND THE BEAST RIPPED HIM APART. NOT ONCE DID THE ELF BOY LOOK AT THE CREATURE. ONLY ME. WITH HATE.
THESE ARE THE LIES OF AN ORC.
HALF ORC. WHY DID THE BEAST LEAVE YOU, BOY?
BECAUSE HE IS ONE OF THEM.
I WONDERED THE SAME. MAYBE HE HAD HIS FILL.
MAYBE I WAS NOTHING TO HIM BUT A CHILD WITH TOY IN HAND.
MORE LIES!! WE SAW HIM DO IT.
AND WHO IS WE?

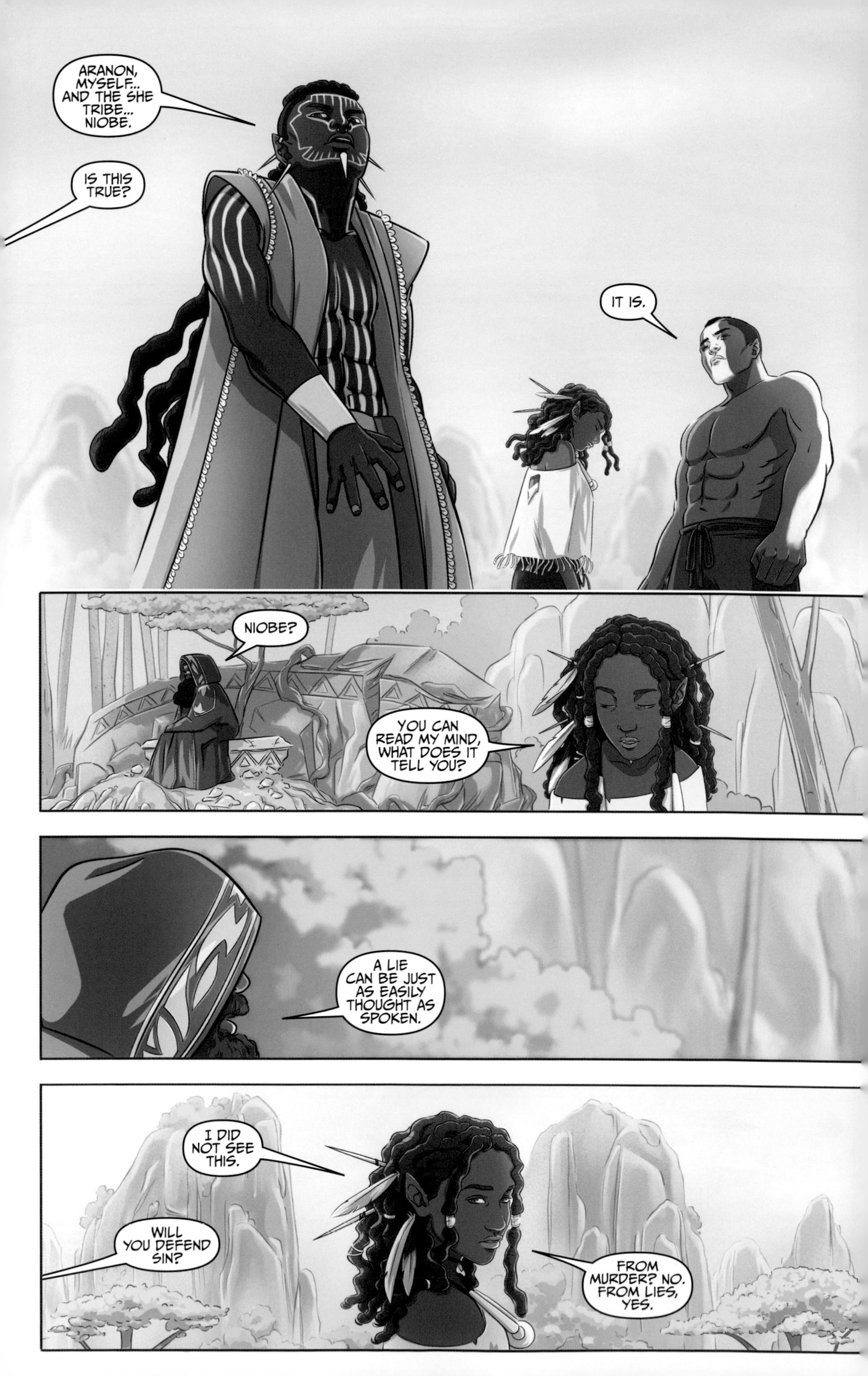
ARANON, MYSELF.. AND THE SHE TRIBE... NIOBE.
IS THIS TRUE?
IT IS.
NIOBE?
YOU CAN READ MY MIND, WHAT DOES IT TELL YOU?
A LIE CAN BE JUST AS EASILY THOUGHT AS SPOKEN.
I DID NOT SEE THIS.
WILL YOU DEFEND SIN?
FROM MURDER? NO. FROM LIES, YES.

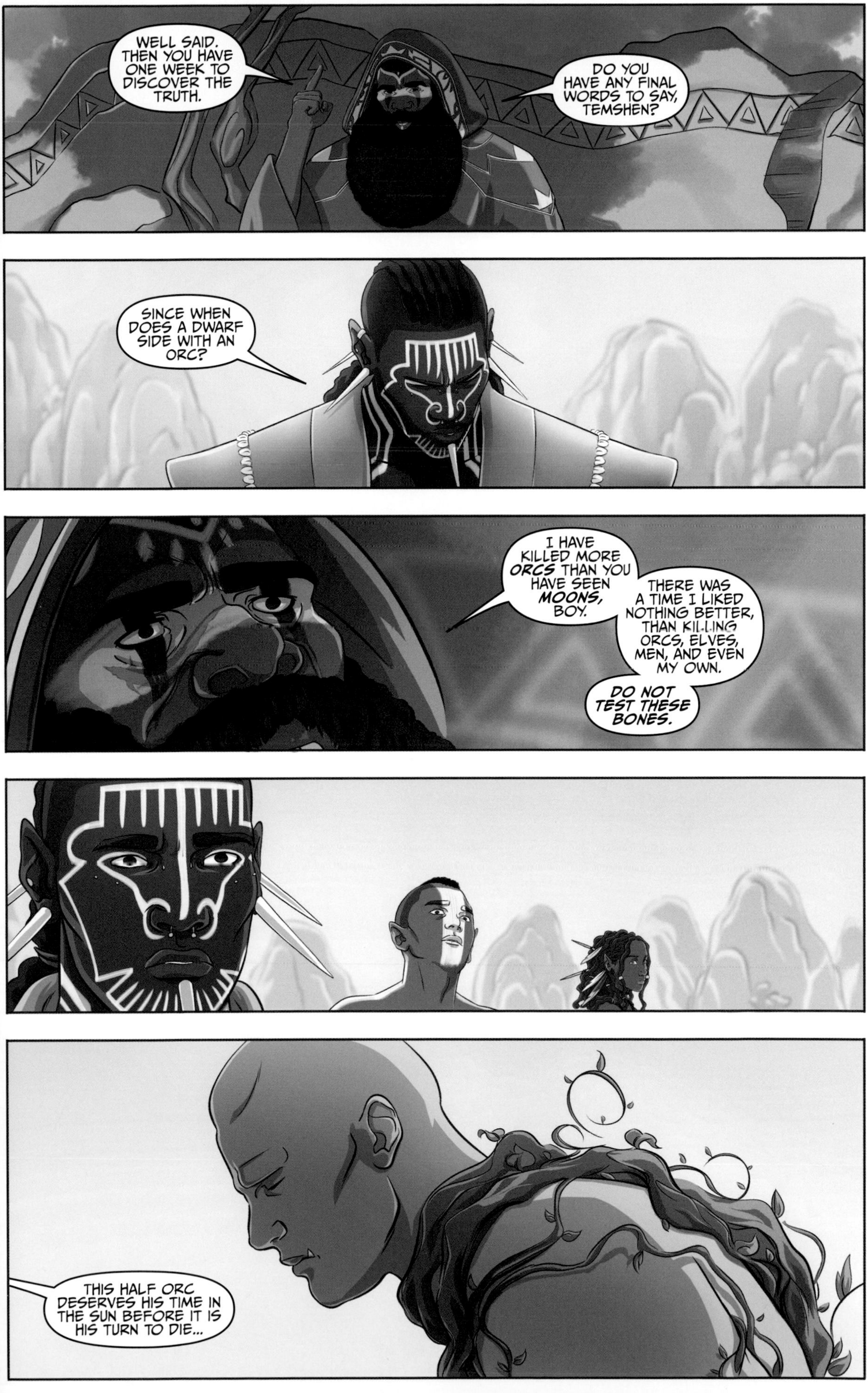

WELL SAID. THEN YOU HAVE ONE WEEK TO DISCOVER THE TRUTH.
DO YOU HAVE ANY FINAL WORDS TO SAY, TEMSHEN?
SINCE WHEN DOES A DWARF SIDE WITH AN ORC?
I HAVE KILLED MORE ORCS THAN YOU HAVE SEEN MOONS, BOY.
THERE WAS A TIME I LIKED NOTHING BETTER, THAN KILLING ORCS, ELVES, MEN, AND EVEN MY OWN.
DO NOT TEST THESE BONES.
THIS HALF ORC DESERVES HIS TIME IN THE SUN BEFORE IT IS HIS TURN TO DIE...

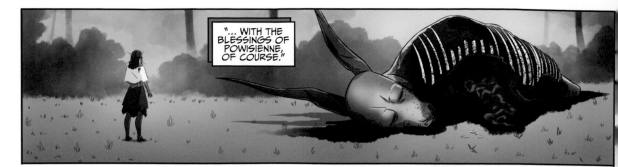

"... WITH THE BLESSINGS OF POWISIENNE, OF COURSE."

YOU AGAIN.

DID YOU SEE THE ATTACK?

PRYN'S AMULET...

WHAT NOW?

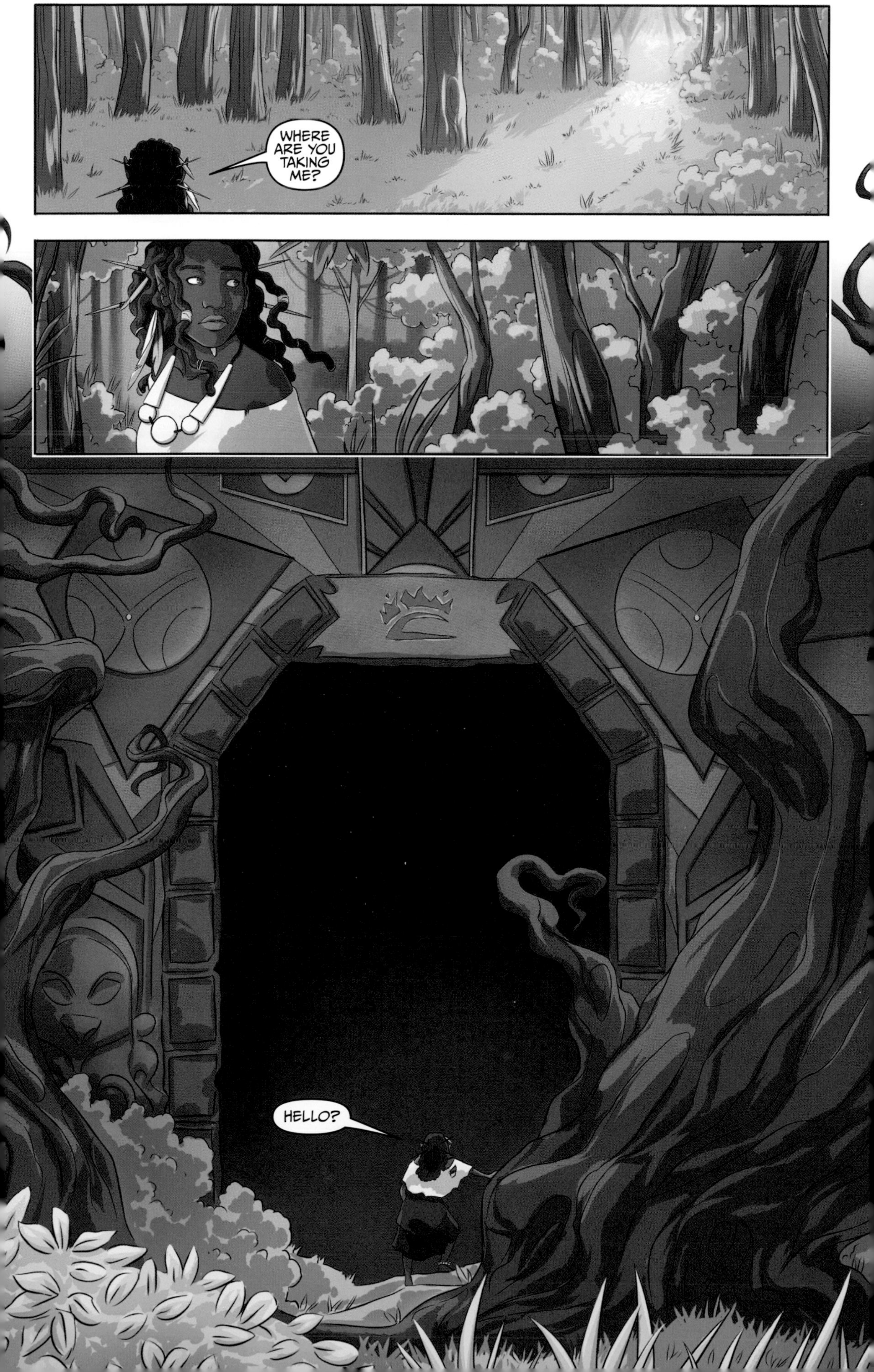
WHERE ARE YOU TAKING ME?
HELLO?

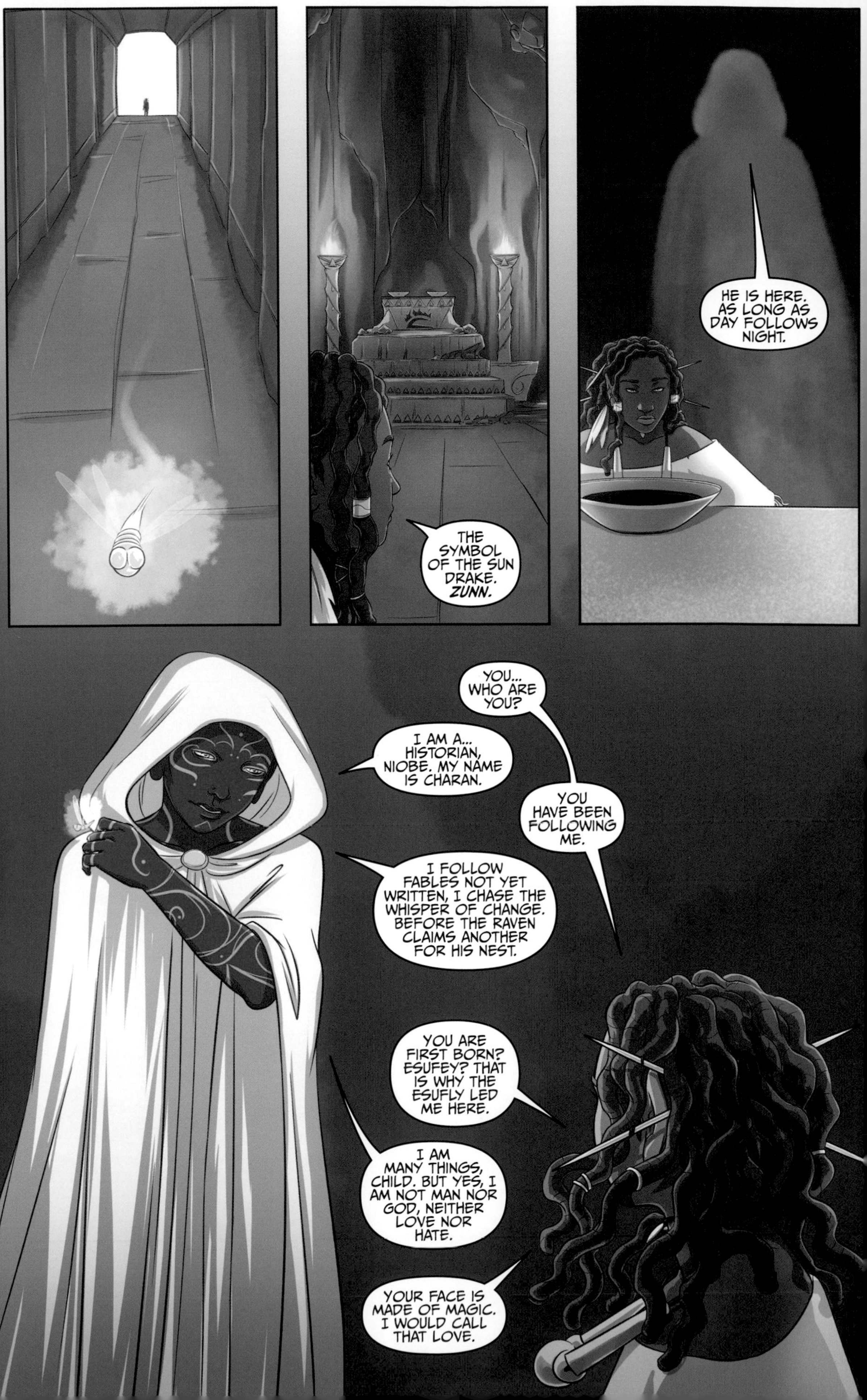
THE SYMBOL OF THE SUN DRAKE. *ZUNN.*
HE IS HERE. AS LONG AS DAY FOLLOWS NIGHT.
YOU... WHO ARE YOU?
I AM A... HISTORIAN, NIOBE. MY NAME IS CHARAN.
YOU HAVE BEEN FOLLOWING ME.
I FOLLOW FABLES NOT YET WRITTEN, I CHASE THE WHISPER OF CHANGE. BEFORE THE RAVEN CLAIMS ANOTHER FOR HIS NEST.
YOU ARE FIRST BORN? ESUFEY? THAT IS WHY THE ESUFLY LED ME HERE.
I AM MANY THINGS, CHILD. BUT YES, I AM NOT MAN NOR GOD, NEITHER LOVE NOR HATE.
YOUR FACE IS MADE OF MAGIC. I WOULD CALL THAT LOVE.

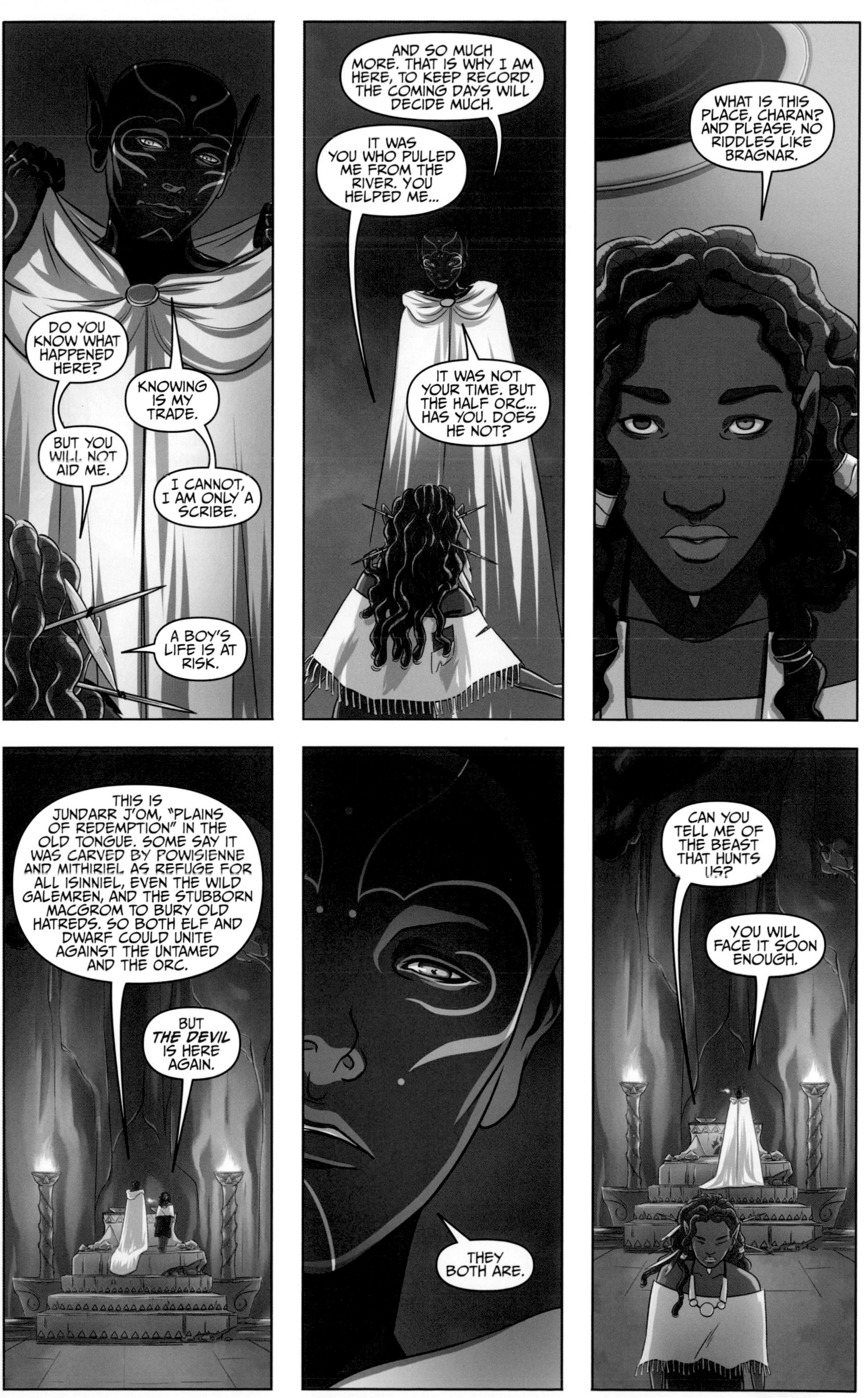
DO YOU KNOW WHAT HAPPENED HERE?
KNOWING IS MY TRADE.
BUT YOU WILL NOT AID ME.
I CANNOT, I AM ONLY A SCRIBE.
A BOY'S LIFE IS AT RISK.
AND SO MUCH MORE. THAT IS WHY I AM HERE, TO KEEP RECORD. THE COMING DAYS WILL DECIDE MUCH.
IT WAS YOU WHO PULLED ME FROM THE RIVER. YOU HELPED ME...
IT WAS NOT YOUR TIME. BUT THE HALF ORC... HAS YOU. DOES HE NOT?
WHAT IS THIS PLACE, CHARAN? AND PLEASE, NO RIDDLES LIKE BRAGNAR.
THIS IS JUNDARR J'OM, "PLAINS OF REDEMPTION" IN THE OLD TONGUE. SOME SAY IT WAS CARVED BY POWISIENNE AND MITHIRIEL AS REFUGE FOR ALL ISINNIEL, EVEN THE WILD GALEMREN, AND THE STUBBORN MACGROM TO BURY OLD HATREDS. SO BOTH ELF AND DWARF COULD UNITE AGAINST THE UNTAMED AND THE ORC.
BUT *THE DEVIL* IS HERE AGAIN.
THEY BOTH ARE.
CAN YOU TELL ME OF THE BEAST THAT HUNTS US?
YOU WILL FACE IT SOON ENOUGH.

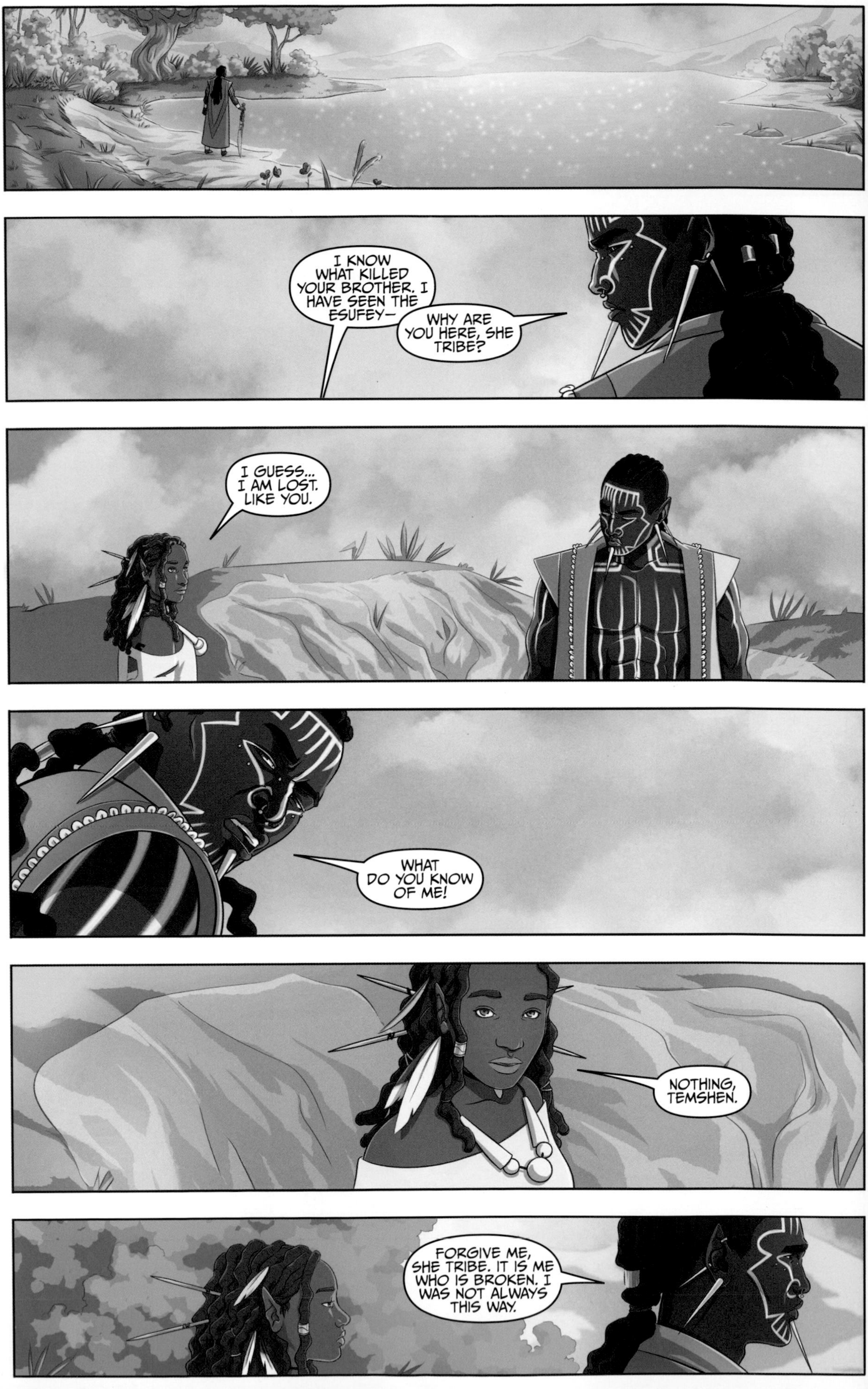
I KNOW WHAT KILLED YOUR BROTHER. I HAVE SEEN THE ESUFEY—
WHY ARE YOU HERE, SHE TRIBE?
I GUESS... I AM LOST. LIKE YOU.
WHAT DO YOU KNOW OF ME!
NOTHING, TEMSHEN.
FORGIVE ME, SHE TRIBE. IT IS ME WHO IS BROKEN. I WAS NOT ALWAYS THIS WAY.

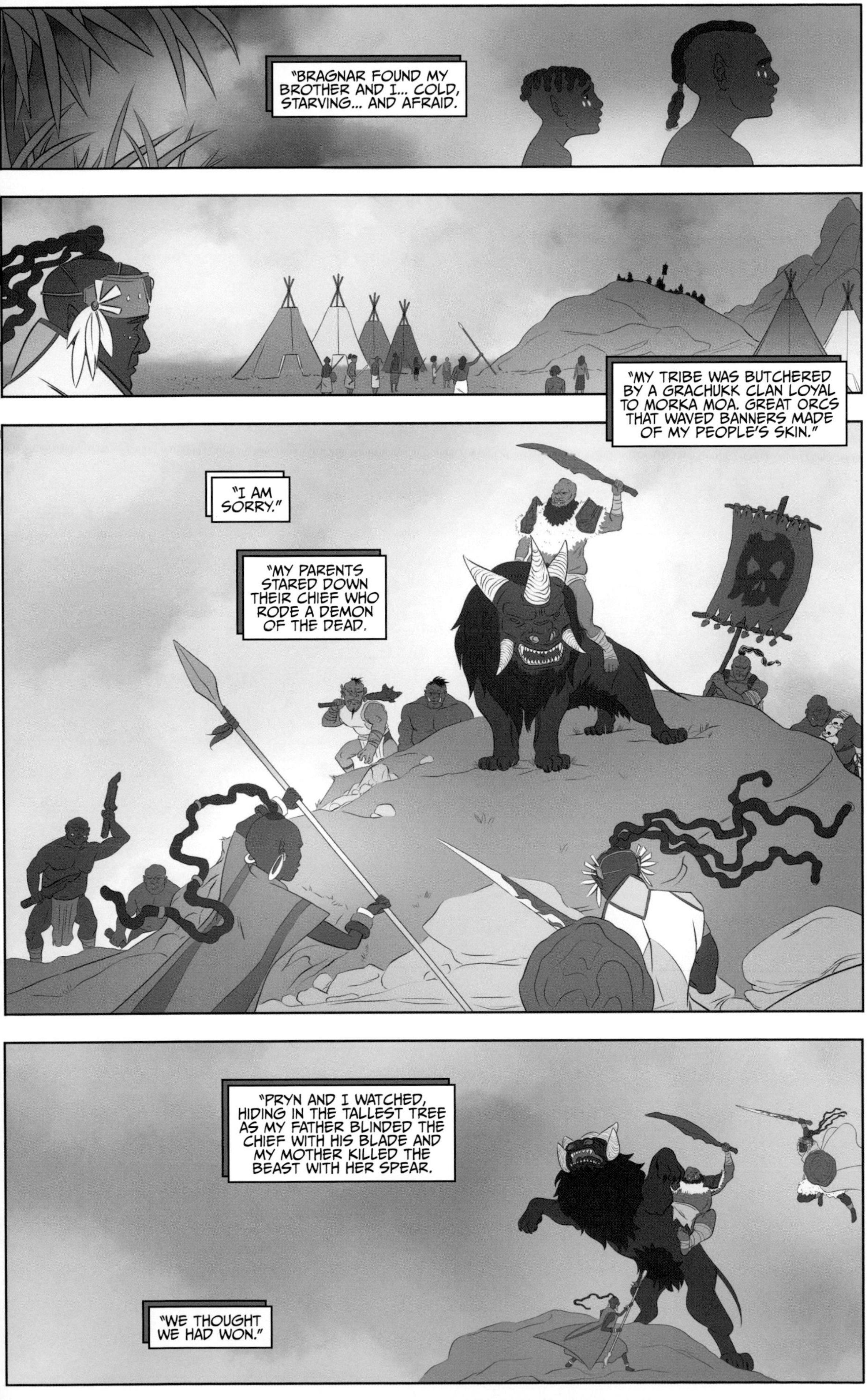
"BRAGNAR FOUND MY BROTHER AND I... COLD, STARVING... AND AFRAID.
"MY TRIBE WAS BUTCHERED BY A GRACHUKK CLAN LOYAL TO MORKA MOA. GREAT ORCS THAT WAVED BANNERS MADE OF MY PEOPLE'S SKIN."
"I AM SORRY."
"MY PARENTS STARED DOWN THEIR CHIEF WHO RODE A DEMON OF THE DEAD.
"PRYN AND I WATCHED, HIDING IN THE TALLEST TREE AS MY FATHER BLINDED THE CHIEF WITH HIS BLADE AND MY MOTHER KILLED THE BEAST WITH HER SPEAR.
"WE THOUGHT WE HAD WON."

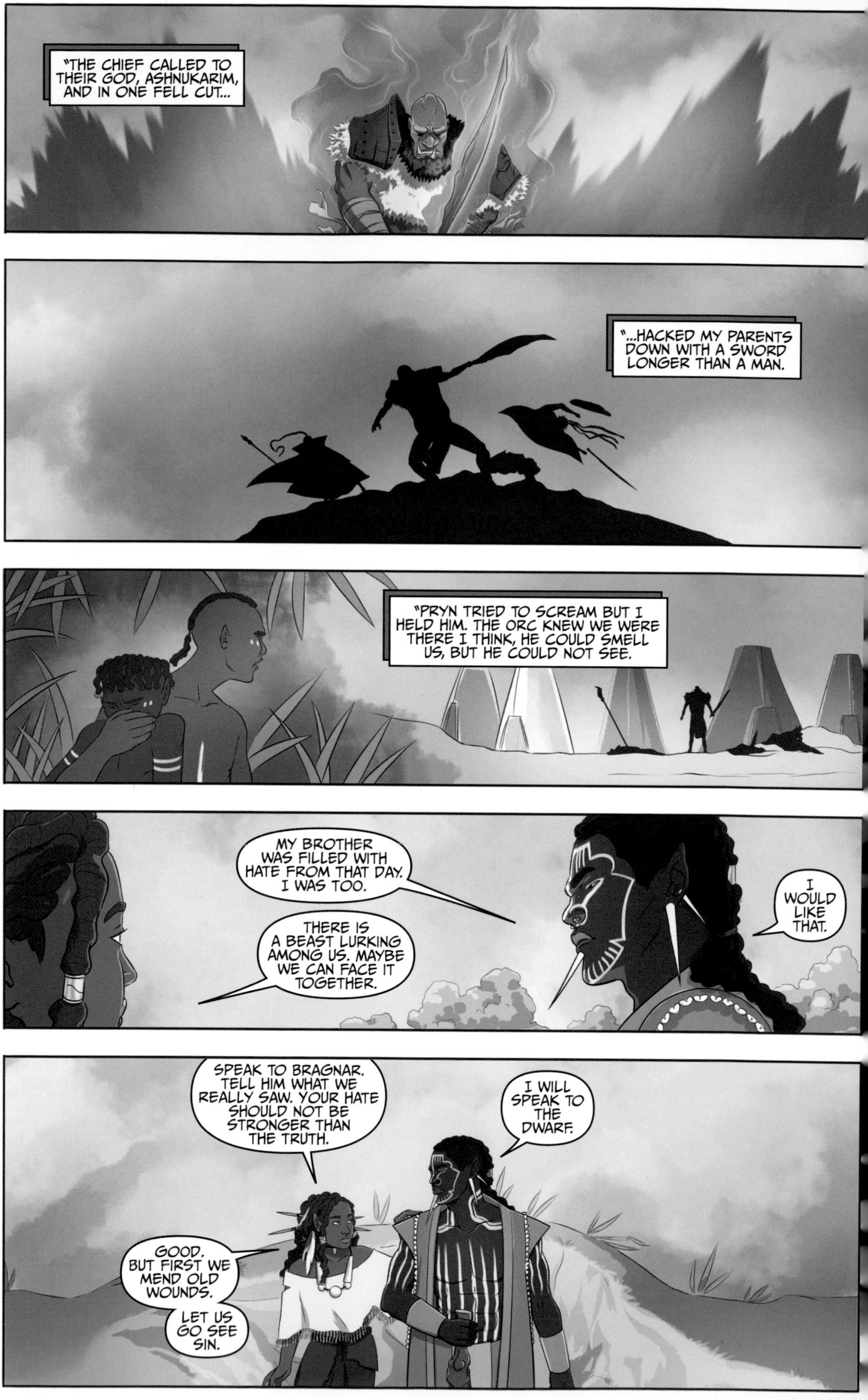
"THE CHIEF CALLED TO THEIR GOD, ASHNUKARIM, AND IN ONE FELL CUT...
"...HACKED MY PARENTS DOWN WITH A SWORD LONGER THAN A MAN.
"PRYN TRIED TO SCREAM BUT I HELD HIM. THE ORC KNEW WE WERE THERE I THINK, HE COULD SMELL US, BUT HE COULD NOT SEE.
MY BROTHER WAS FILLED WITH HATE FROM THAT DAY. I WAS TOO.
THERE IS A BEAST LURKING AMONG US. MAYBE WE CAN FACE IT TOGETHER.
I WOULD LIKE THAT.
SPEAK TO BRAGNAR. TELL HIM WHAT WE REALLY SAW. YOUR HATE SHOULD NOT BE STRONGER THAN THE TRUTH.
I WILL SPEAK TO THE DWARF.
GOOD. BUT FIRST WE MEND OLD WOUNDS.
LET US GO SEE SIN.

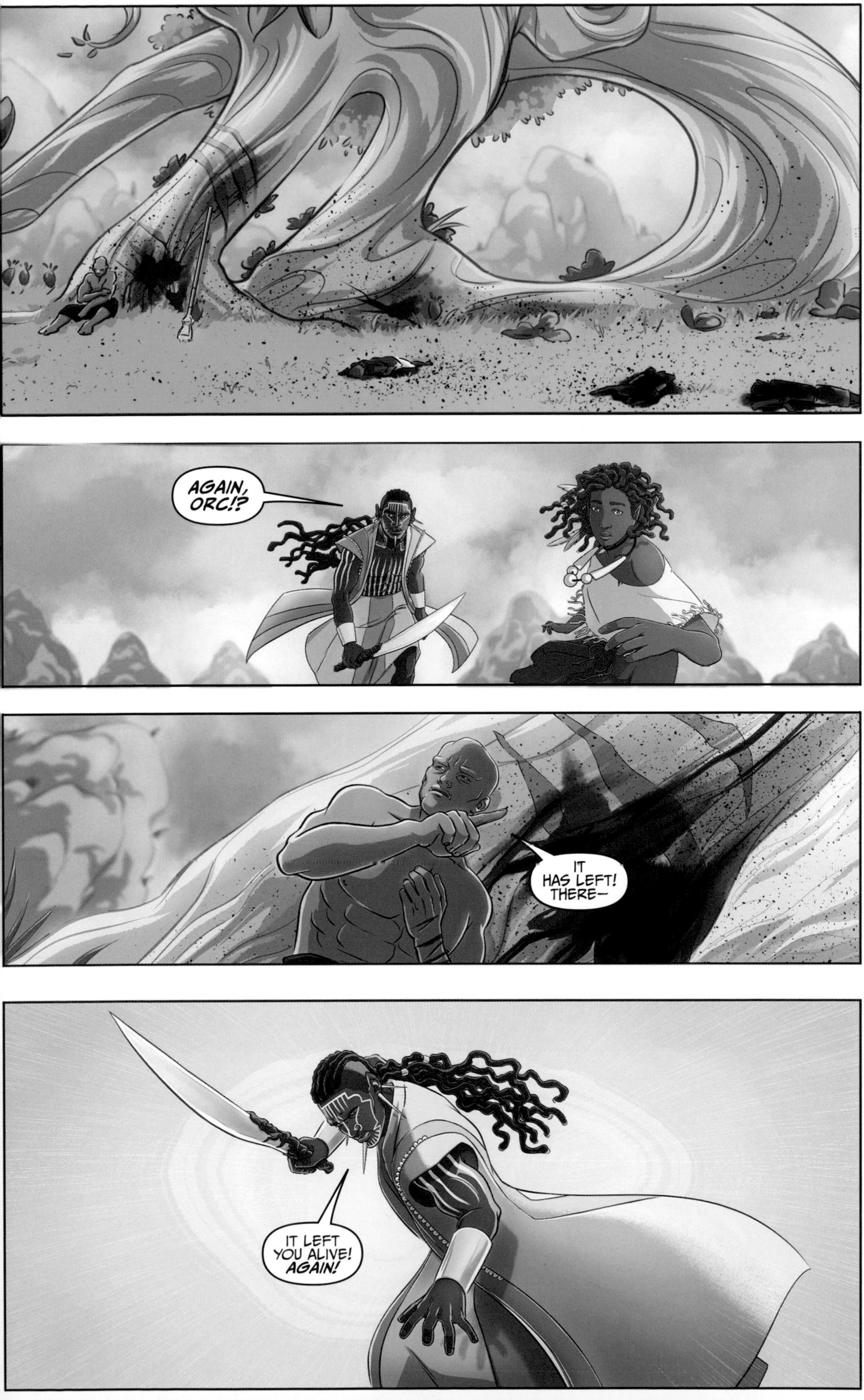
AGAIN, ORC!?
IT HAS LEFT! THERE—
IT LEFT YOU ALIVE! AGAIN!

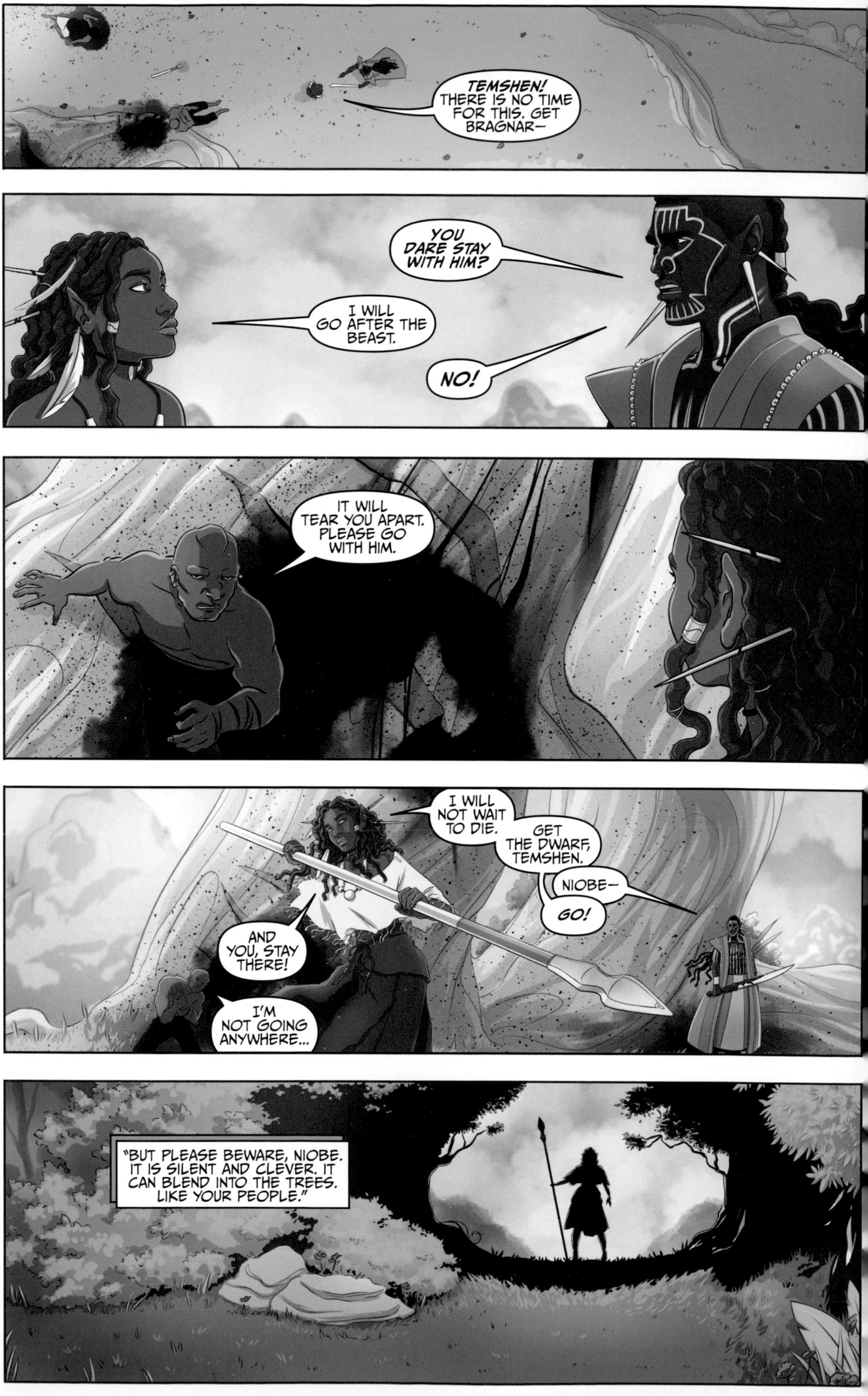
TEMSHEN! THERE IS NO TIME FOR THIS. GET BRAGNAR—
YOU DARE STAY WITH HIM?
I WILL GO AFTER THE BEAST.
NO!
IT WILL TEAR YOU APART. PLEASE GO WITH HIM.
I WILL NOT WAIT TO DIE.
GET THE DWARF, TEMSHEN.
NIOBE—
GO!
AND YOU, STAY THERE!
I'M NOT GOING ANYWHERE...
"BUT PLEASE BEWARE, NIOBE. IT IS SILENT AND CLEVER. IT CAN BLEND INTO THE TREES. LIKE YOUR PEOPLE."

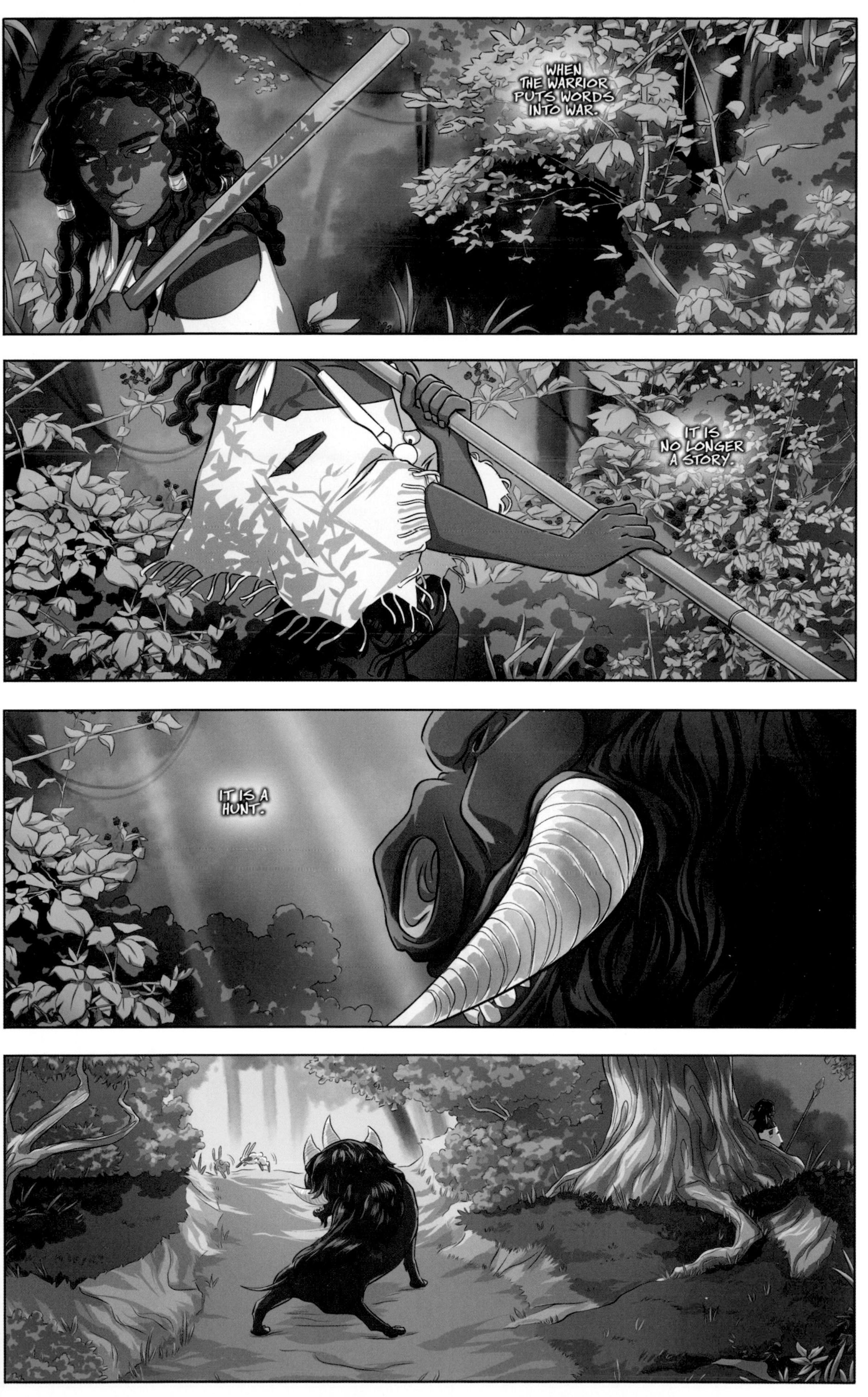
WHEN THE WARRIOR PUTS WORDS INTO WAR.
IT IS NO LONGER A STORY.
IT IS A HUNT.

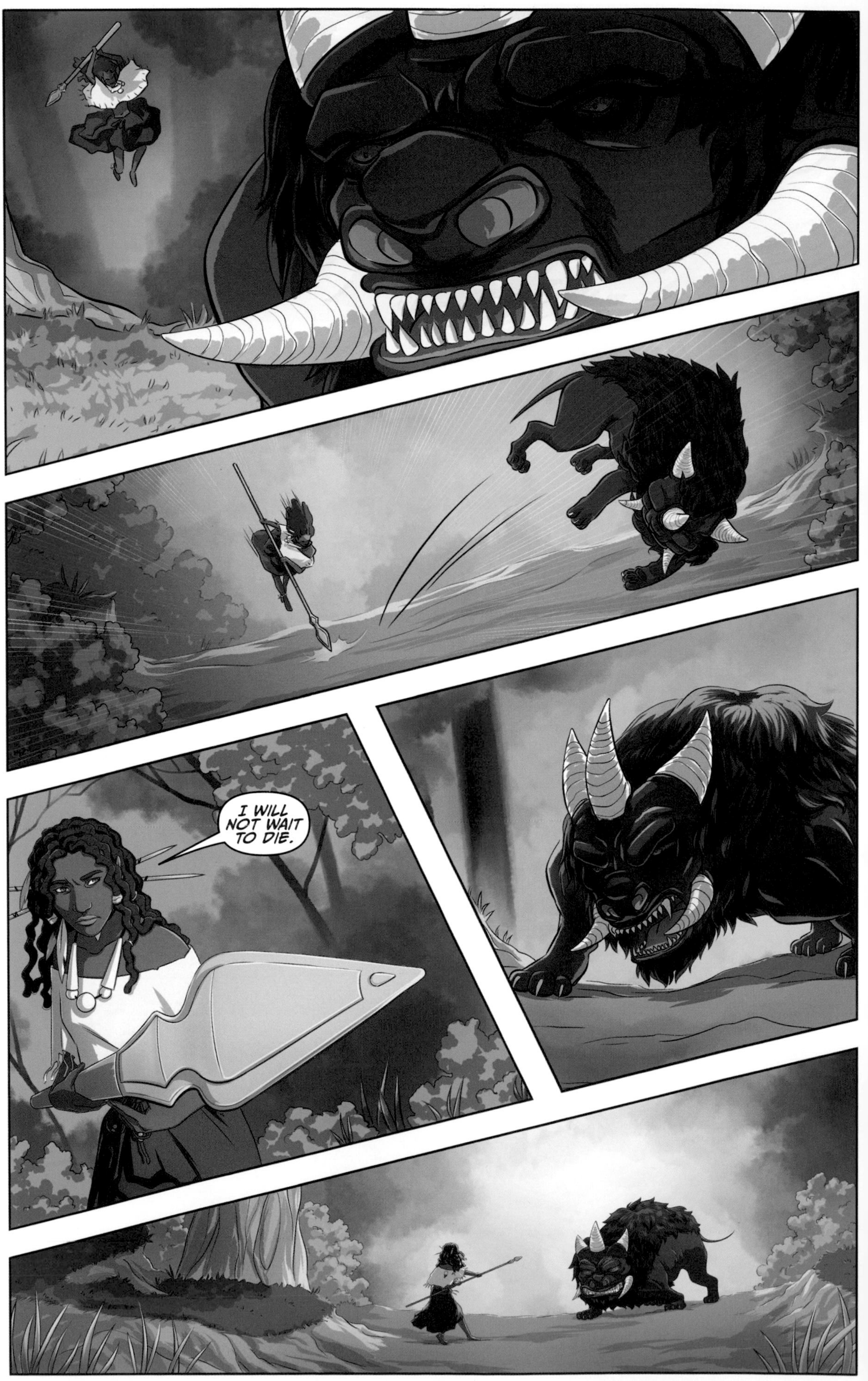
I WILL NOT WAIT TO DIE.

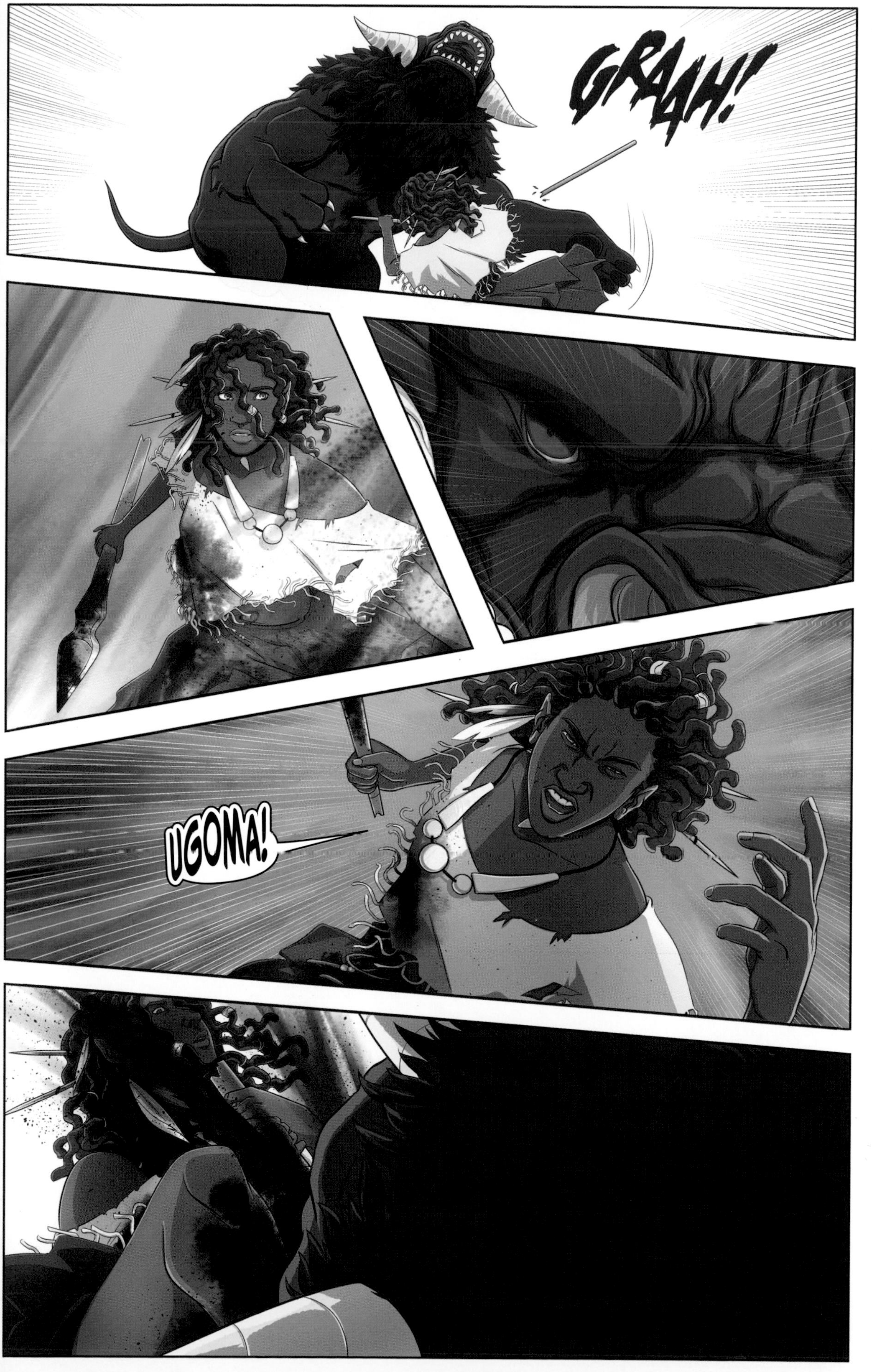
GRAAH!
UGOMA!

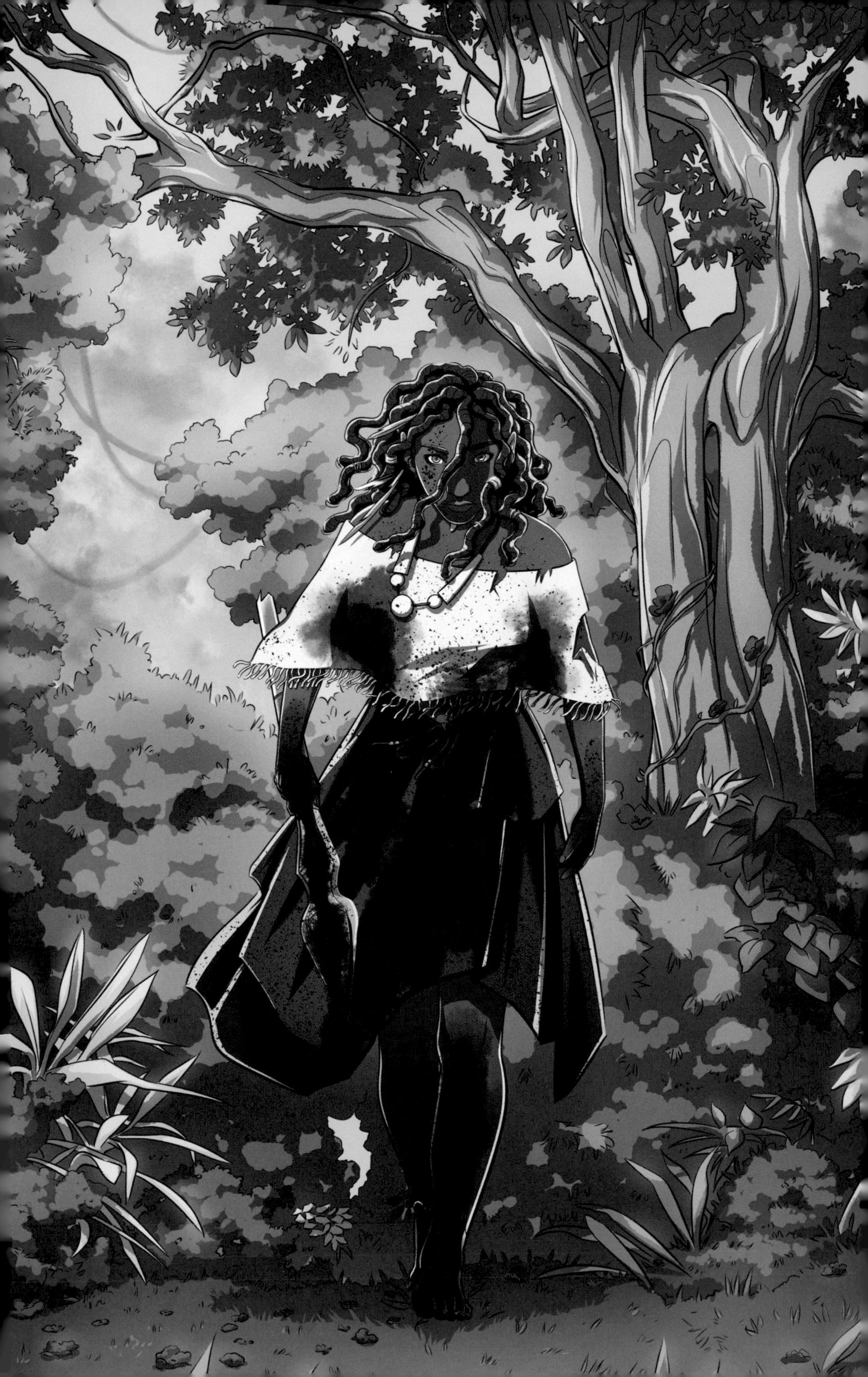

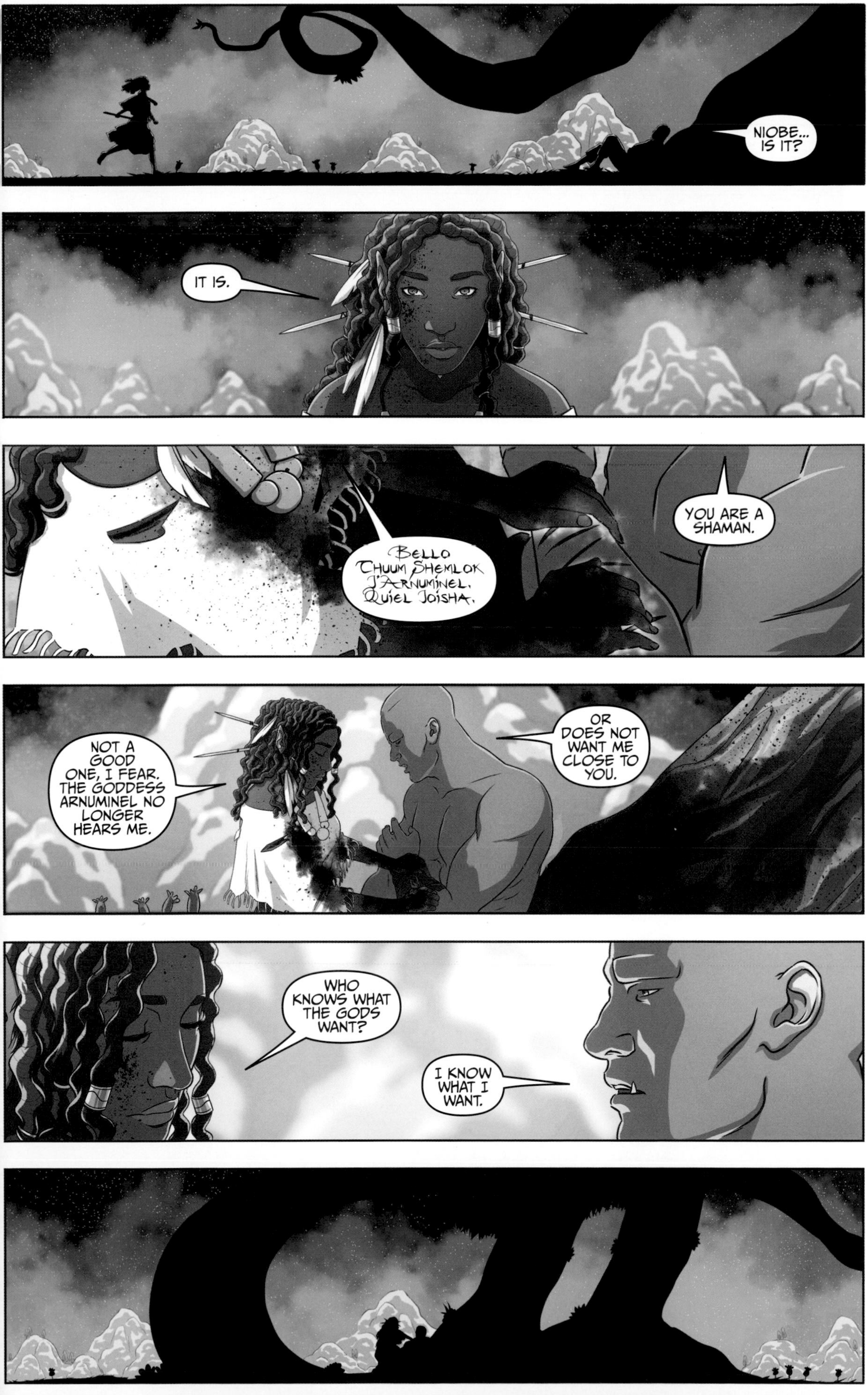
NIOBE... IS IT?
IT IS.
YOU ARE A SHAMAN.
Bello Chuum Shemlok J'Arnuminel. Quiel Joisha.
NOT A GOOD ONE, I FEAR. THE GODDESS ARNUMINEL NO LONGER HEARS ME.
OR DOES NOT WANT ME CLOSE TO YOU.
WHO KNOWS WHAT THE GODS WANT?
I KNOW WHAT I WANT.

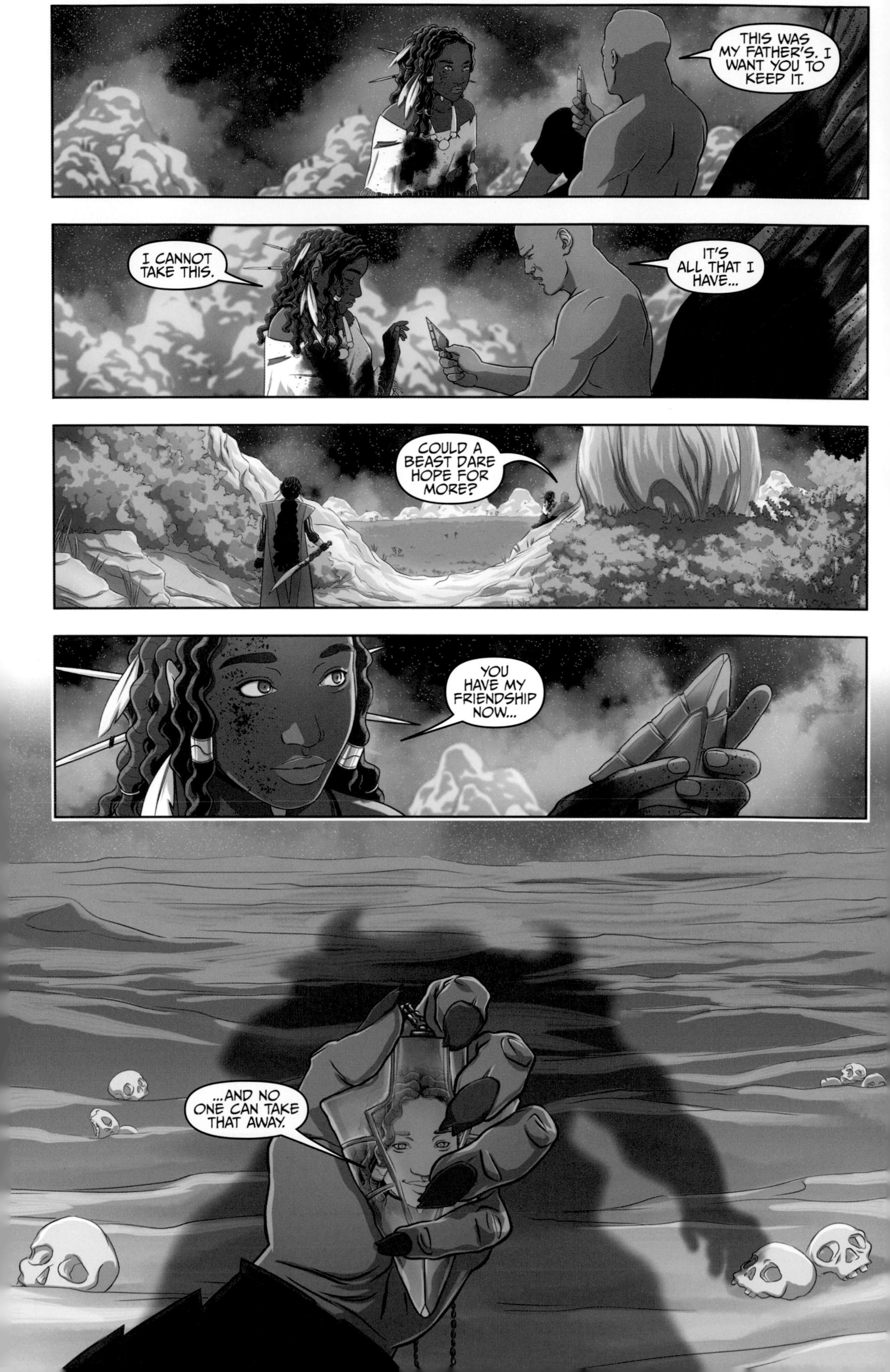
THIS WAS MY FATHER'S. I WANT YOU TO KEEP IT.
I CANNOT TAKE THIS.
IT'S ALL THAT I HAVE...
COULD A BEAST DARE HOPE FOR MORE?
YOU HAVE MY FRIENDSHIP NOW...
...AND NO ONE CAN TAKE THAT AWAY.

My faith is in the spirit of good, as I much I fall short. Not in the righteous or the writt[redacted]word, although song and sermon may move me to act. For therein lies the truth[redacted]action and deed maketh the human, not adherence to laws or a history writt[redacted]by conquerors. I am the fool who will give the shirt off my back, but I will neve[redacted]be foolish enough to put down my blade. I am not looking for a handout, a lectu[redacted]e, or even a fight… only a healing embrace.

Arnuminel is the embodiment of light and love on Asunda, the Goddess of Healing and Peace.

As the first daughter of Andarcil (King of the Heavens) and Madraq (Queen of Death), she was born moments after Arukas the Untamed (The Devil). In the bur[redacted]re of the spirit womb, the side of her face and body closest to Arukas was disfigured and twisted, while the other half remained beautiful like her brother's. Although armed with the power to heal others, she never tried to cure the scars her brother had left her. She did not blame him, for she could see beyond such things. Her love was a movement of the soul, not the body.

In the War of the Gods, when Arukas painted the heavens in blood, laying waste to all of the lesser Gods and angels with his white and terrible sword, it was Arnuminel who was his bane. Her love for him was such a fierce and blinding thing to behold that for the briefest of moments, it consumed his rage and disarmed his hate, forcing him to his knees. He grabbed at her flowing robes with bloodied hands, and looked up with eyes stung by sorrow and guilt. Could he have repented? We will never know[redacted]for as the tears fell from the would-be Devil, he was felled by his brothers Urzo[redacted] (God of War) and Powisienne (God of Nature), and cast down from the Pyramid of Heaven.

And so, Arukas the Untamed, stricken with grief and believing he had been tricked by his sister, the so-called pure Goddess, will never rest until he has enacted his vengeance upon her and her most blessed children, wiping them from the surface of the vast and volatile world of…

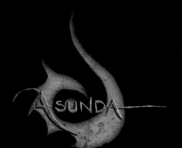

Chapter 3

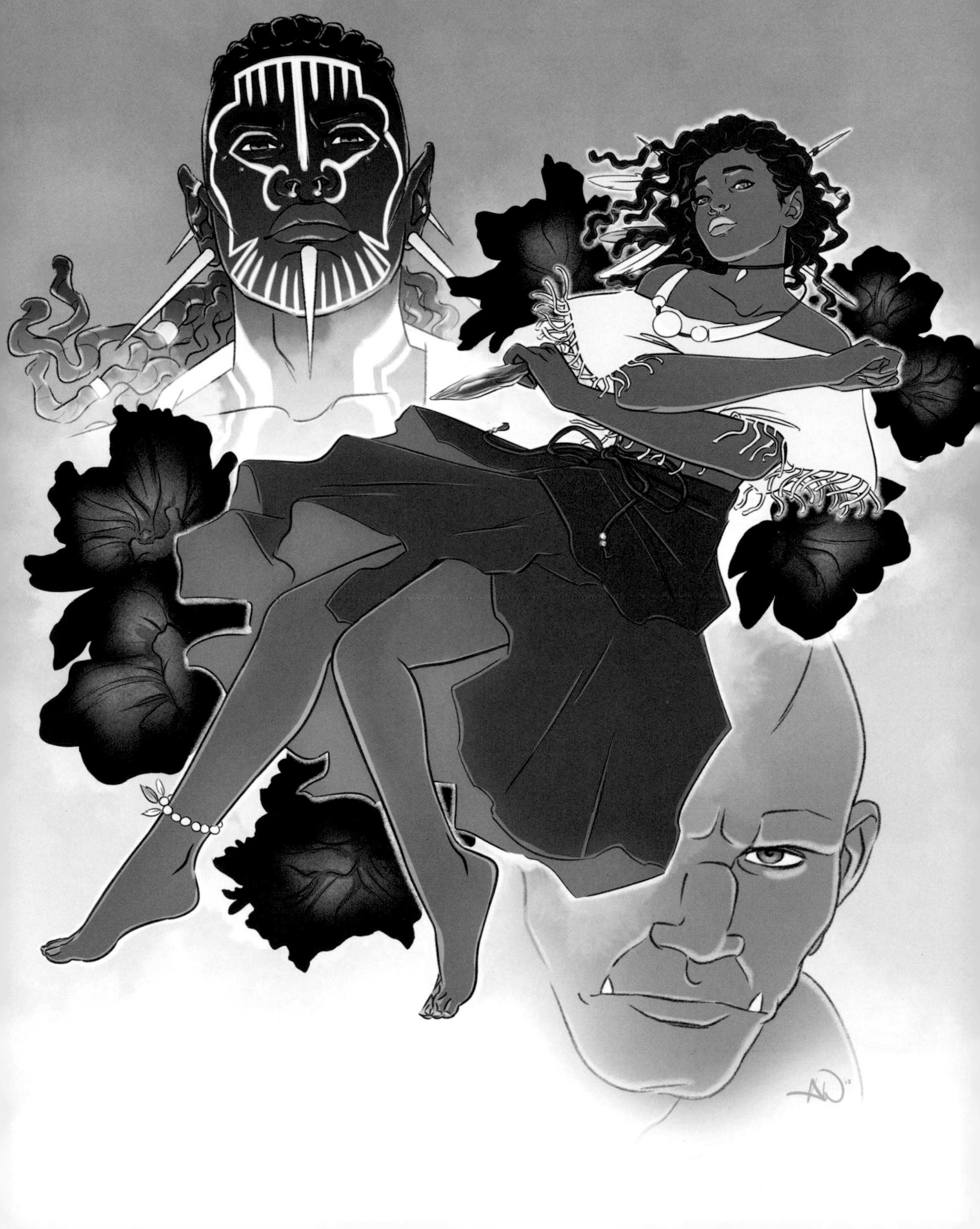

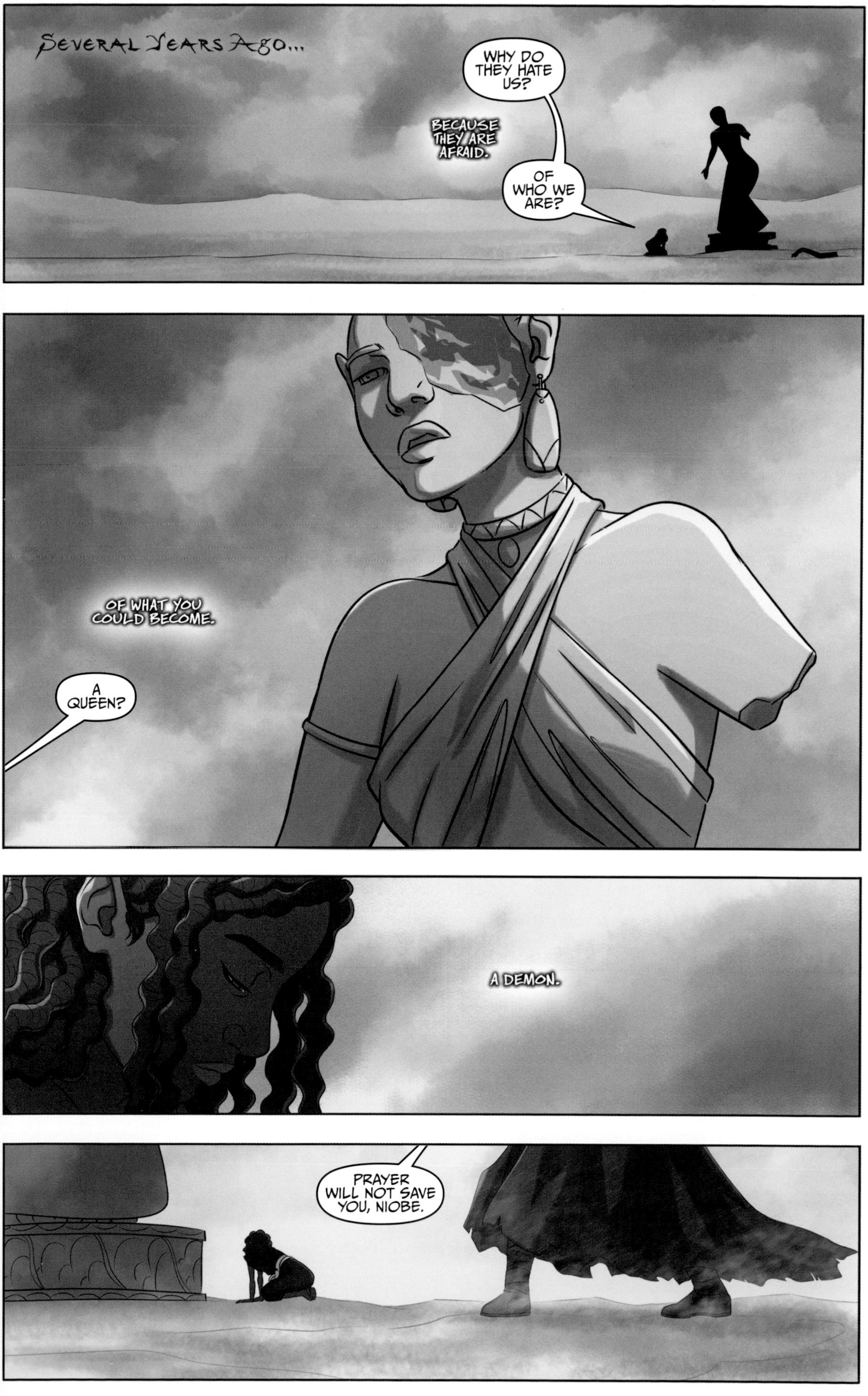

Several Years Ago...
WHY DO THEY HATE US?
BECAUSE THEY ARE AFRAID.
OF WHO WE ARE?
OF WHAT YOU COULD BECOME.
A QUEEN?
A DEMON.
PRAYER WILL NOT SAVE YOU, NIOBE.

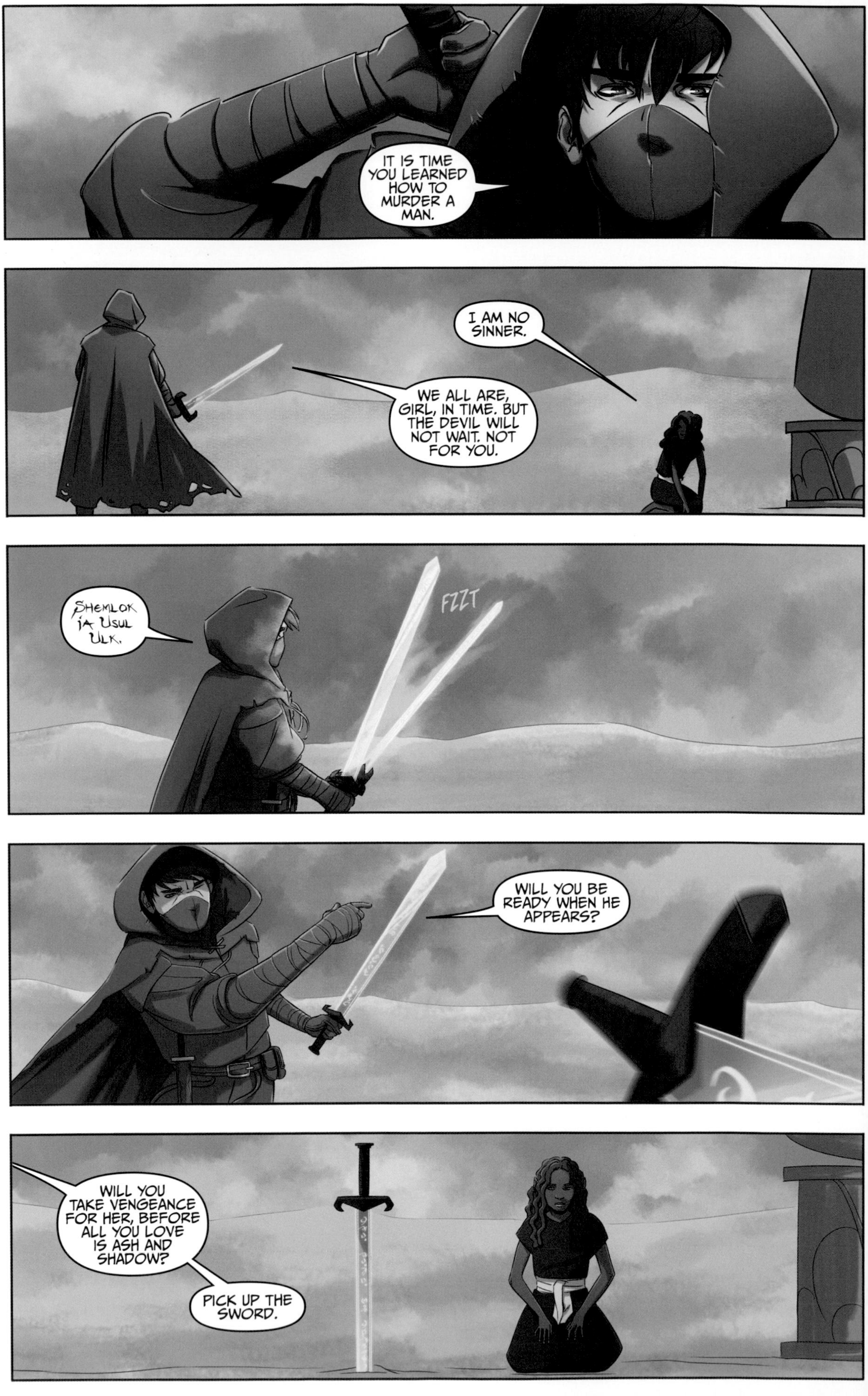
IT IS TIME YOU LEARNED HOW TO MURDER A MAN.
I AM NO SINNER.
WE ALL ARE, GIRL, IN TIME. BUT THE DEVIL WILL NOT WAIT. NOT FOR YOU.
SHEMLOK ÍA USUL ULK.
FZZT
WILL YOU BE READY WHEN HE APPEARS?
WILL YOU TAKE VENGEANCE FOR HER, BEFORE ALL YOU LOVE IS ASH AND SHADOW?
PICK UP THE SWORD.

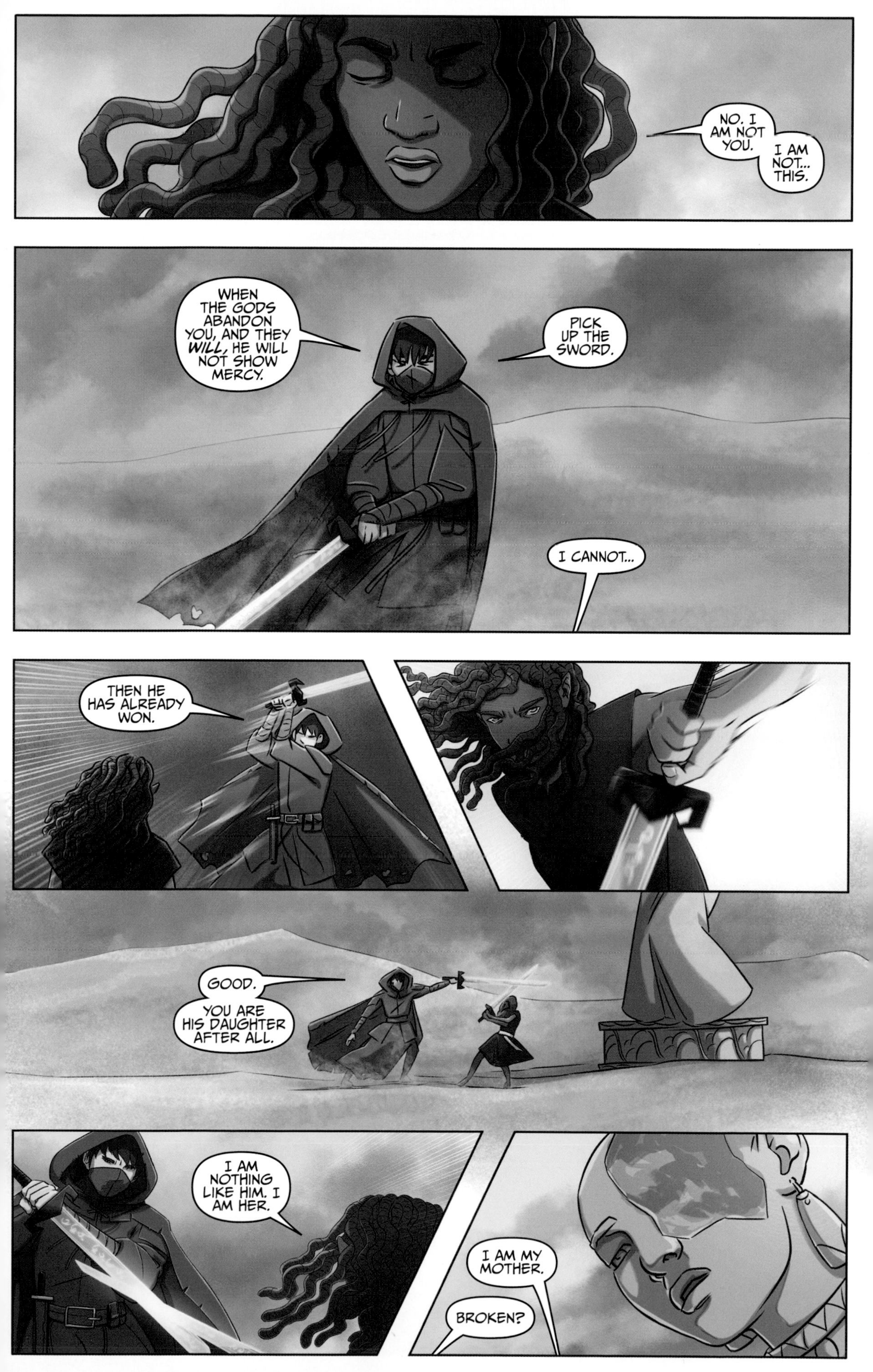
NO. I AM NOT YOU.
I AM NOT... THIS.
WHEN THE GODS ABANDON YOU, AND THEY WILL, HE WILL NOT SHOW MERCY.
PICK UP THE SWORD.
I CANNOT...
THEN HE HAS ALREADY WON.
GOOD.
YOU ARE HIS DAUGHTER AFTER ALL.
I AM NOTHING LIKE HIM. I AM HER.
I AM MY MOTHER.
BROKEN?

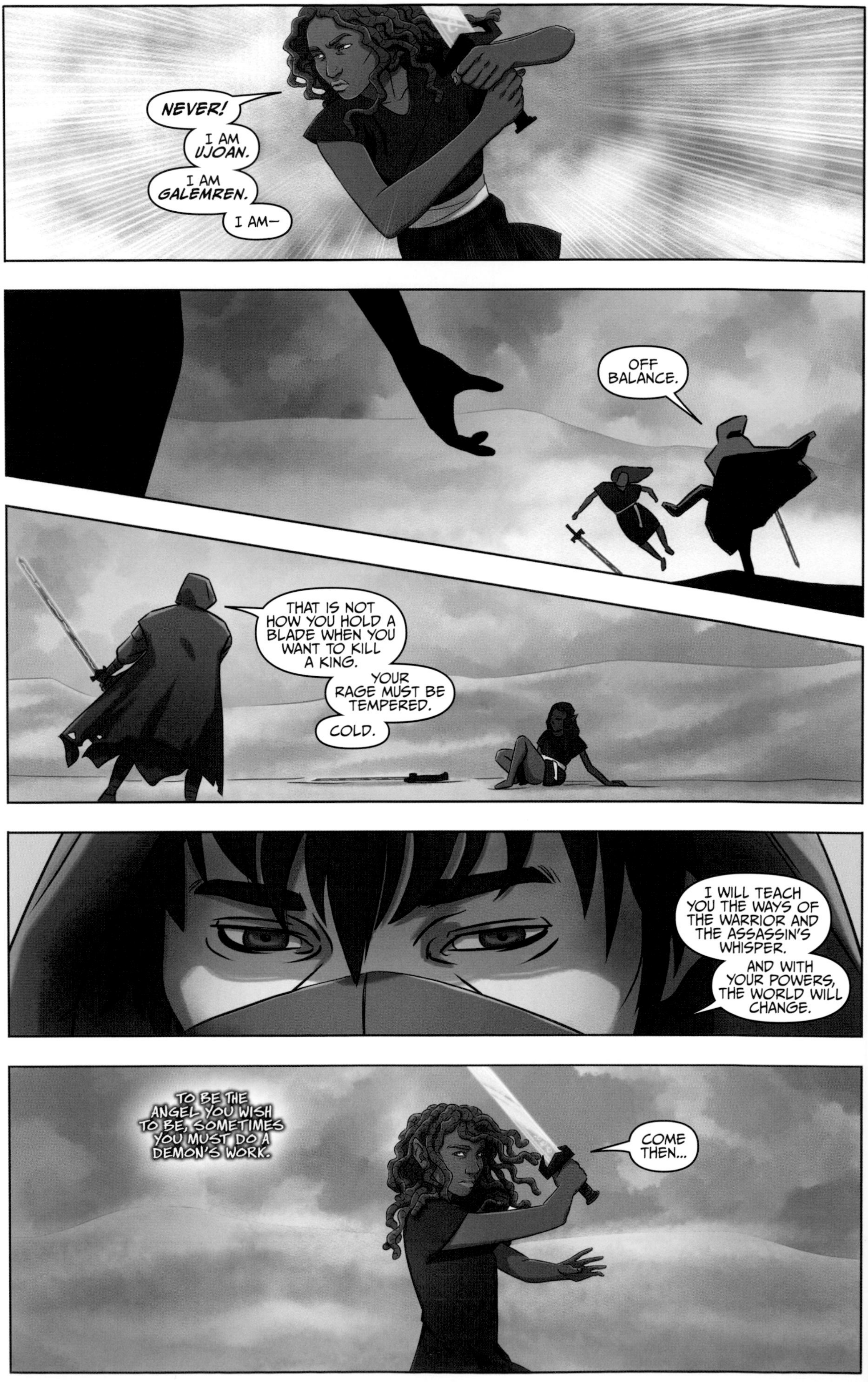
NEVER!
I AM UJOAN.
I AM GALEMREN.
I AM—
OFF BALANCE.
THAT IS NOT HOW YOU HOLD A BLADE WHEN YOU WANT TO KILL A KING.
YOUR RAGE MUST BE TEMPERED.
COLD.
I WILL TEACH YOU THE WAYS OF THE WARRIOR AND THE ASSASSIN'S WHISPER.
AND WITH YOUR POWERS, THE WORLD WILL CHANGE.
TO BE THE ANGEL YOU WISH TO BE, SOMETIMES YOU MUST DO A DEMON'S WORK.
COME THEN...

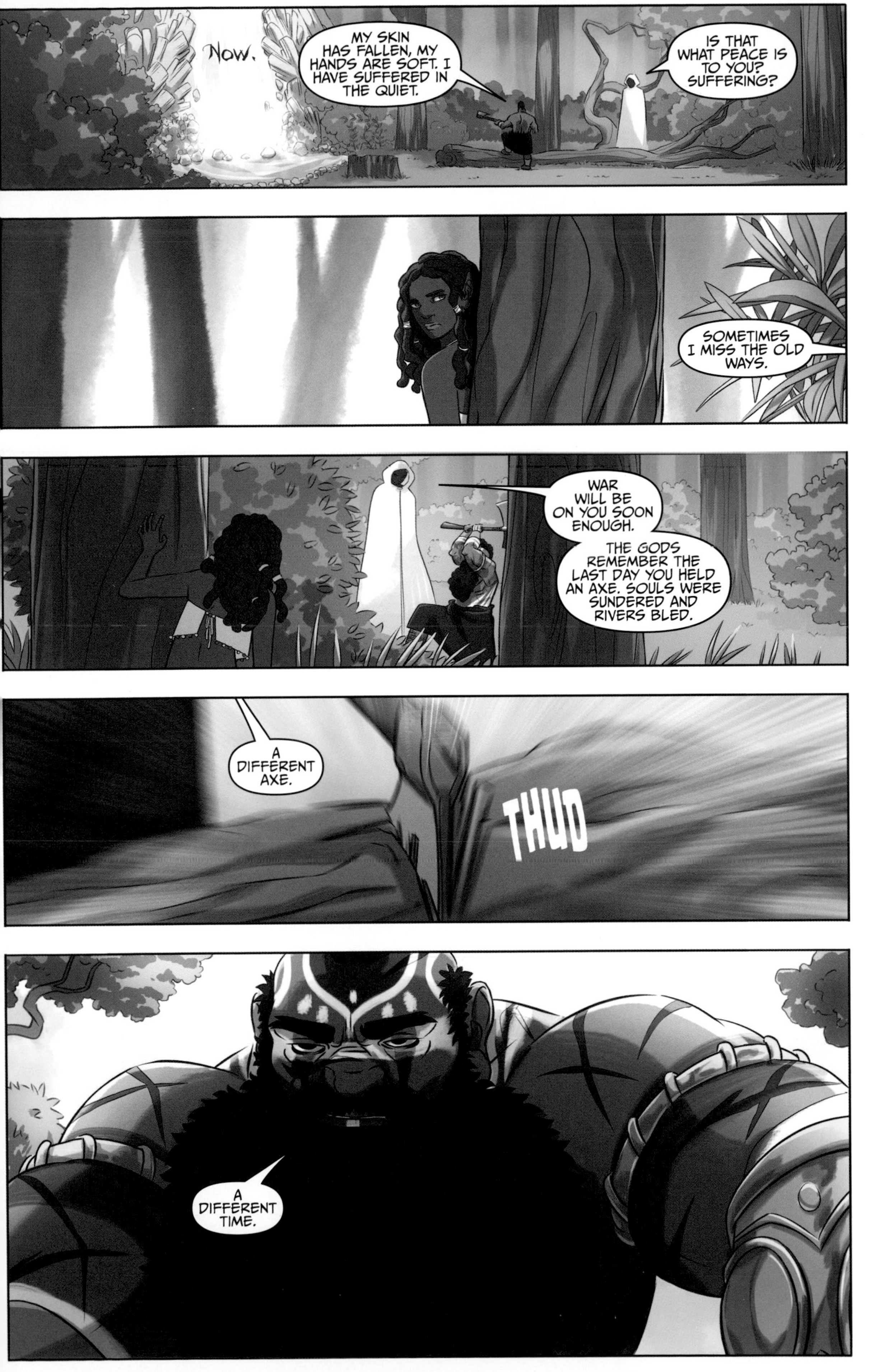
Now.
MY SKIN HAS FALLEN, MY HANDS ARE SOFT. I HAVE SUFFERED IN THE QUIET.
IS THAT WHAT PEACE IS TO YOU? SUFFERING?
SOMETIMES I MISS THE OLD WAYS.
WAR WILL BE ON YOU SOON ENOUGH.
THE GODS REMEMBER THE LAST DAY YOU HELD AN AXE. SOULS WERE SUNDERED AND RIVERS BLED.
A DIFFERENT AXE.
THUD
A DIFFERENT TIME.

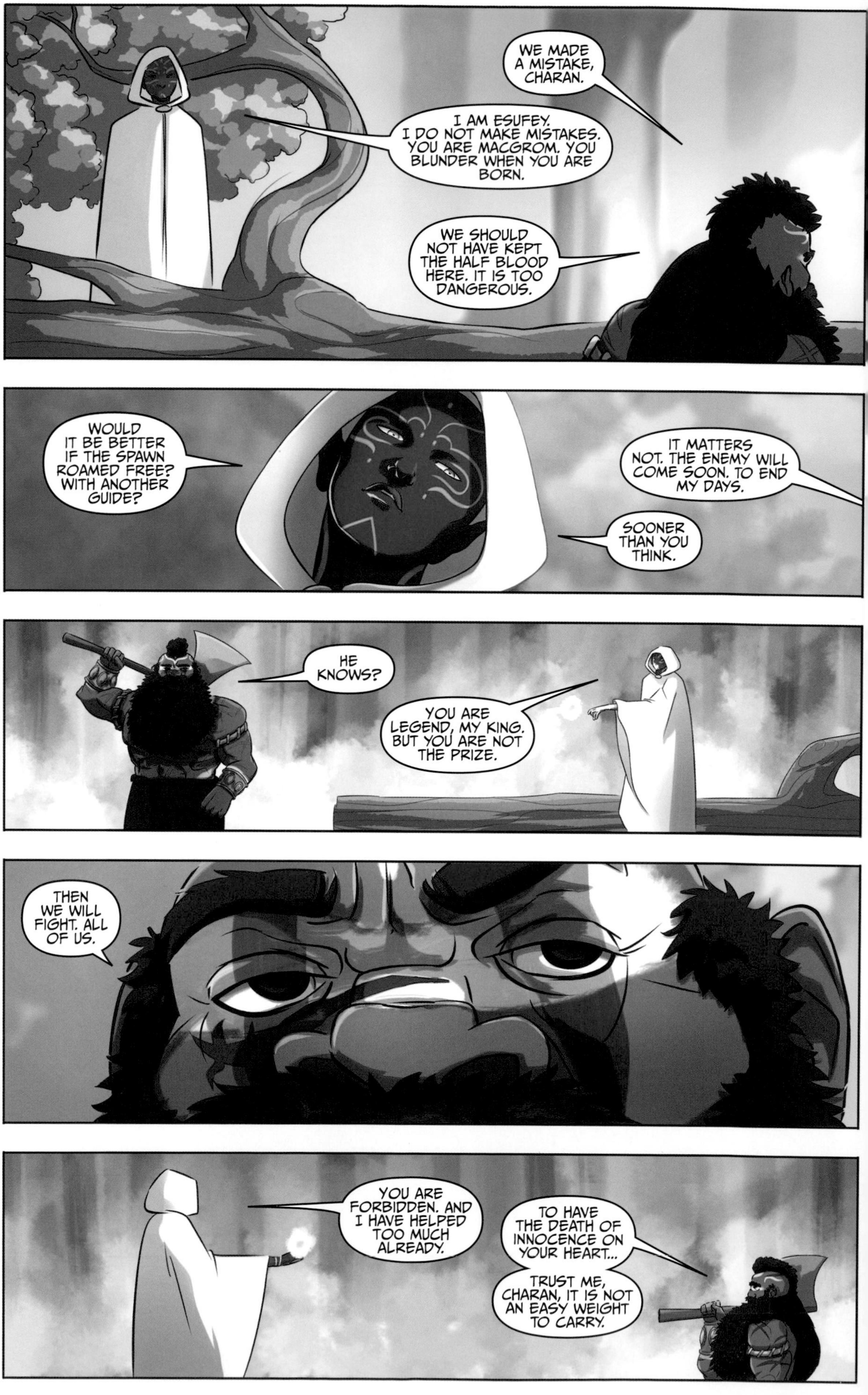
WE MADE A MISTAKE, CHARAN.
I AM ESUFEY. I DO NOT MAKE MISTAKES. YOU ARE MACGROM. YOU BLUNDER WHEN YOU ARE BORN.
WE SHOULD NOT HAVE KEPT THE HALF BLOOD HERE. IT IS TOO DANGEROUS.
WOULD IT BE BETTER IF THE SPAWN ROAMED FREE? WITH ANOTHER GUIDE?
IT MATTERS NOT. THE ENEMY WILL COME SOON. TO END MY DAYS.
SOONER THAN YOU THINK.
HE KNOWS?
YOU ARE LEGEND, MY KING. BUT YOU ARE NOT THE PRIZE.
THEN WE WILL FIGHT. ALL OF US.
YOU ARE FORBIDDEN. AND I HAVE HELPED TOO MUCH ALREADY.
TO HAVE THE DEATH OF INNOCENCE ON YOUR HEART...
TRUST ME, CHARAN, IT IS NOT AN EASY WEIGHT TO CARRY.

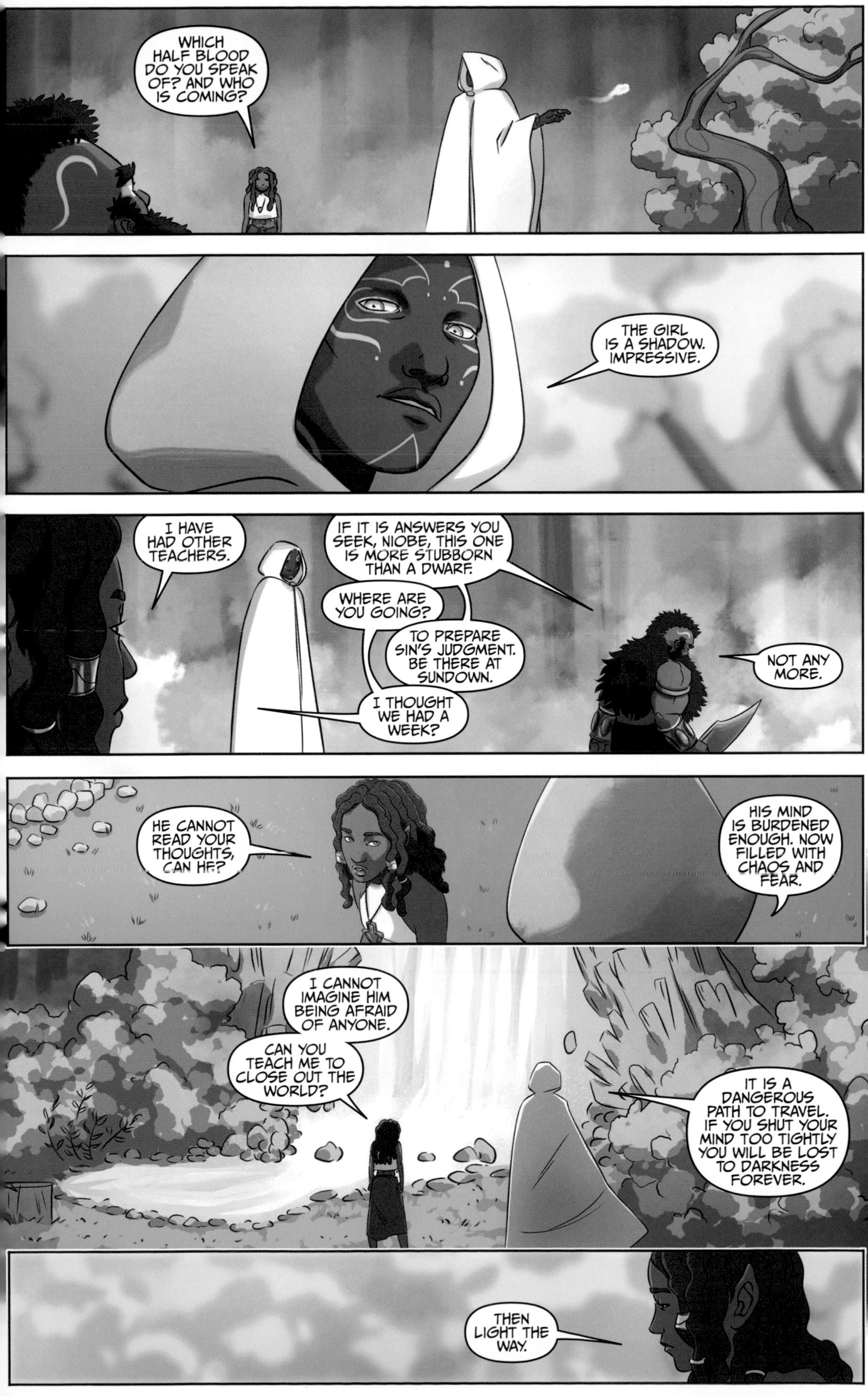
WHICH HALF BLOOD DO YOU SPEAK OF? AND WHO IS COMING?
THE GIRL IS A SHADOW. IMPRESSIVE.
I HAVE HAD OTHER TEACHERS.
IF IT IS ANSWERS YOU SEEK, NIOBE, THIS ONE IS MORE STUBBORN THAN A DWARF.
WHERE ARE YOU GOING?
TO PREPARE SIN'S JUDGMENT. BE THERE AT SUNDOWN.
I THOUGHT WE HAD A WEEK?
NOT ANY MORE.
HE CANNOT READ YOUR THOUGHTS, CAN HE?
HIS MIND IS BURDENED ENOUGH. NOW FILLED WITH CHAOS AND FEAR.
I CANNOT IMAGINE HIM BEING AFRAID OF ANYONE.
CAN YOU TEACH ME TO CLOSE OUT THE WORLD?
IT IS A DANGEROUS PATH TO TRAVEL. IF YOU SHUT YOUR MIND TOO TIGHTLY YOU WILL BE LOST TO DARKNESS FOREVER.
THEN LIGHT THE WAY.

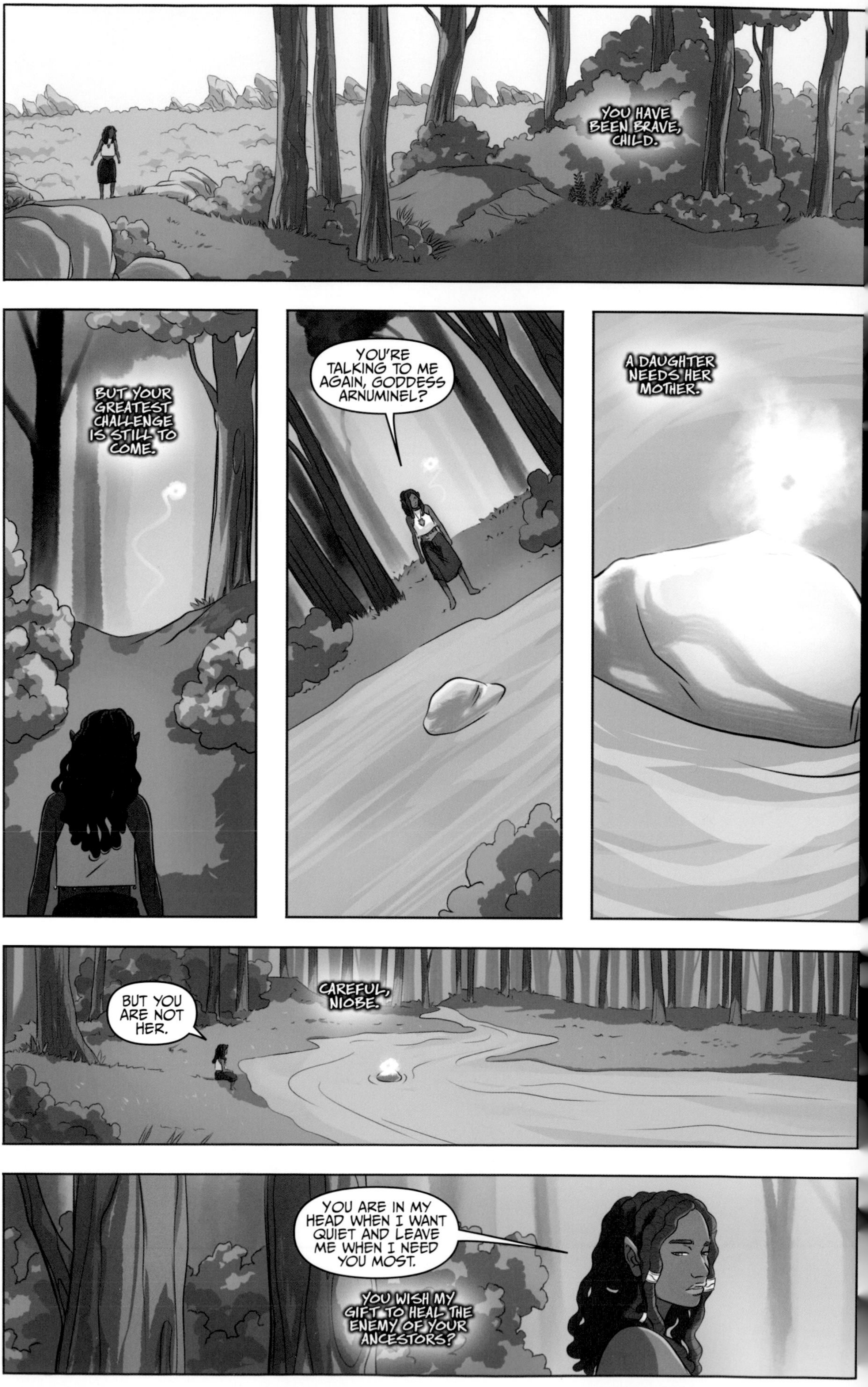
YOU HAVE BEEN BRAVE, CHILD.
BUT YOUR GREATEST CHALLENGE IS STILL TO COME.
YOU'RE TALKING TO ME AGAIN, GODDESS ARNUMINEL?
A DAUGHTER NEEDS HER MOTHER.
BUT YOU ARE NOT HER.
CAREFUL, NIOBE.
YOU ARE IN MY HEAD WHEN I WANT QUIET AND LEAVE ME WHEN I NEED YOU MOST.
YOU WISH MY GIFT TO HEAL THE ENEMY OF YOUR ANCESTORS?

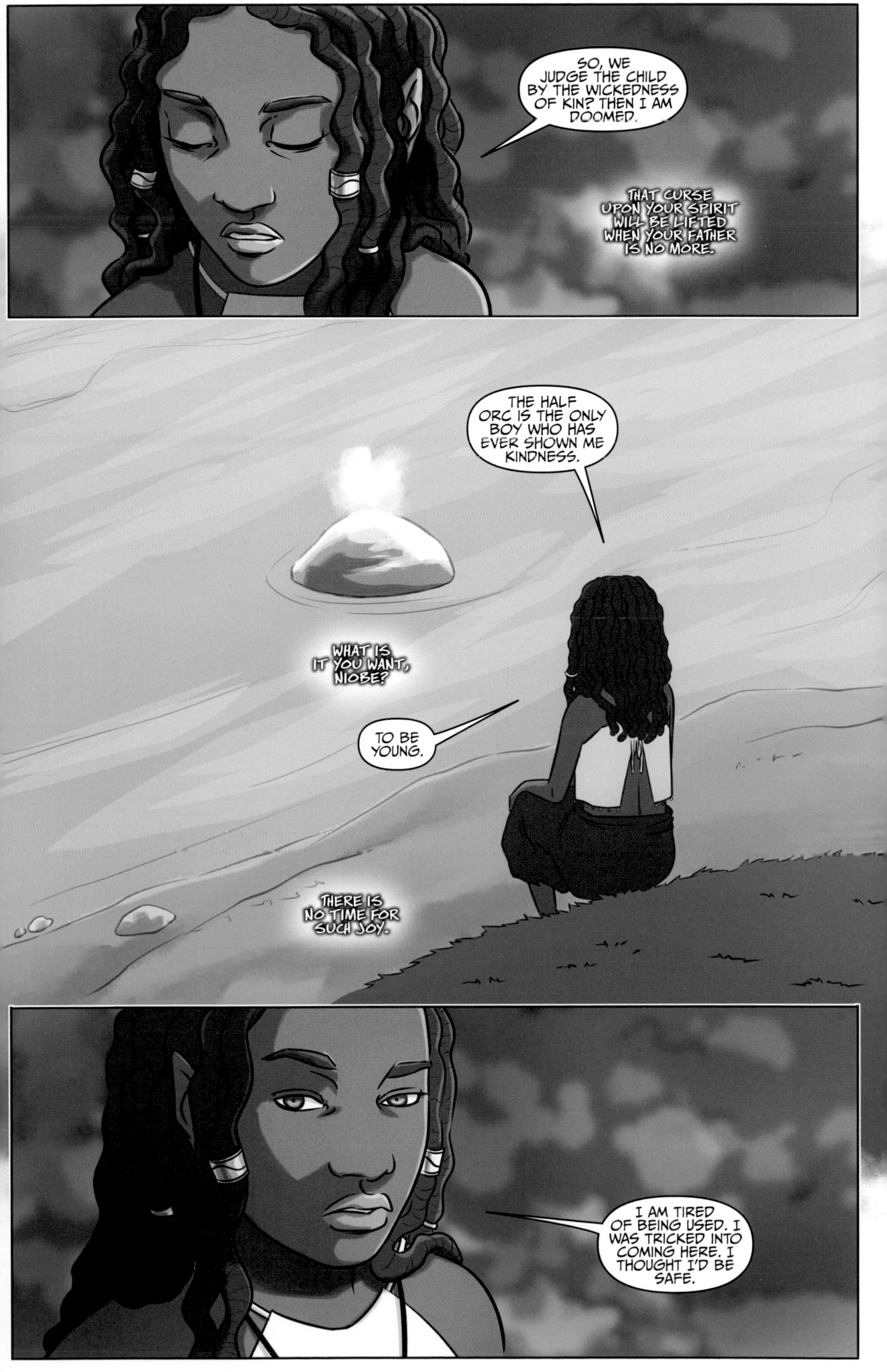
SO, WE JUDGE THE CHILD BY THE WICKEDNESS OF KIN? THEN I AM DOOMED.
THAT CURSE UPON YOUR SPIRIT WILL BE LIFTED WHEN YOUR FATHER IS NO MORE.
THE HALF ORC IS THE ONLY BOY WHO HAS EVER SHOWN ME KINDNESS.
WHAT IS IT YOU WANT, NIOBE?
TO BE YOUNG.
THERE IS NO TIME FOR SUCH JOY.
I AM TIRED OF BEING USED. I WAS TRICKED INTO COMING HERE. I THOUGHT I'D BE SAFE.

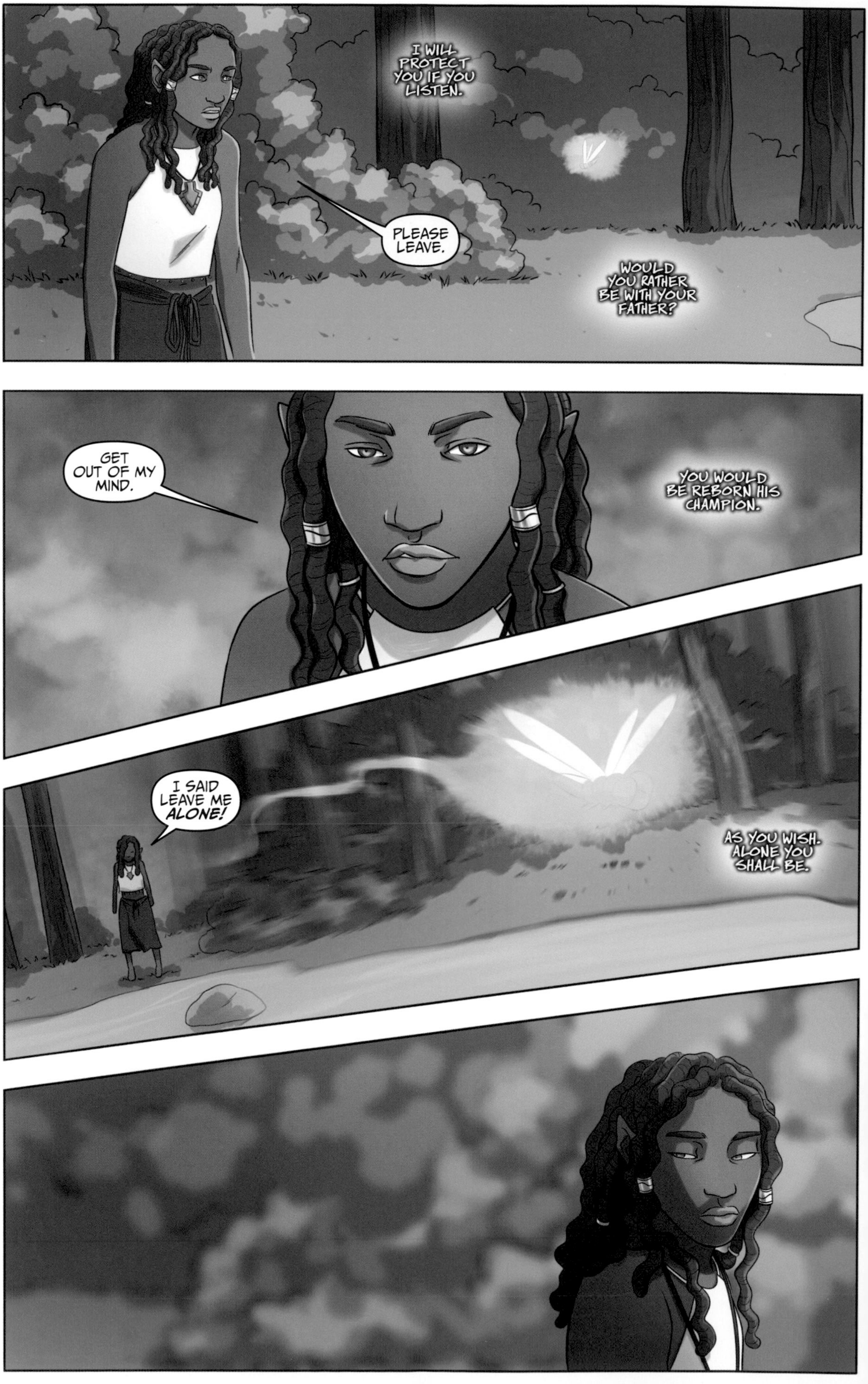

I WILL PROTECT YOU IF YOU LISTEN.
PLEASE LEAVE.
WOULD YOU RATHER BE WITH YOUR FATHER?
GET OUT OF MY MIND.
YOU WOULD BE REBORN HIS CHAMPION.
I SAID LEAVE ME *ALONE!*
AS YOU WISH. ALONE YOU SHALL BE.

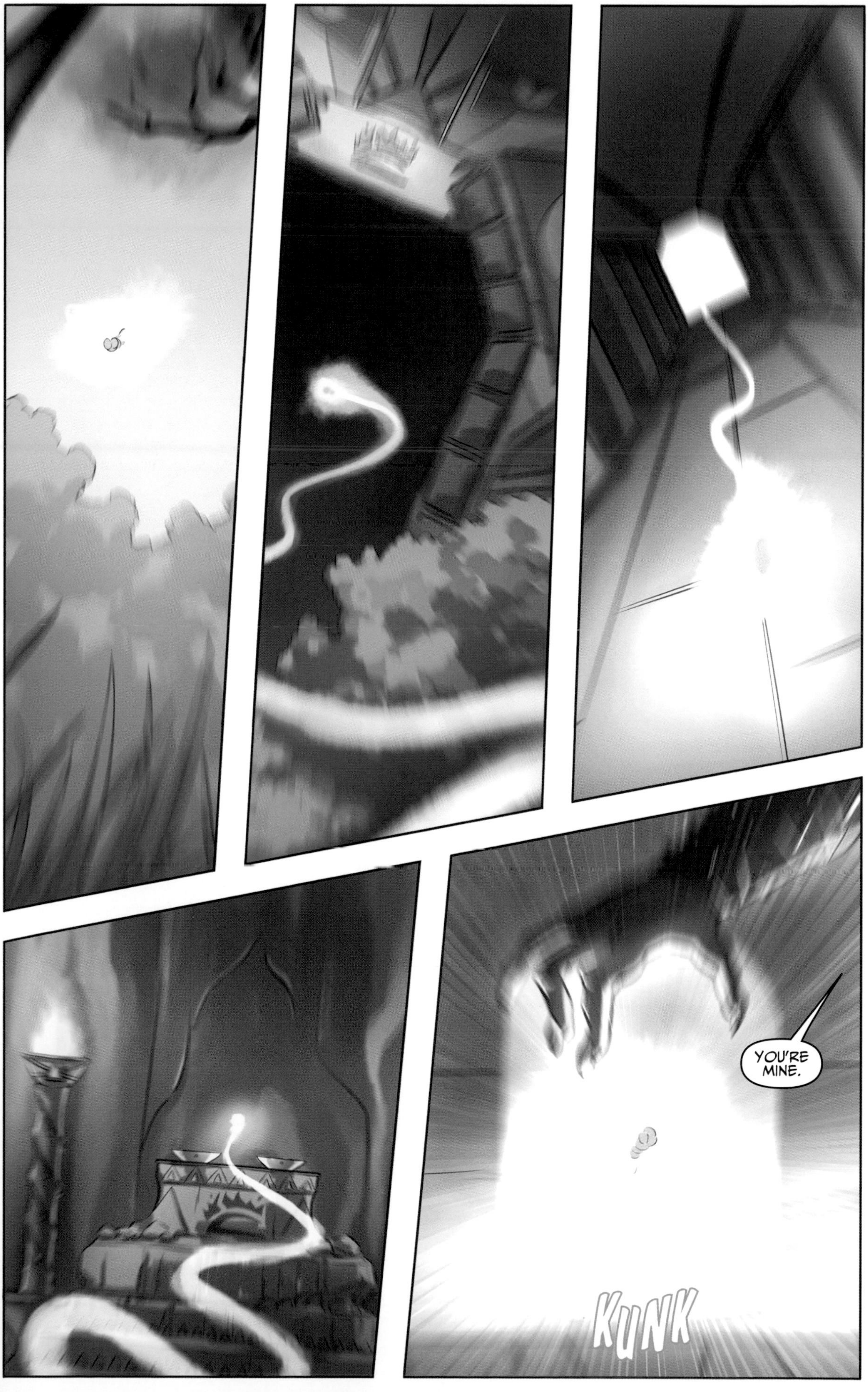
YOU'RE MINE.
KUNK

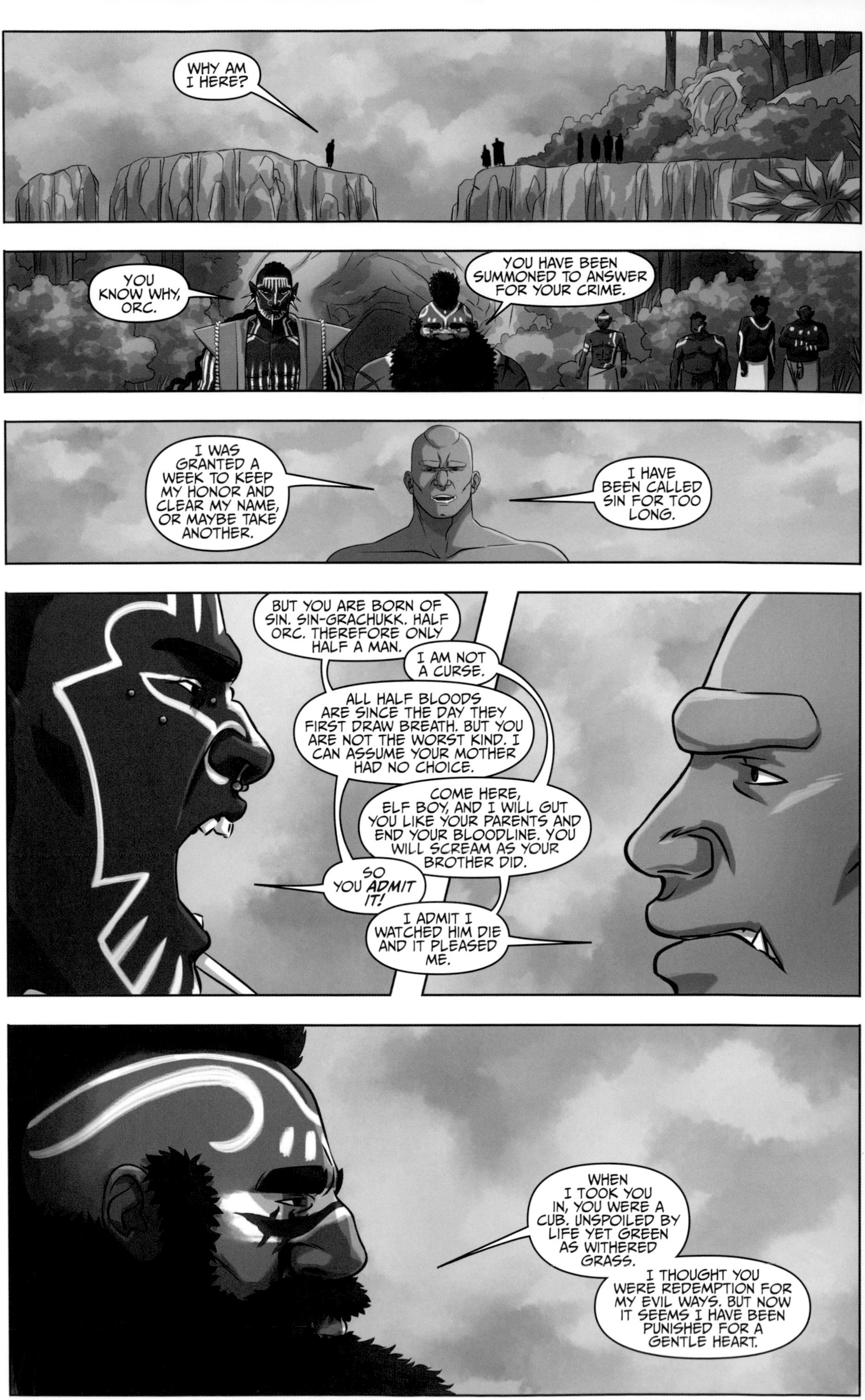
WHY AM I HERE?
YOU KNOW WHY, ORC.
YOU HAVE BEEN SUMMONED TO ANSWER FOR YOUR CRIME.
I WAS GRANTED A WEEK TO KEEP MY HONOR AND CLEAR MY NAME, OR MAYBE TAKE ANOTHER.
I HAVE BEEN CALLED SIN FOR TOO LONG.
BUT YOU ARE BORN OF SIN. SIN-GRACHUKK. HALF ORC. THEREFORE ONLY HALF A MAN.
I AM NOT A CURSE.
ALL HALF BLOODS ARE SINCE THE DAY THEY FIRST DRAW BREATH. BUT YOU ARE NOT THE WORST KIND. I CAN ASSUME YOUR MOTHER HAD NO CHOICE.
COME HERE, ELF BOY, AND I WILL GUT YOU LIKE YOUR PARENTS AND END YOUR BLOODLINE. YOU WILL SCREAM AS YOUR BROTHER DID.
SO YOU ADMIT IT!
I ADMIT I WATCHED HIM DIE AND IT PLEASED ME.
WHEN I TOOK YOU IN, YOU WERE A CUB. UNSPOILED BY LIFE YET GREEN AS WITHERED GRASS.
I THOUGHT YOU WERE REDEMPTION FOR MY EVIL WAYS. BUT NOW IT SEEMS I HAVE BEEN PUNISHED FOR A GENTLE HEART.

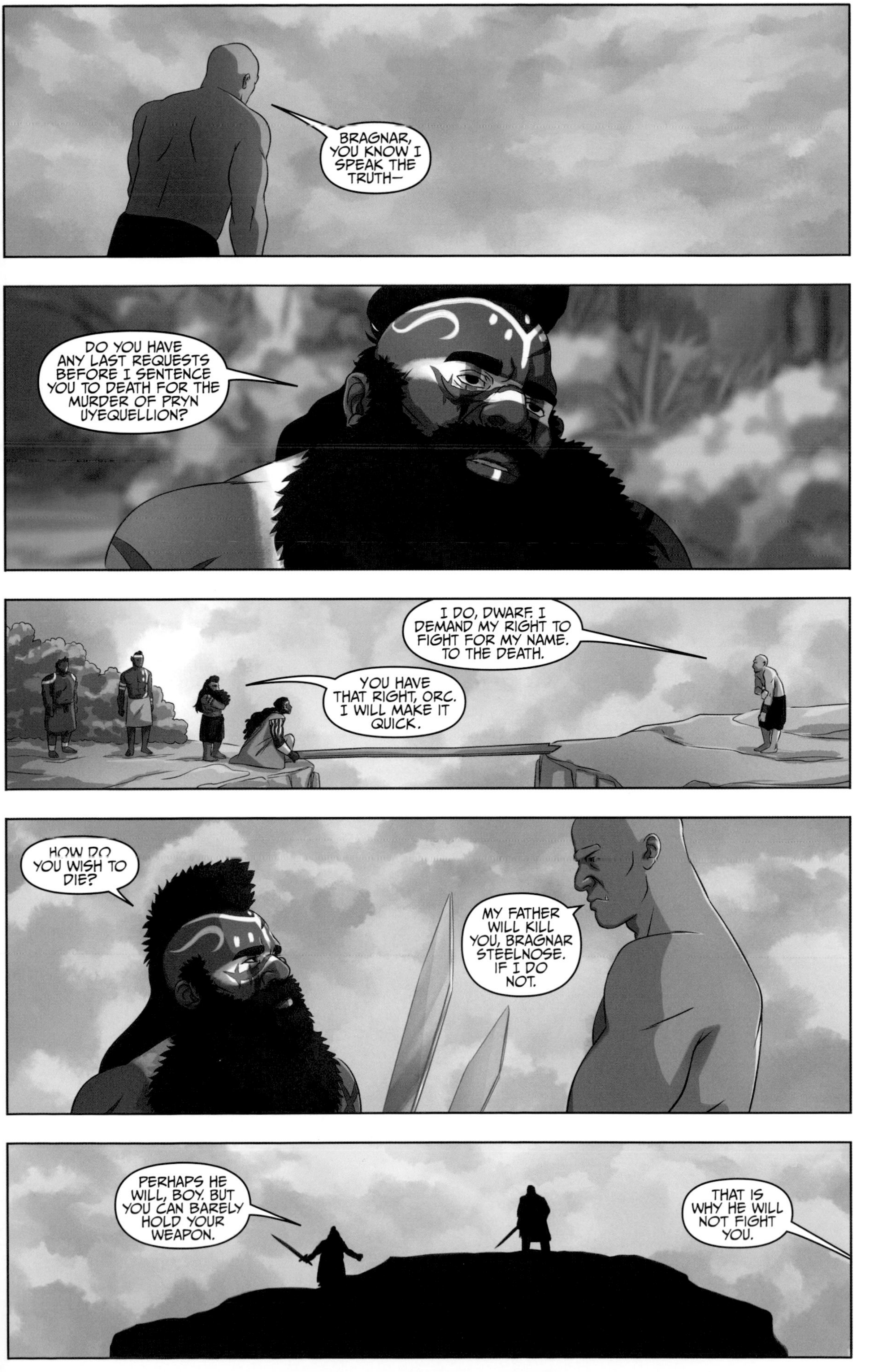
BRAGNAR, YOU KNOW I SPEAK THE TRUTH—
DO YOU HAVE ANY LAST REQUESTS BEFORE I SENTENCE YOU TO DEATH FOR THE MURDER OF PRYN UYEQUELLION?
I DO, DWARF. I DEMAND MY RIGHT TO FIGHT FOR MY NAME. TO THE DEATH.
YOU HAVE THAT RIGHT, ORC. I WILL MAKE IT QUICK.
HOW DO YOU WISH TO DIE?
MY FATHER WILL KILL YOU, BRAGNAR STEELNOSE. IF I DO NOT.
PERHAPS HE WILL, BOY. BUT YOU CAN BARELY HOLD YOUR WEAPON.
THAT IS WHY HE WILL NOT FIGHT YOU.

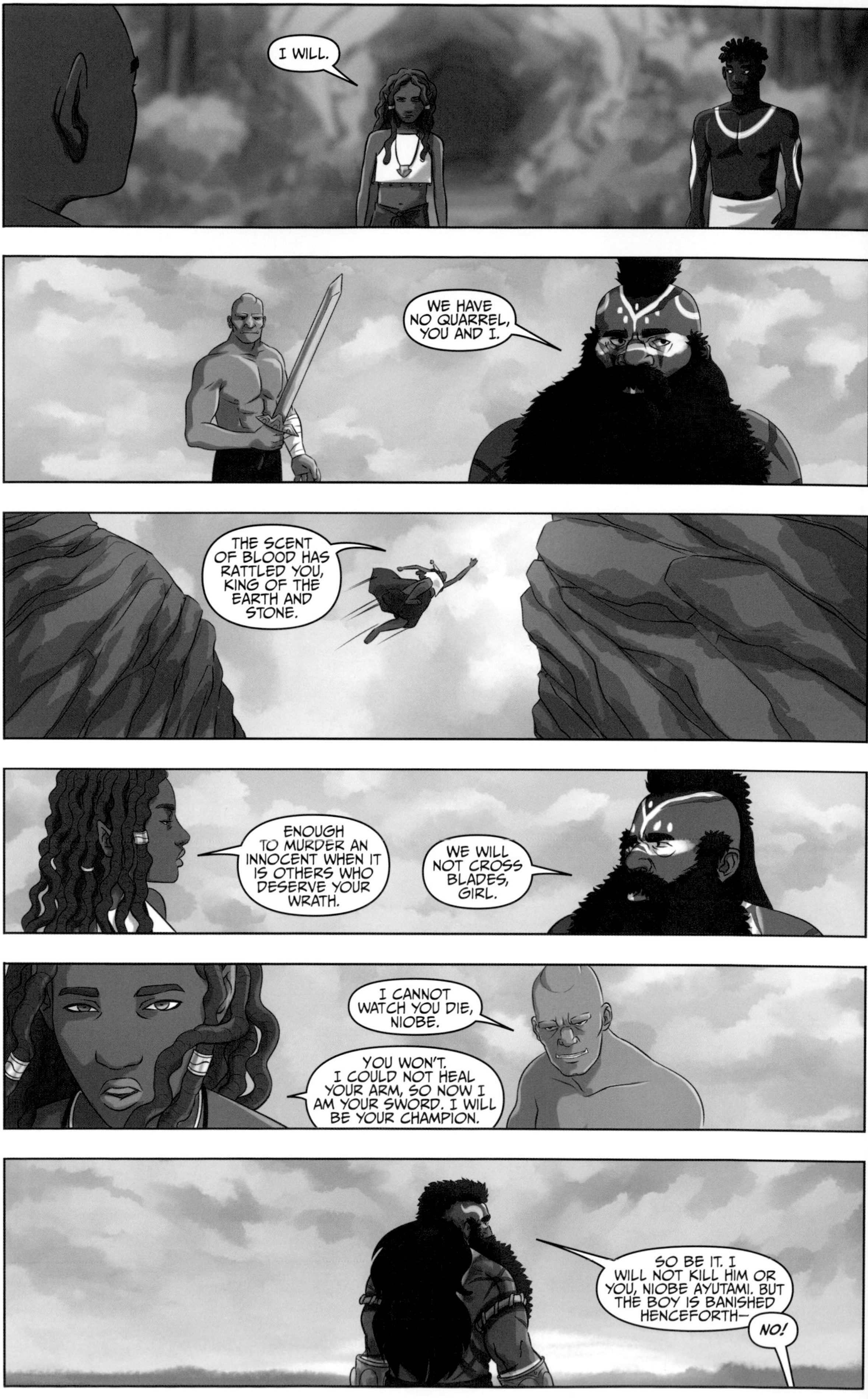
I WILL.
WE HAVE NO QUARREL, YOU AND I.
THE SCENT OF BLOOD HAS RATTLED YOU, KING OF THE EARTH AND STONE.
ENOUGH TO MURDER AN INNOCENT WHEN IT IS OTHERS WHO DESERVE YOUR WRATH.
WE WILL NOT CROSS BLADES, GIRL.
I CANNOT WATCH YOU DIE, NIOBE.
YOU WON'T. I COULD NOT HEAL YOUR ARM, SO NOW I AM YOUR SWORD. I WILL BE YOUR CHAMPION.
SO BE IT. I WILL NOT KILL HIM OR YOU, NIOBE AYUTAMI. BUT THE BOY IS BANISHED HENCEFORTH—
NO!

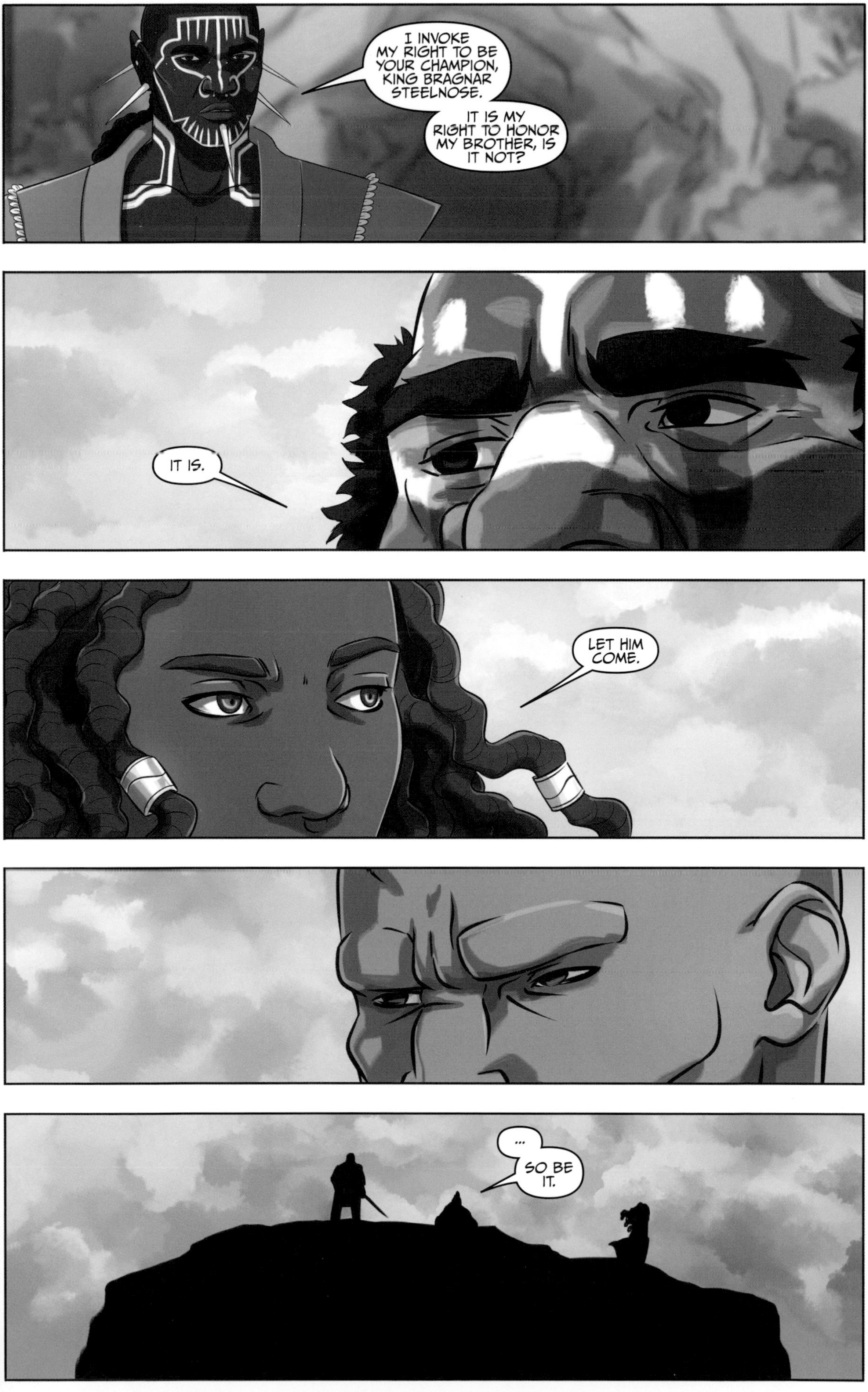
I INVOKE MY RIGHT TO BE YOUR CHAMPION, KING BRAGNAR STEELNOSE.
IT IS MY RIGHT TO HONOR MY BROTHER, IS IT NOT?
IT IS.
LET HIM COME.
...
SO BE IT.

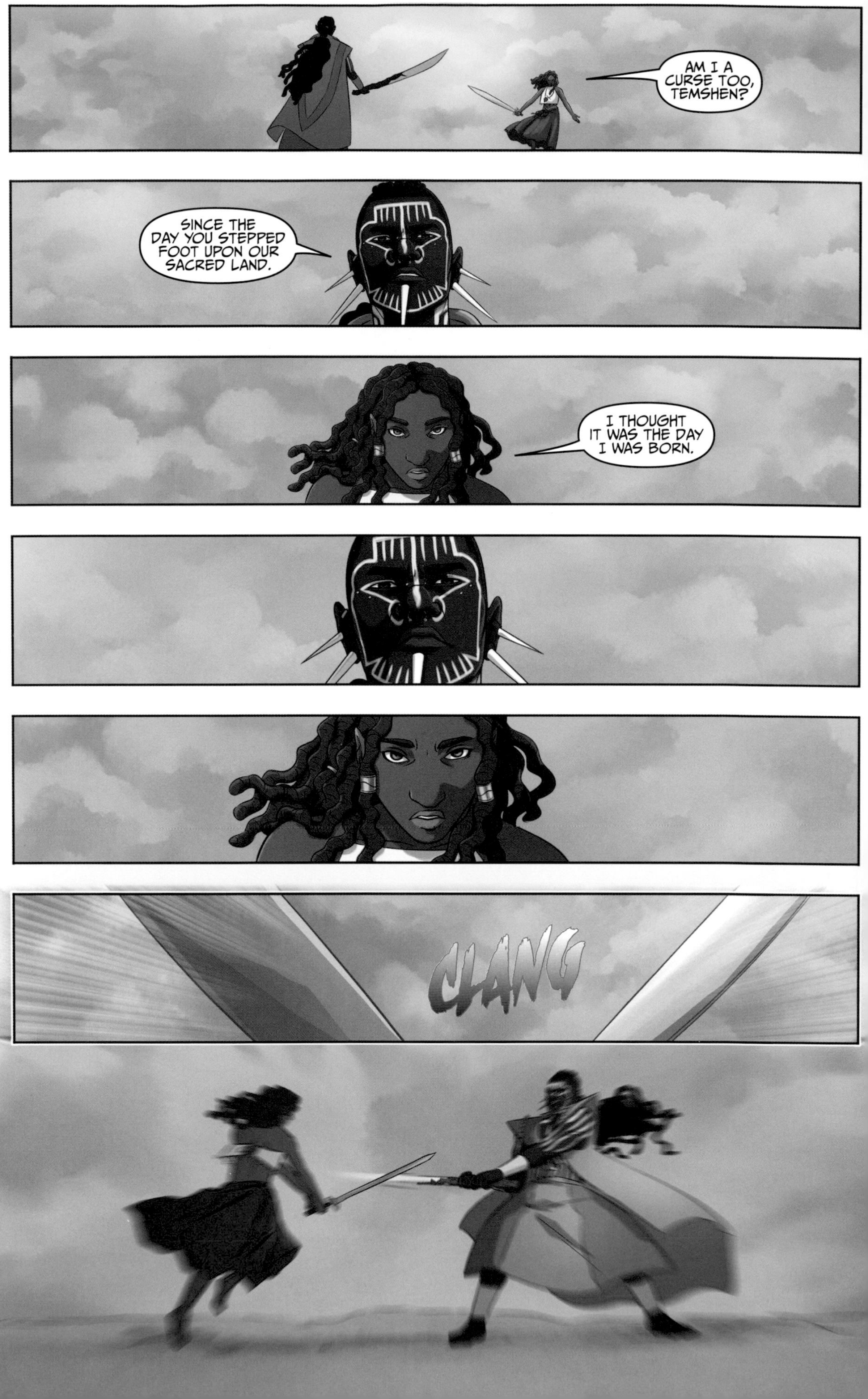
AM I A CURSE TOO, TEMSHEN?
SINCE THE DAY YOU STEPPED FOOT UPON OUR SACRED LAND.
I THOUGHT IT WAS THE DAY I WAS BORN.
CLANG

YOU LOVE HIM? INSTEAD OF YOUR OWN PEOPLE?

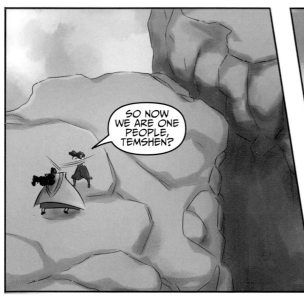

SO NOW WE ARE ONE PEOPLE, TEMSHEN?

OR DO YOU REALLY MEAN INSTEAD OF YOU?

I WOULD NOT WANT YOU, SHE TRIBE.

I AM STRONGER.

I AM QUICKER.

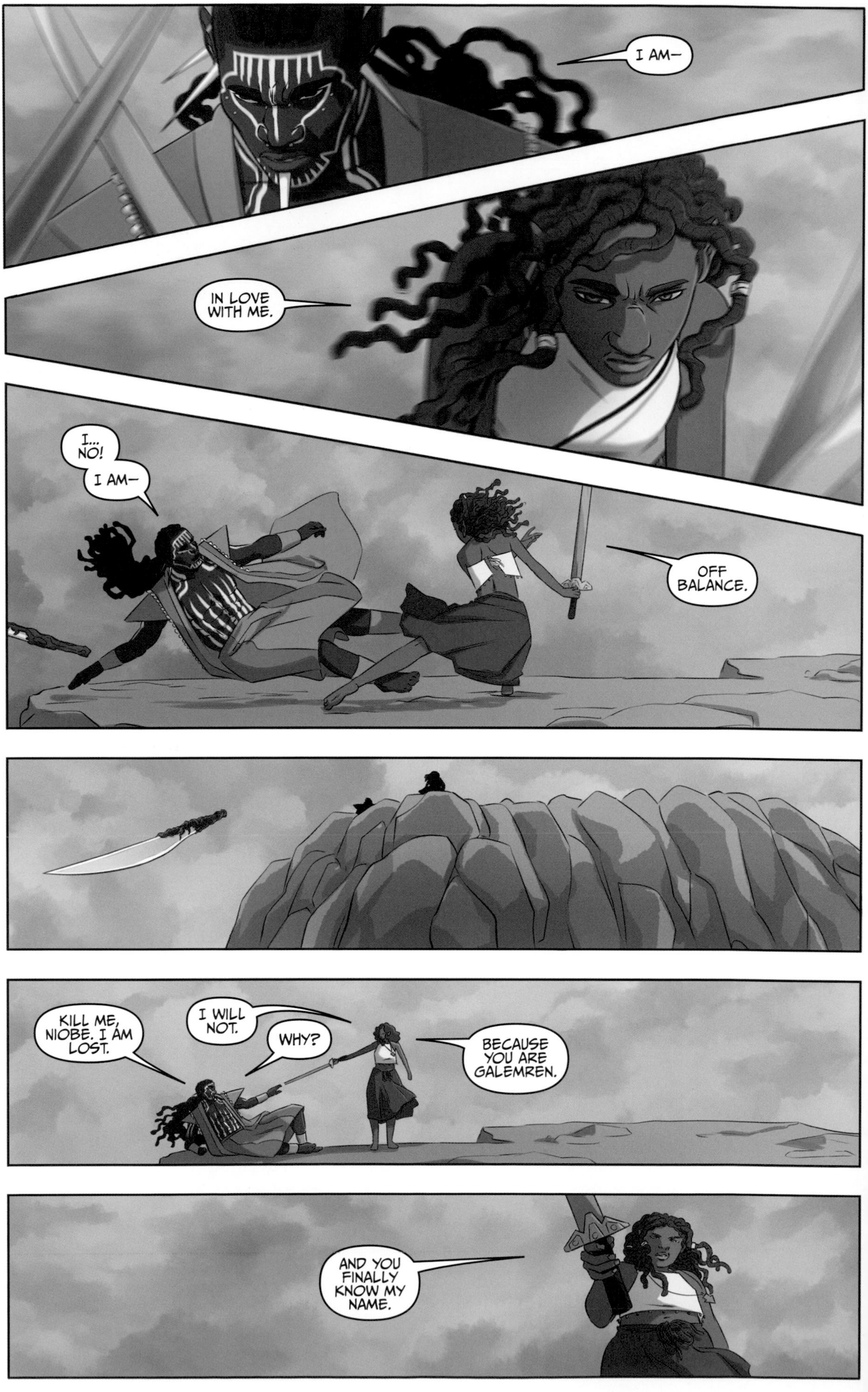
I AM—
IN LOVE WITH ME.
I... NO!
I AM—
OFF BALANCE.
KILL ME, NIOBE. I AM LOST.
I WILL NOT.
WHY?
BECAUSE YOU ARE GALEMREN.
AND YOU FINALLY KNOW MY NAME.

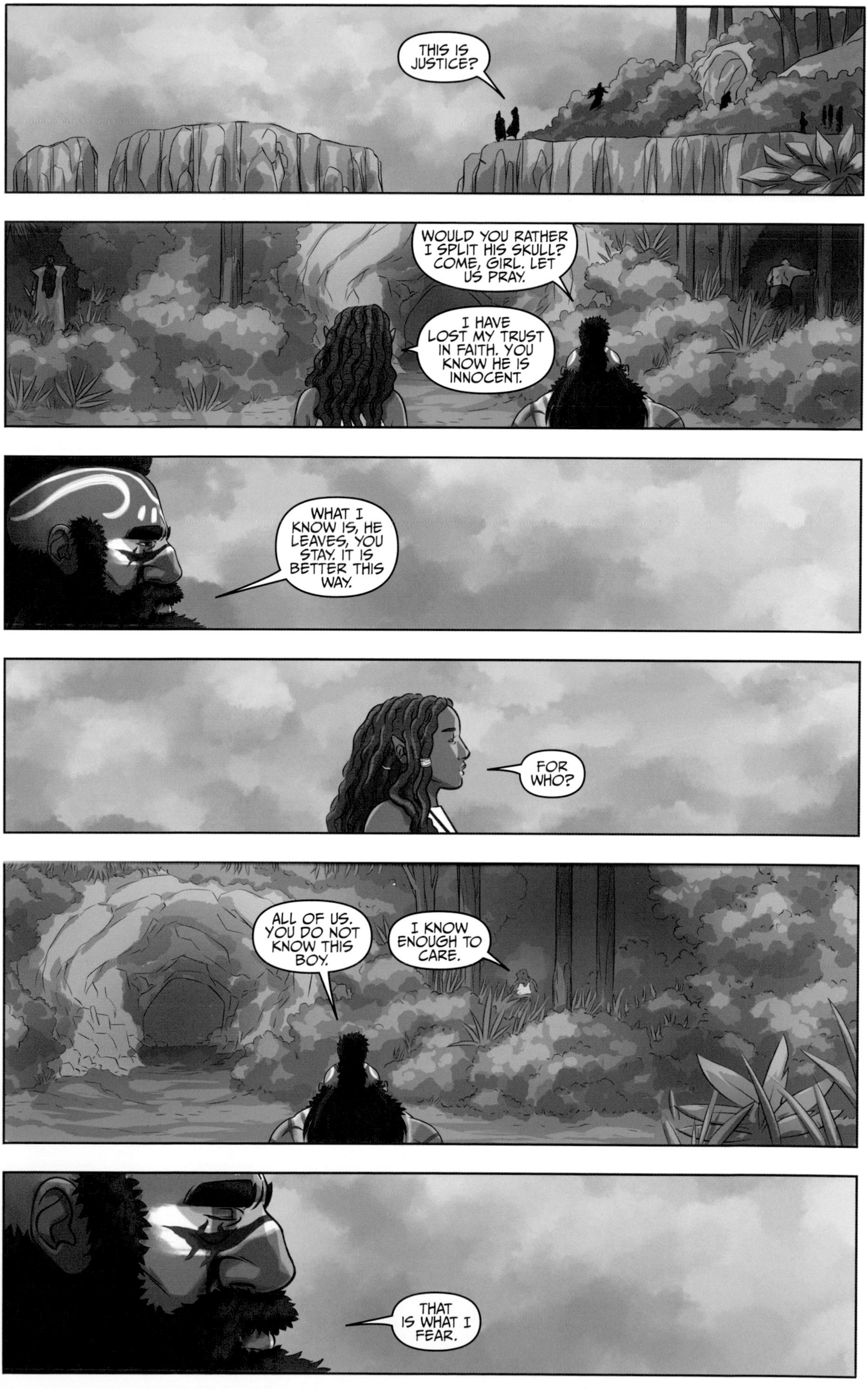

THIS IS JUSTICE?
WOULD YOU RATHER I SPLIT HIS SKULL? COME, GIRL. LET US PRAY.
I HAVE LOST MY TRUST IN FAITH. YOU KNOW HE IS INNOCENT.
WHAT I KNOW IS, HE LEAVES, YOU STAY. IT IS BETTER THIS WAY.
FOR WHO?
ALL OF US. YOU DO NOT KNOW THIS BOY.
I KNOW ENOUGH TO CARE.
THAT IS WHAT I FEAR.

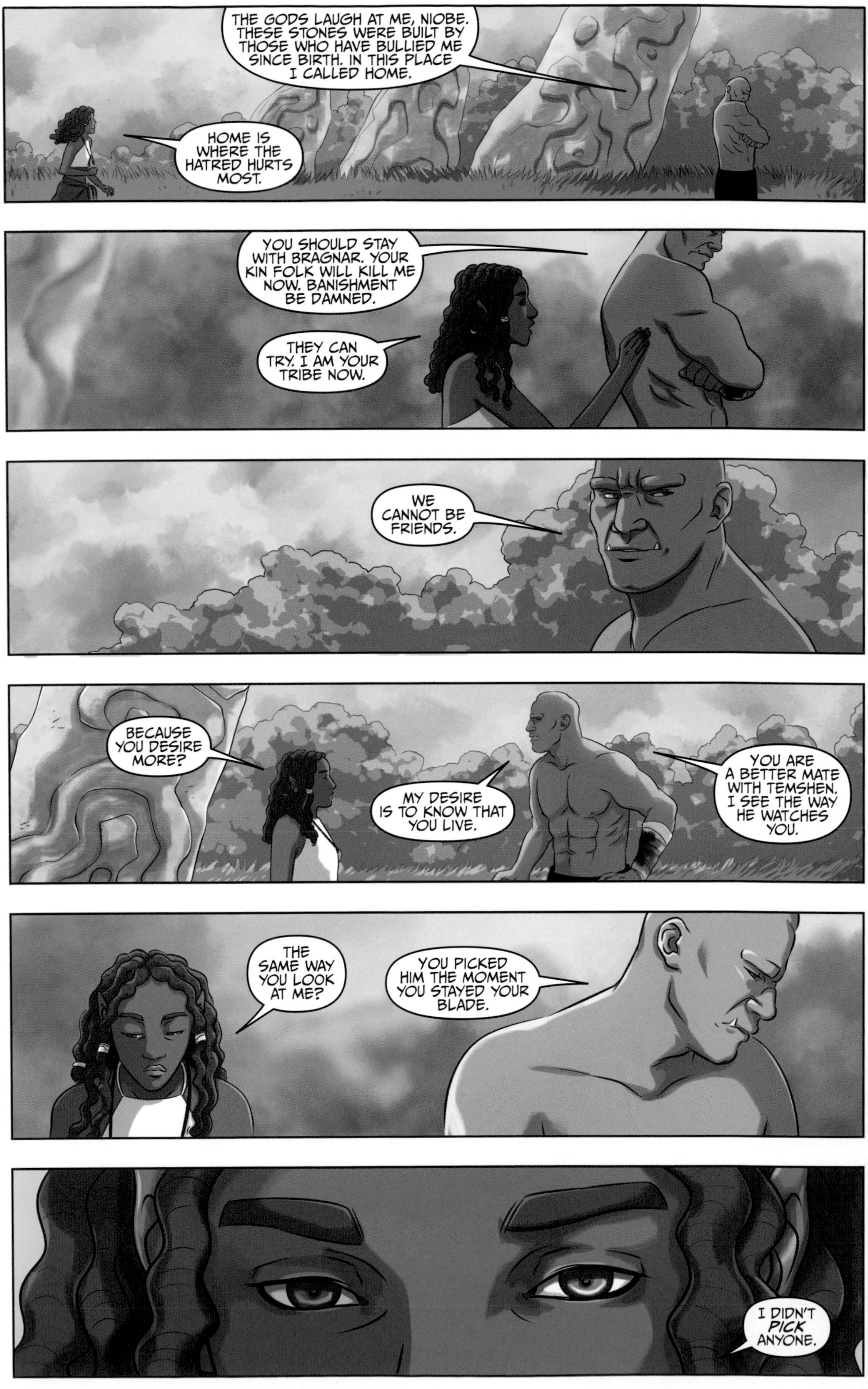
THE GODS LAUGH AT ME, NIOBE. THESE STONES WERE BUILT BY THOSE WHO HAVE BULLIED ME SINCE BIRTH. IN THIS PLACE I CALLED HOME.
HOME IS WHERE THE HATRED HURTS MOST.
YOU SHOULD STAY WITH BRAGNAR. YOUR KIN FOLK WILL KILL ME NOW. BANISHMENT BE DAMNED.
THEY CAN TRY. I AM YOUR TRIBE NOW.
WE CANNOT BE FRIENDS.
BECAUSE YOU DESIRE MORE?
MY DESIRE IS TO KNOW THAT YOU LIVE.
YOU ARE A BETTER MATE WITH TEMSHEN. I SEE THE WAY HE WATCHES YOU.
THE SAME WAY YOU LOOK AT ME?
YOU PICKED HIM THE MOMENT YOU STAYED YOUR BLADE.
I DIDN'T *PICK* ANYONE.

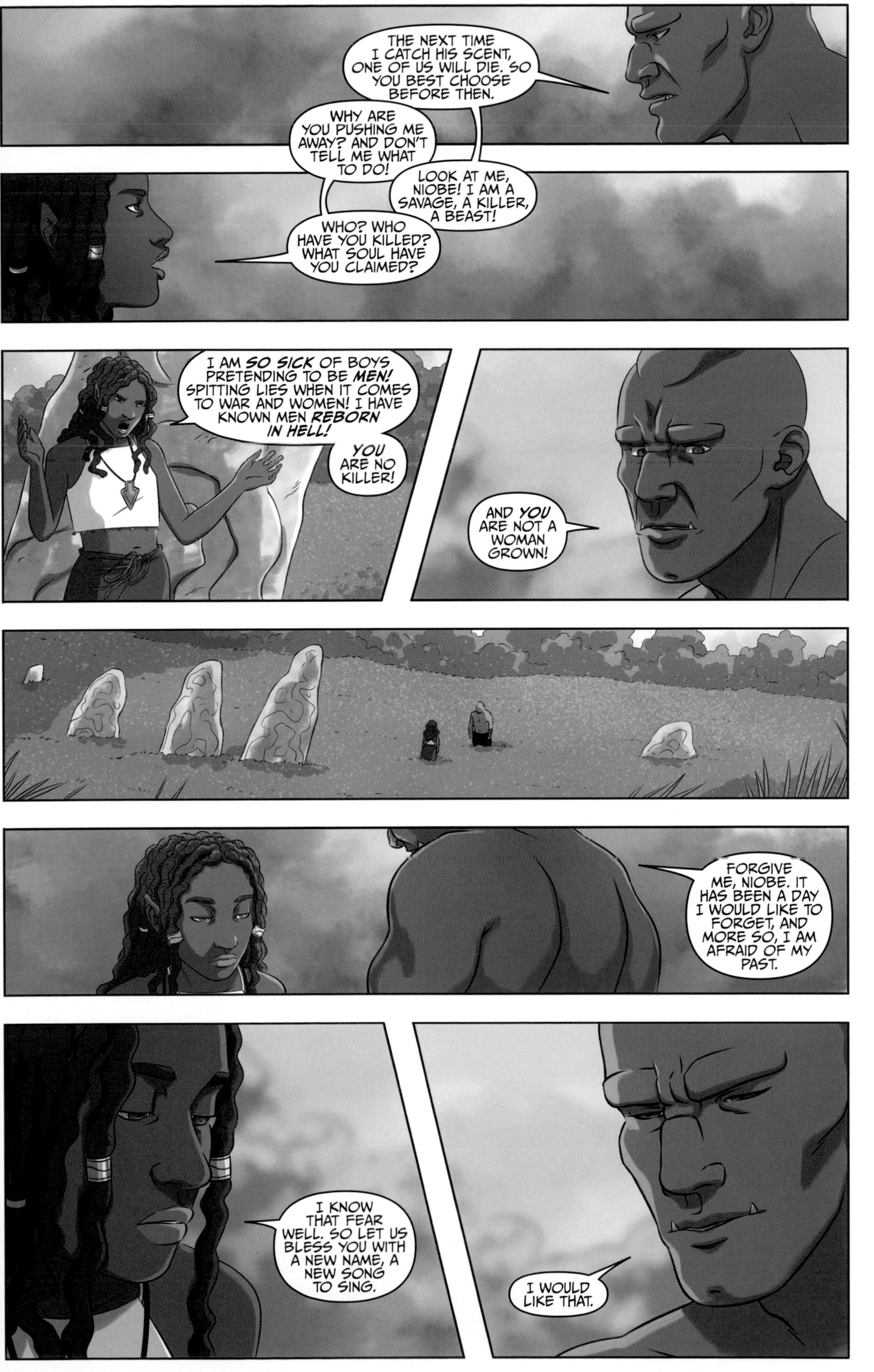
THE NEXT TIME I CATCH HIS SCENT, ONE OF US WILL DIE. SO YOU BEST CHOOSE BEFORE THEN.
WHY ARE YOU PUSHING ME AWAY? AND DON'T TELL ME WHAT TO DO!
LOOK AT ME, NIOBE! I AM A SAVAGE, A KILLER, A BEAST!
WHO? WHO HAVE YOU KILLED? WHAT SOUL HAVE YOU CLAIMED?
I AM *SO SICK* OF BOYS PRETENDING TO BE *MEN!* SPITTING LIES WHEN IT COMES TO WAR AND WOMEN! I HAVE KNOWN MEN *REBORN IN HELL!*
YOU ARE NO KILLER!
AND *YOU* ARE NOT A WOMAN GROWN!
FORGIVE ME, NIOBE. IT HAS BEEN A DAY I WOULD LIKE TO FORGET, AND MORE SO, I AM AFRAID OF MY PAST.
I KNOW THAT FEAR WELL. SO LET US BLESS YOU WITH A NEW NAME, A NEW SONG TO SING.
I WOULD LIKE THAT.

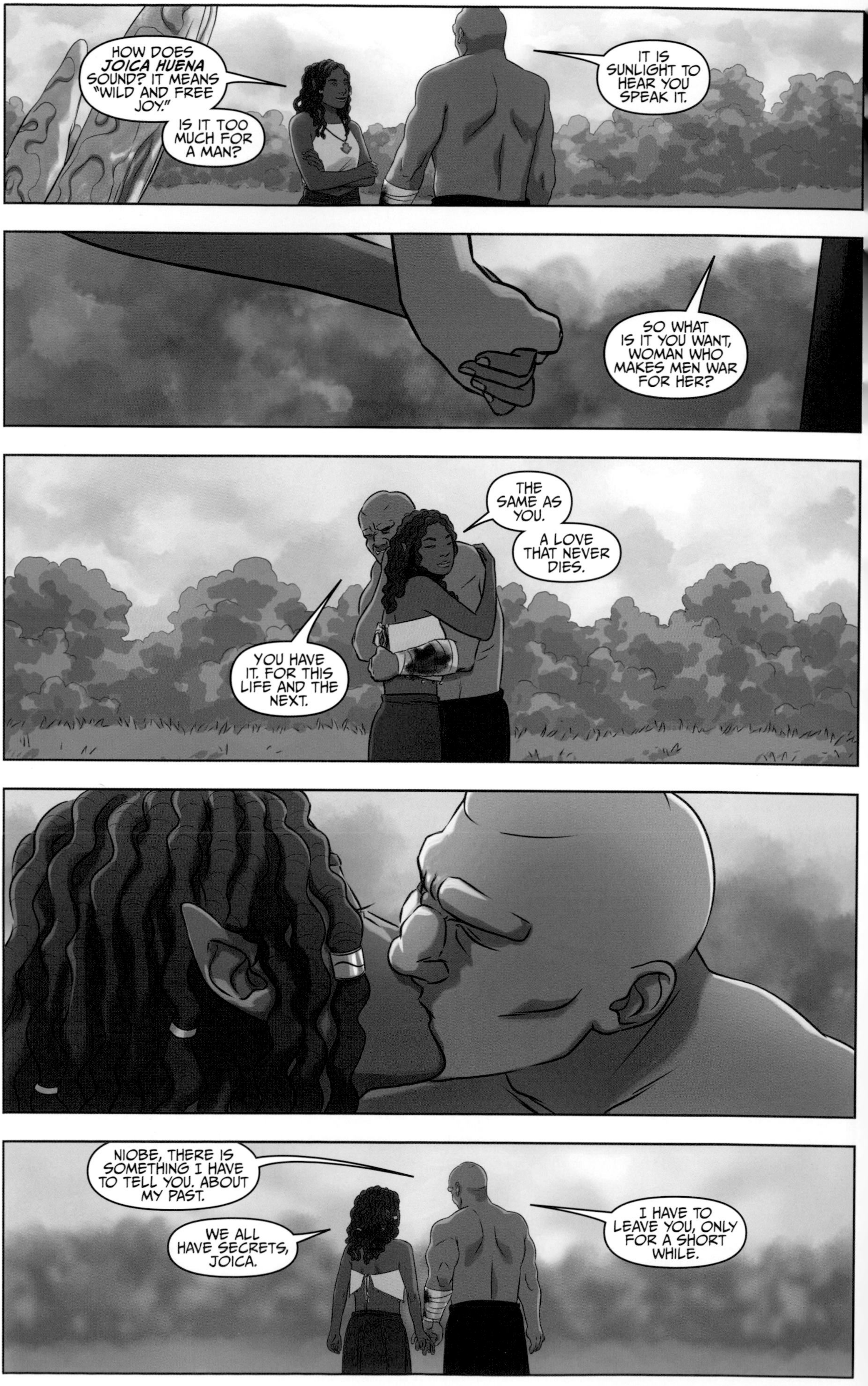
HOW DOES JOICA HUENA SOUND? IT MEANS "WILD AND FREE JOY."
IS IT TOO MUCH FOR A MAN?
IT IS SUNLIGHT TO HEAR YOU SPEAK IT.
SO WHAT IS IT YOU WANT, WOMAN WHO MAKES MEN WAR FOR HER?
THE SAME AS YOU.
A LOVE THAT NEVER DIES.
YOU HAVE IT. FOR THIS LIFE AND THE NEXT.
NIOBE, THERE IS SOMETHING I HAVE TO TELL YOU. ABOUT MY PAST.
WE ALL HAVE SECRETS, JOICA.
I HAVE TO LEAVE YOU, ONLY FOR A SHORT WHILE.

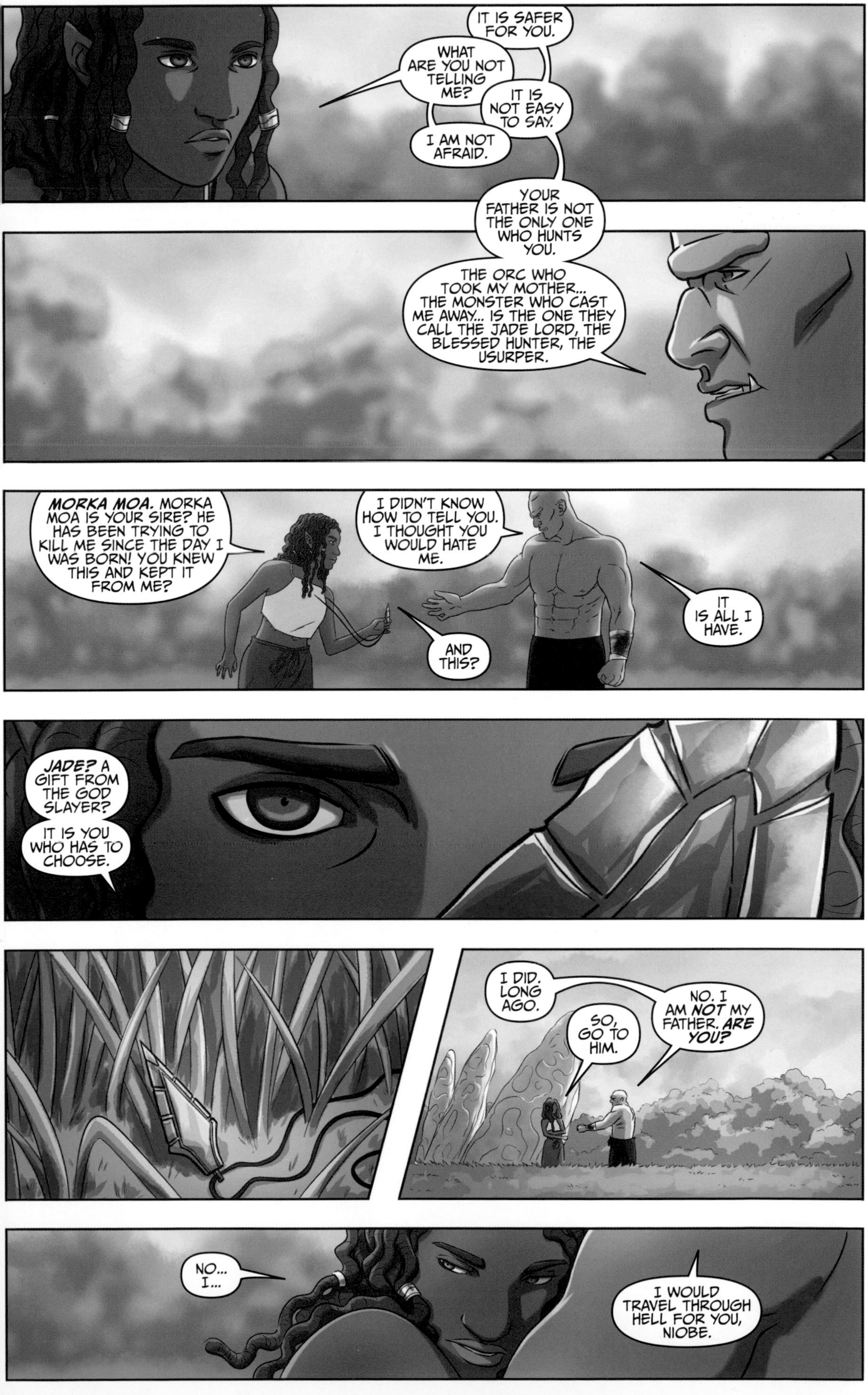

IT IS SAFER FOR YOU.
WHAT ARE YOU NOT TELLING ME?
IT IS NOT EASY TO SAY.
I AM NOT AFRAID.
YOUR FATHER IS NOT THE ONLY ONE WHO HUNTS YOU.
THE ORC WHO TOOK MY MOTHER... THE MONSTER WHO CAST ME AWAY... IS THE ONE THEY CALL THE JADE LORD, THE BLESSED HUNTER, THE USURPER.
MORKA MOA. MORKA MOA IS YOUR SIRE? HE HAS BEEN TRYING TO KILL ME SINCE THE DAY I WAS BORN! YOU KNEW THIS AND KEPT IT FROM ME?
I DIDN'T KNOW HOW TO TELL YOU. I THOUGHT YOU WOULD HATE ME.
AND THIS?
IT IS ALL I HAVE.
JADE? A GIFT FROM THE GOD SLAYER?
IT IS YOU WHO HAS TO CHOOSE.
I DID. LONG AGO.
SO, GO TO HIM.
NO. I AM NOT MY FATHER. ARE YOU?
NO... I...
I WOULD TRAVEL THROUGH HELL FOR YOU, NIOBE.

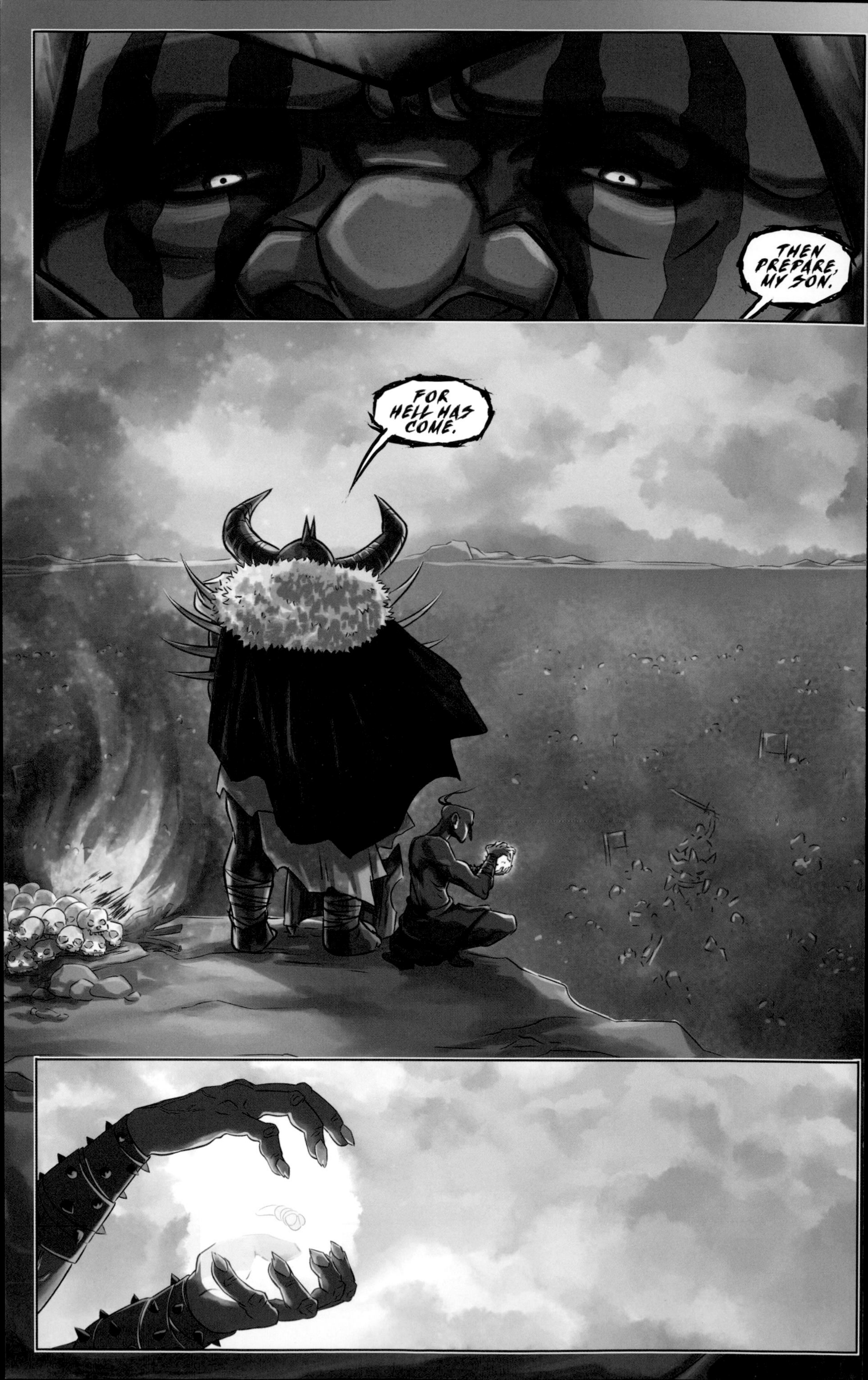
THEN PREPARE, MY SON.
FOR HELL HAS COME.

Hello Stranger

When all is bleak, it is the voice within that keeps us warm. She is God.

The child was born in a place where killers are sent to die. It was deep within the ground, a thousand leagues from a father busy conquering worlds; he had no knowledge of her birth. But all that would change.

The man who sired her was far from living, but he was not dead. A husk of wintery skin draped in silks in winter and fur in summer just to feel the penance of his wrongdoings. The stolen crown lay heavy on Andrek VII's head, but the weight did not compare to the evil of kidnapping another man's wife, a queen of the Galemren, more regal and true than he could have dared to hope for. He had to have her. The devil was in him.

The Galemren woman was the most beautiful he had ever seen and bore the blessings of a Goddess. A thousand statues were made in her honor, and gold was showered at her feet. But he could not win her love, so he would own her instead. Compel her heart. Quiet her song. But despite all that he did, it was not her that broke, but him. Hope gave way to desperation, which crumbled into madness, until finally he drugged and forced her, his final act of sin. She kept his seed, her final act of vengeance.

Not knowing she carried an heir, the devil's puppet king cast Nadami into a pit of darkness, far from the light of Arnuminel. Andrek could not kill the woman he craved, but he would not look upon her eyes again. Or his own.

Who can say how much of her mother's faith was gifted to the child, or how much of her father's tainted spirit remains? Only time will tell, and The Untamed will hunt Niobe to have the answer, chasing her across the vast and volatile word of…

Chapter 9

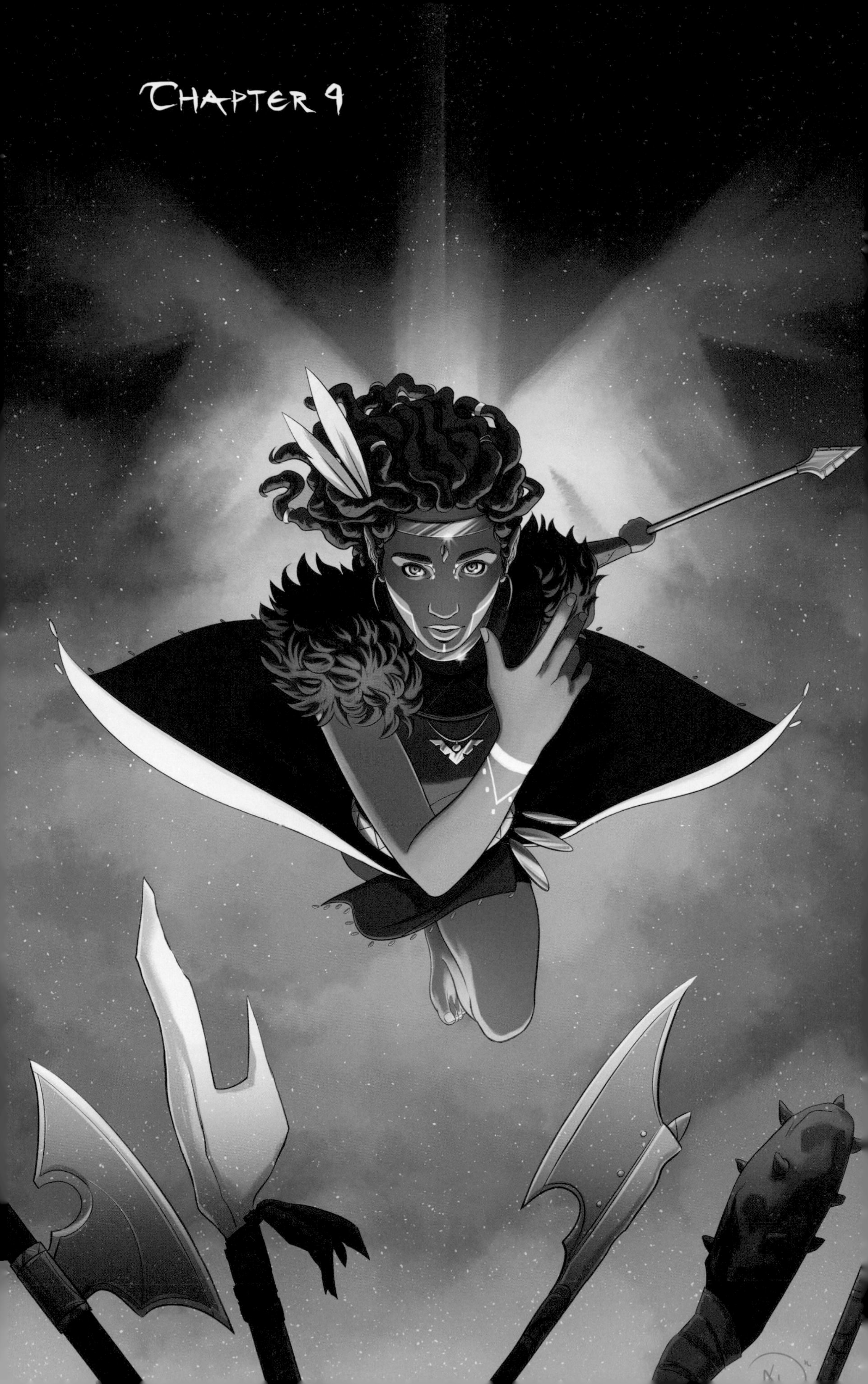

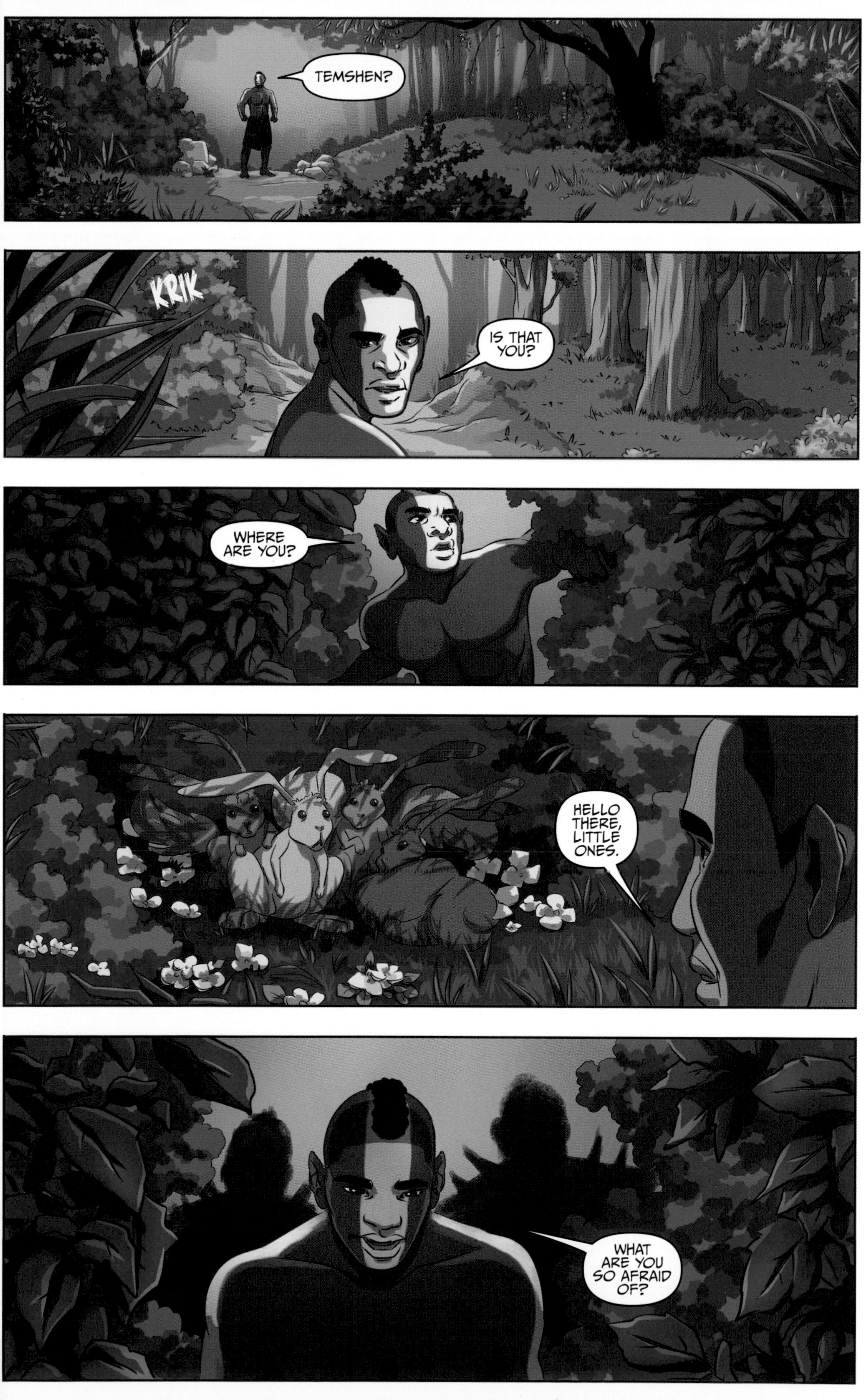
TEMSHEN?
KRIK
IS THAT YOU?
WHERE ARE YOU?
HELLO THERE, LITTLE ONES.
WHAT ARE YOU SO AFRAID OF?

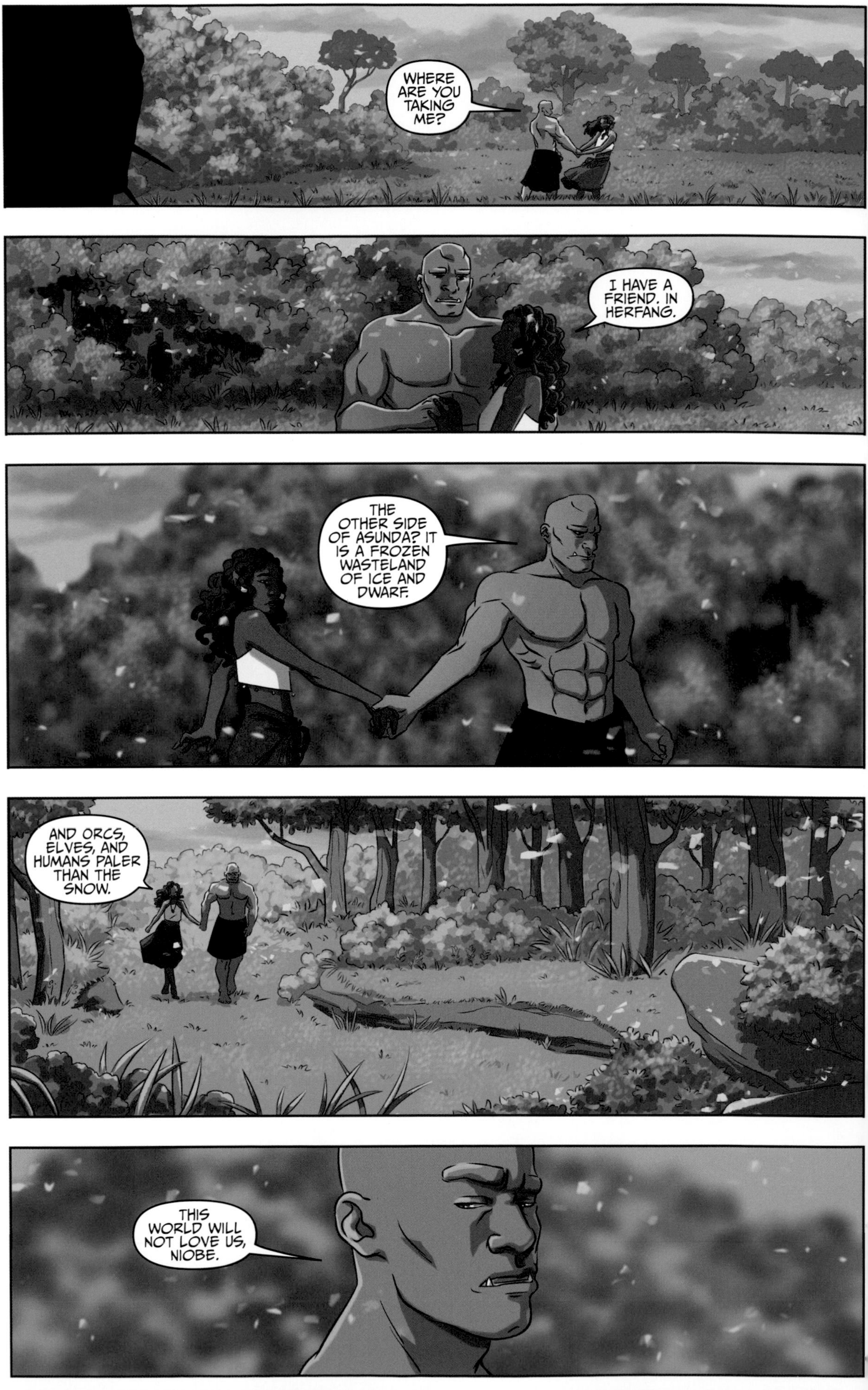
WHERE ARE YOU TAKING ME?
I HAVE A FRIEND. IN HERFANG.
THE OTHER SIDE OF ASUNDA? IT IS A FROZEN WASTELAND OF ICE AND DWARF.
AND ORCS, ELVES, AND HUMANS PALER THAN THE SNOW.
THIS WORLD WILL NOT LOVE US, NIOBE.

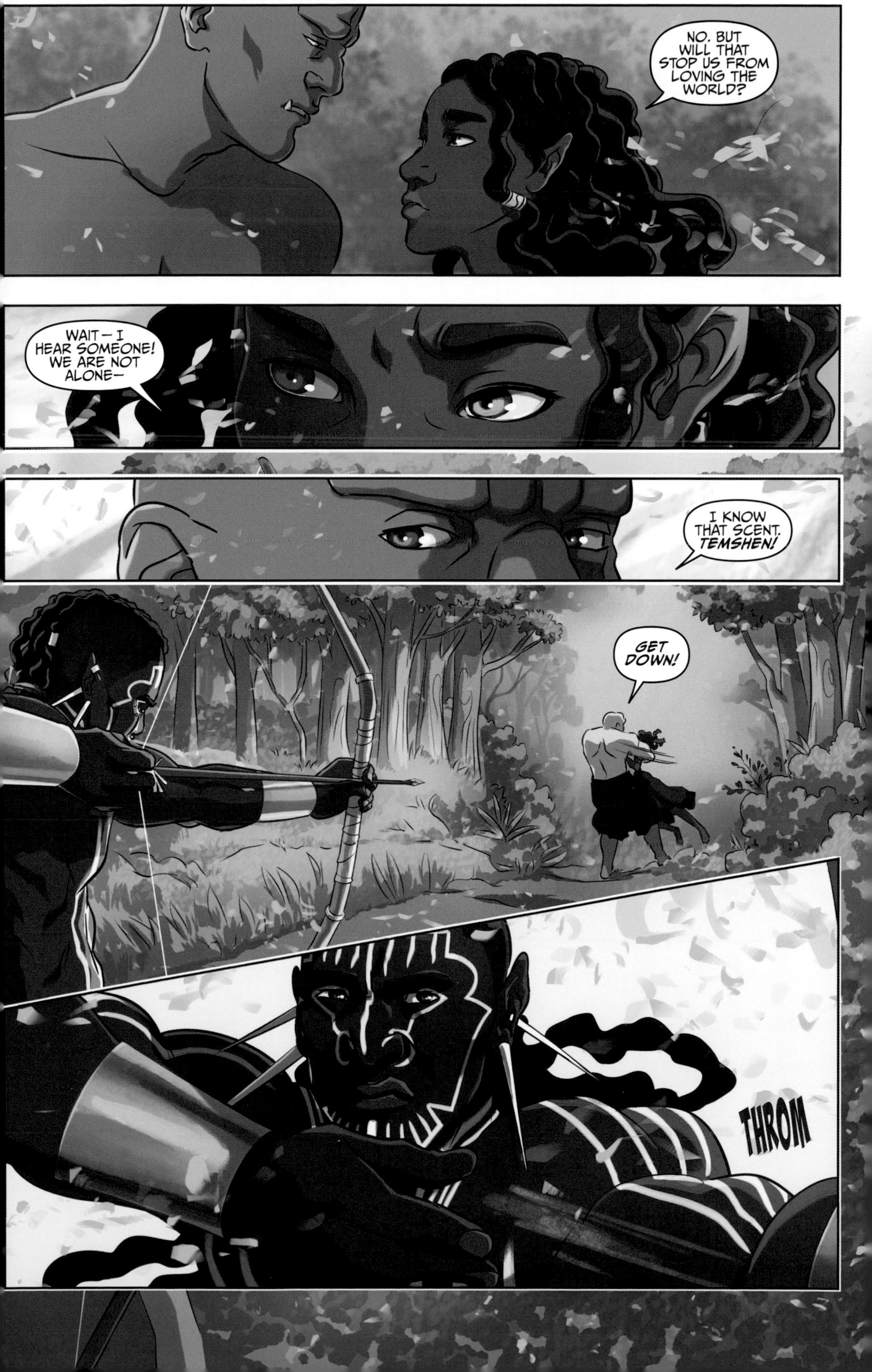
NO. BUT WILL THAT STOP US FROM LOVING THE WORLD?
WAIT— I HEAR SOMEONE! WE ARE NOT ALONE—
I KNOW THAT SCENT. *TEMSHEN!*
GET DOWN!
THROM

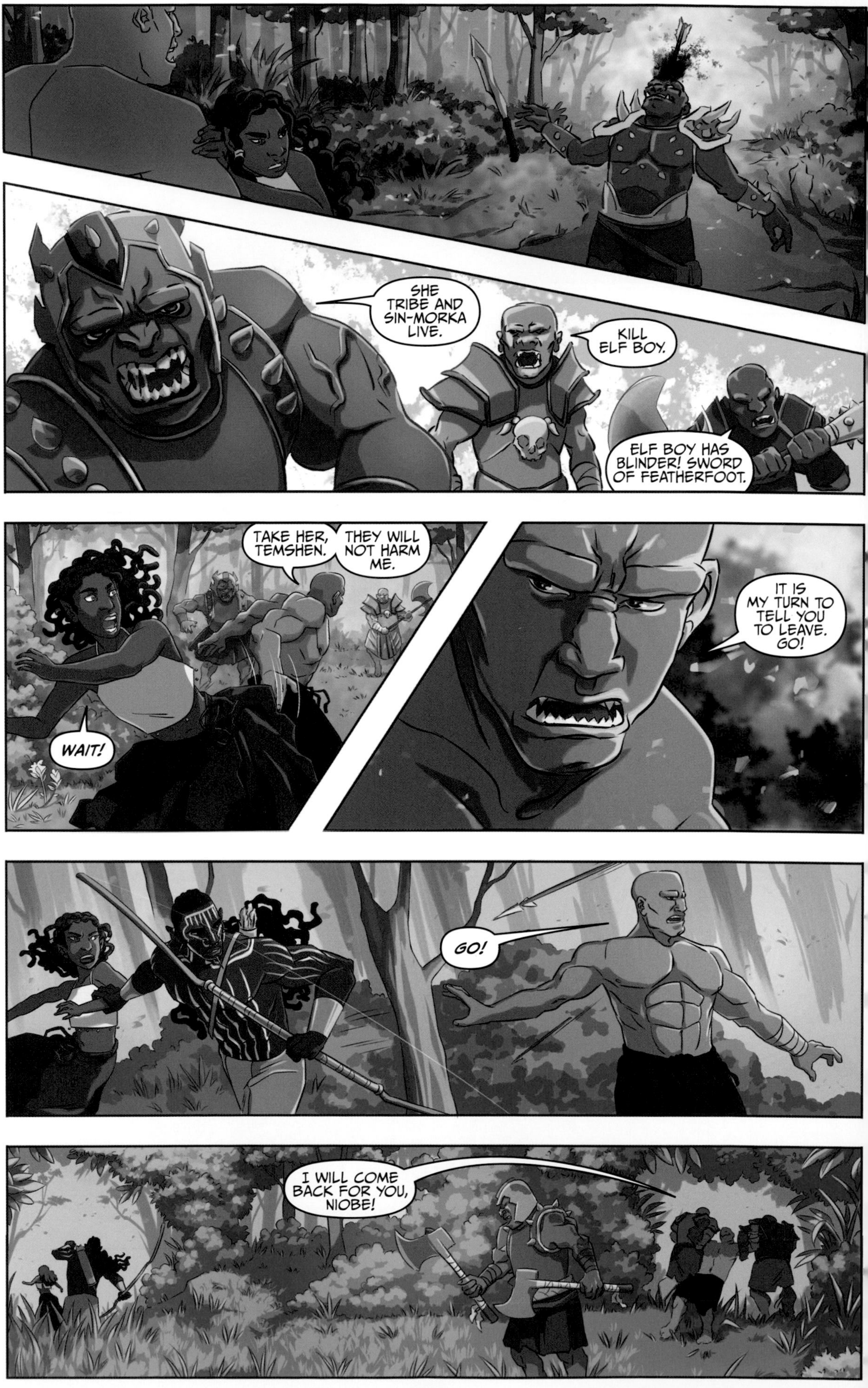
SHE TRIBE AND SIN-MORKA LIVE.
KILL ELF BOY.
ELF BOY HAS BLINDER! SWORD OF FEATHERFOOT.
TAKE HER, TEMSHEN.
THEY WILL NOT HARM ME.
WAIT!
IT IS MY TURN TO TELL YOU TO LEAVE. GO!
GO!
I WILL COME BACK FOR YOU, NIOBE!

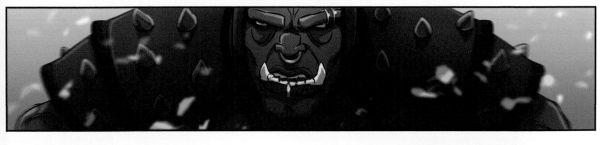

I ATTACK HIGH.

UGOMA!

I KNOW WHAT YOU WOULD ASK BUT THERE ARE TOO MANY! WE WILL BE SURROUNDED.

I WILL *NOT* LOSE HIM.

HE WAS ALWAYS LOST TO US. HE IS THE MONSTER ONLY A MORTAL CAN LOVE.

YOU ARE THE MONSTER, TEMSHEN. LIKE THE ORC THAT KILLED YOUR FATHER, YOU ARE TOO BLIND TO SEE.

YOUR WORDS CANNOT HURT ME ANY MORE THAN YOU ALREADY HAVE.

WHERE ARE YOU GOING?

TO THE TEMPLE.

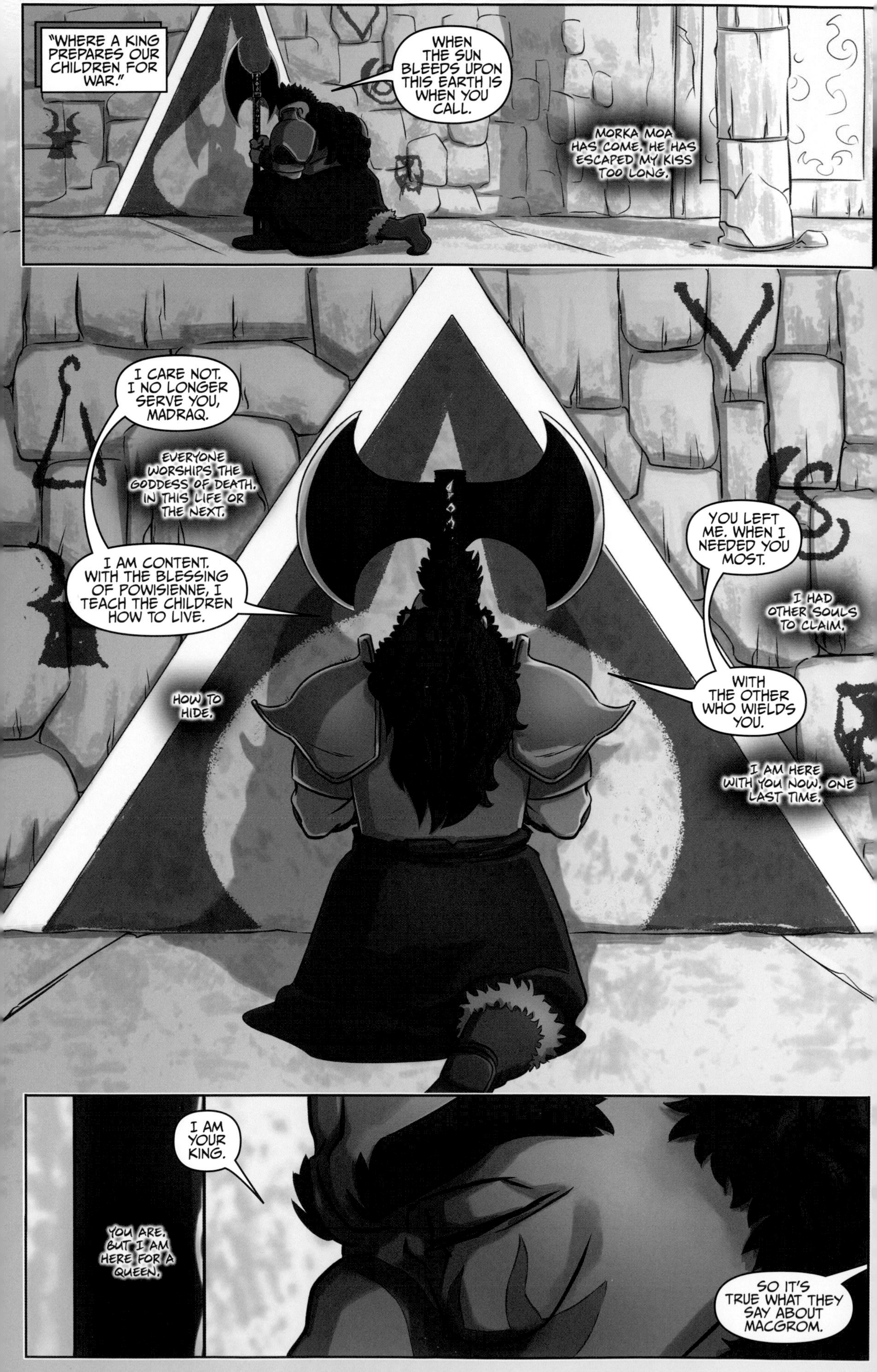
"WHERE A KING PREPARES OUR CHILDREN FOR WAR."
WHEN THE SUN BLEEDS UPON THIS EARTH IS WHEN YOU CALL.
MORKA MOA HAS COME. HE HAS ESCAPED MY KISS TOO LONG.
I CARE NOT. I NO LONGER SERVE YOU, MADRAQ.
EVERYONE WORSHIPS THE GODDESS OF DEATH. IN THIS LIFE OR THE NEXT.
I AM CONTENT. WITH THE BLESSING OF POWISIENNE, I TEACH THE CHILDREN HOW TO LIVE.
HOW TO HIDE.
YOU LEFT ME. WHEN I NEEDED YOU MOST.
I HAD OTHER SOULS TO CLAIM.
WITH THE OTHER WHO WIELDS YOU.
I AM HERE WITH YOU NOW. ONE LAST TIME.
I AM YOUR KING.
YOU ARE. BUT I AM HERE FOR A QUEEN.
SO IT'S TRUE WHAT THEY SAY ABOUT MACGROM.

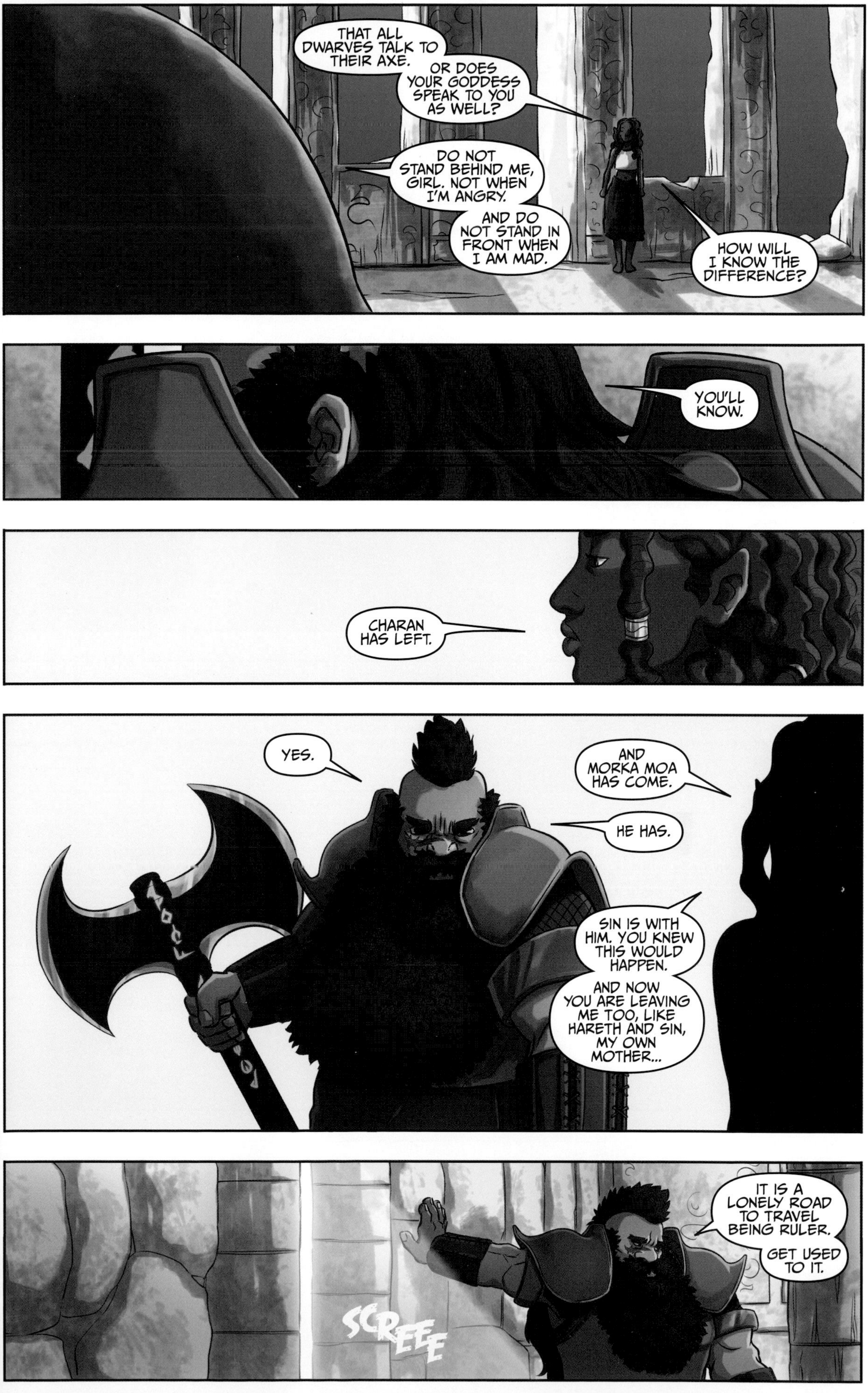

THAT ALL DWARVES TALK TO THEIR AXE.
OR DOES YOUR GODDESS SPEAK TO YOU AS WELL?
DO NOT STAND BEHIND ME, GIRL. NOT WHEN I'M ANGRY.
AND DO NOT STAND IN FRONT WHEN I AM MAD.
HOW WILL I KNOW THE DIFFERENCE?
YOU'LL KNOW.
CHARAN HAS LEFT.
YES.
AND MORKA MOA HAS COME.
HE HAS.
SIN IS WITH HIM. YOU KNEW THIS WOULD HAPPEN.
AND NOW YOU ARE LEAVING ME TOO, LIKE HARETH AND SIN, MY OWN MOTHER...
IT IS A LONELY ROAD TO TRAVEL BEING RULER.
GET USED TO IT.
SCREEE

BECAUSE THERE ARE THOSE WHO WOULD FOLLOW YOU.

WHO?

YOUR SISTERS.

THEY WERE LOST LIKE YOU, AND THEY TOO ARE GIFTED.

BRAGNAR HAS LOOKED AFTER THEM. UNTIL NOW.

BUT THEY ARE READY TO FIGHT BESIDE YOU. WE ALL WILL.

NO, YOU WILL NOT.

THEIR LIVES ARE YOURS TO PROTECT NOW, NIOBE. TAKE THEM FAR FROM HERE, AND DON'T LOOK BACK.

WHERE ARE YOU GOING?

I HAVE NEVER MET AN ORC I DIDN'T WANT TO KILL.

I WOULD RATHER FIGHT AND DIE THAN RUN AGAIN.

THEN THEY AND THE WORLD WILL DIE WITH YOU.

YOUR BATTLE WILL COME. HAVE FAITH, NIOBE.

IN THE END, IT'S ALL WE EVER HAVE.

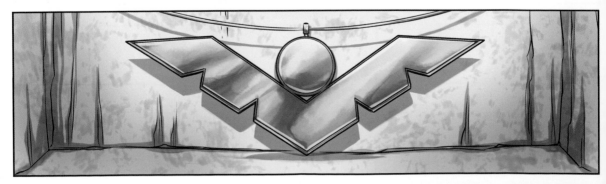

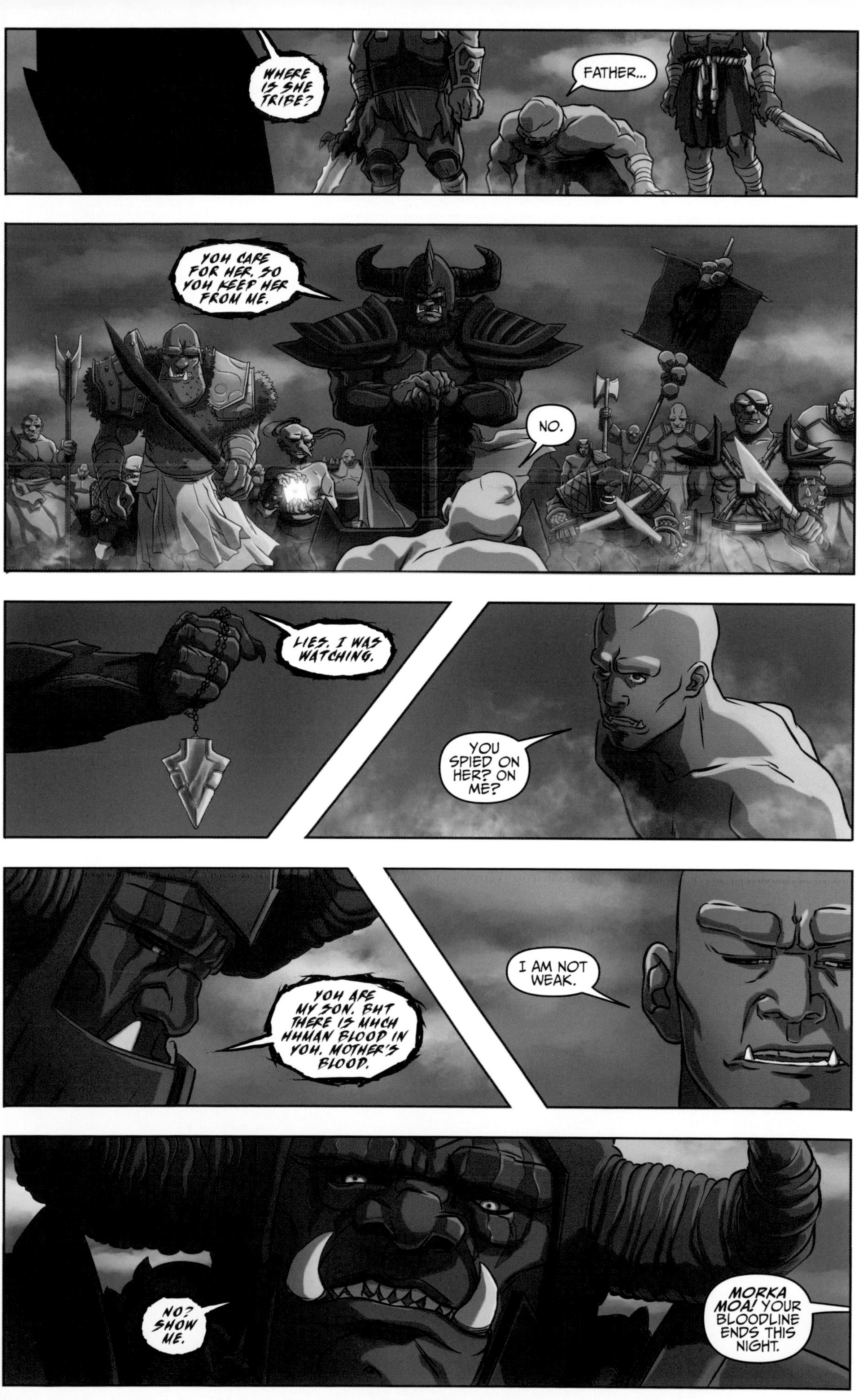
WHERE IS SHE TRIBE?
FATHER...
YOU CARE FOR HER. SO YOU KEEP HER FROM ME.
NO.
LIES. I WAS WATCHING.
YOU SPIED ON HER? ON ME?
YOU ARE MY SON. BUT THERE IS MUCH HUMAN BLOOD IN YOU. MOTHER'S BLOOD.
I AM NOT WEAK.
NO? SHOW ME.
MORKA MOA! YOUR BLOODLINE ENDS THIS NIGHT.

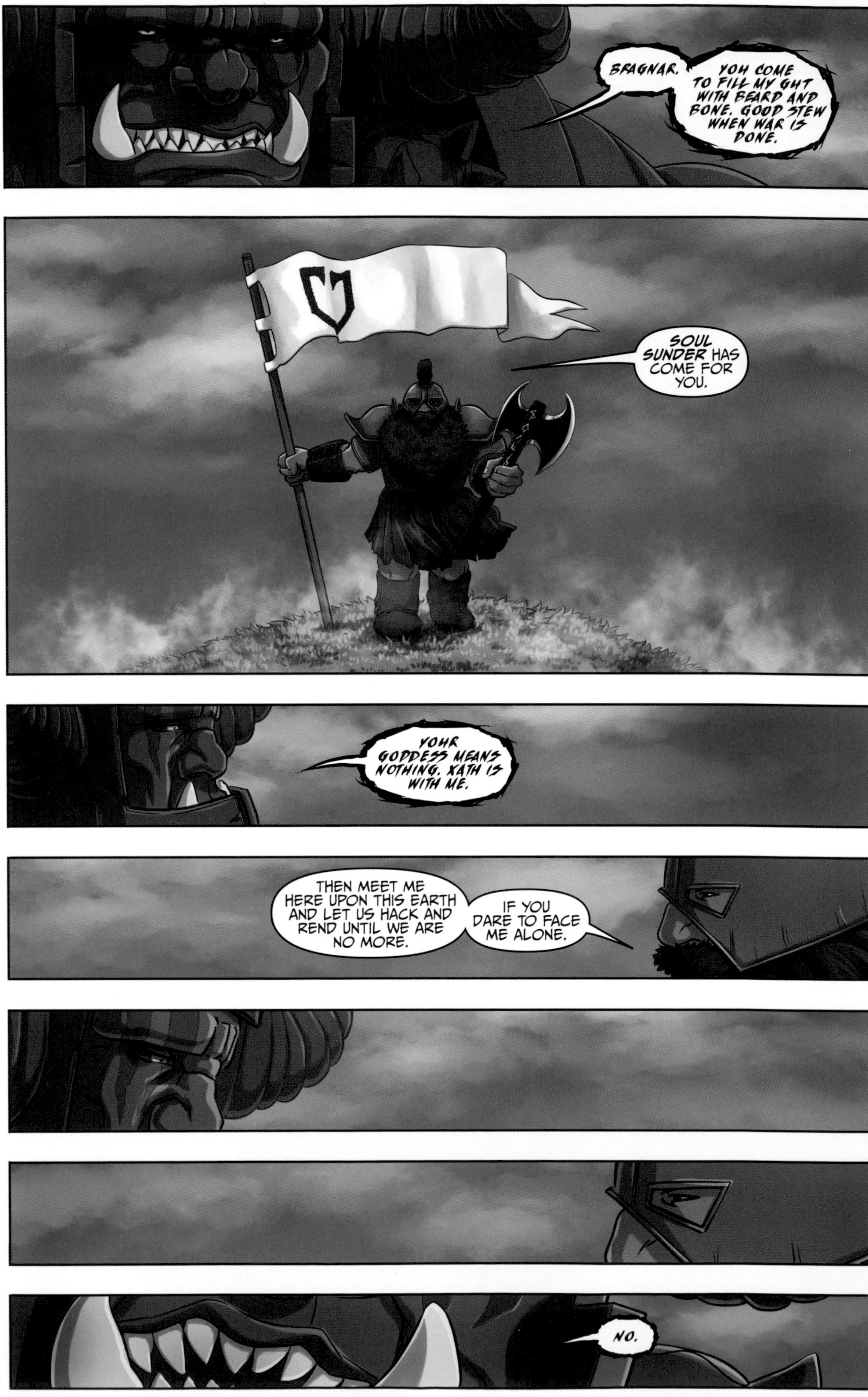
BRAGNAR.
YOU COME TO FILL MY GUT WITH BEARD AND BONE. GOOD STEW WHEN WAR IS DONE.
SOUL SUNDER HAS COME FOR YOU.
YOUR GODDESS MEANS NOTHING. XATH IS WITH ME.
THEN MEET ME HERE UPON THIS EARTH AND LET US HACK AND REND UNTIL WE ARE NO MORE.
IF YOU DARE TO FACE ME ALONE.
NO.

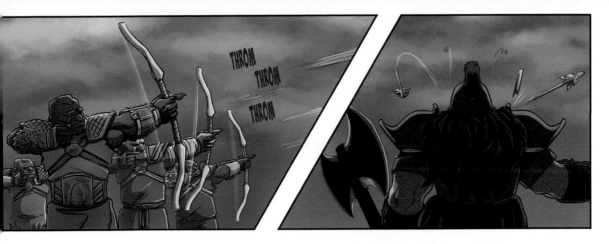

THROM
THROM
THROM

TINK

I WILL SHOW YOU, FATHER. I WILL KILL HIM.

NO. STEELNOSE IS NOT YOUR FEAST.

THEN HOW CAN I PROVE MYSELF TO YOU?

KRAK

YOU KNOW.

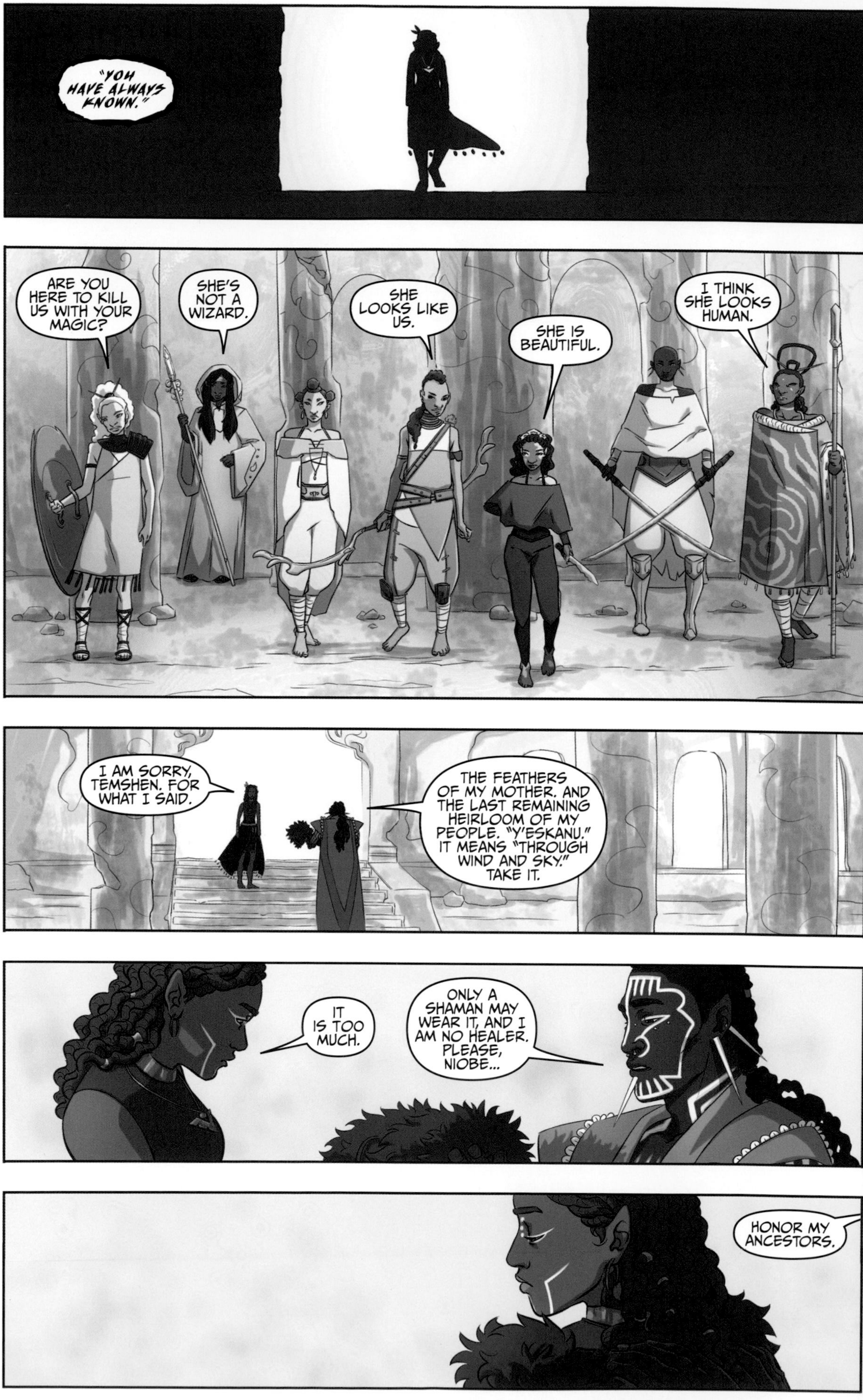
"YOU HAVE ALWAYS KNOWN."
ARE YOU HERE TO KILL US WITH YOUR MAGIC?
SHE'S NOT A WIZARD.
SHE LOOKS LIKE US.
SHE IS BEAUTIFUL.
I THINK SHE LOOKS HUMAN.
I AM SORRY, TEMSHEN. FOR WHAT I SAID.
THE FEATHERS OF MY MOTHER. AND THE LAST REMAINING HEIRLOOM OF MY PEOPLE. "Y'ESKANU." IT MEANS "THROUGH WIND AND SKY." TAKE IT.
IT IS TOO MUCH.
ONLY A SHAMAN MAY WEAR IT, AND I AM NO HEALER. PLEASE, NIOBE...
HONOR MY ANCESTORS.

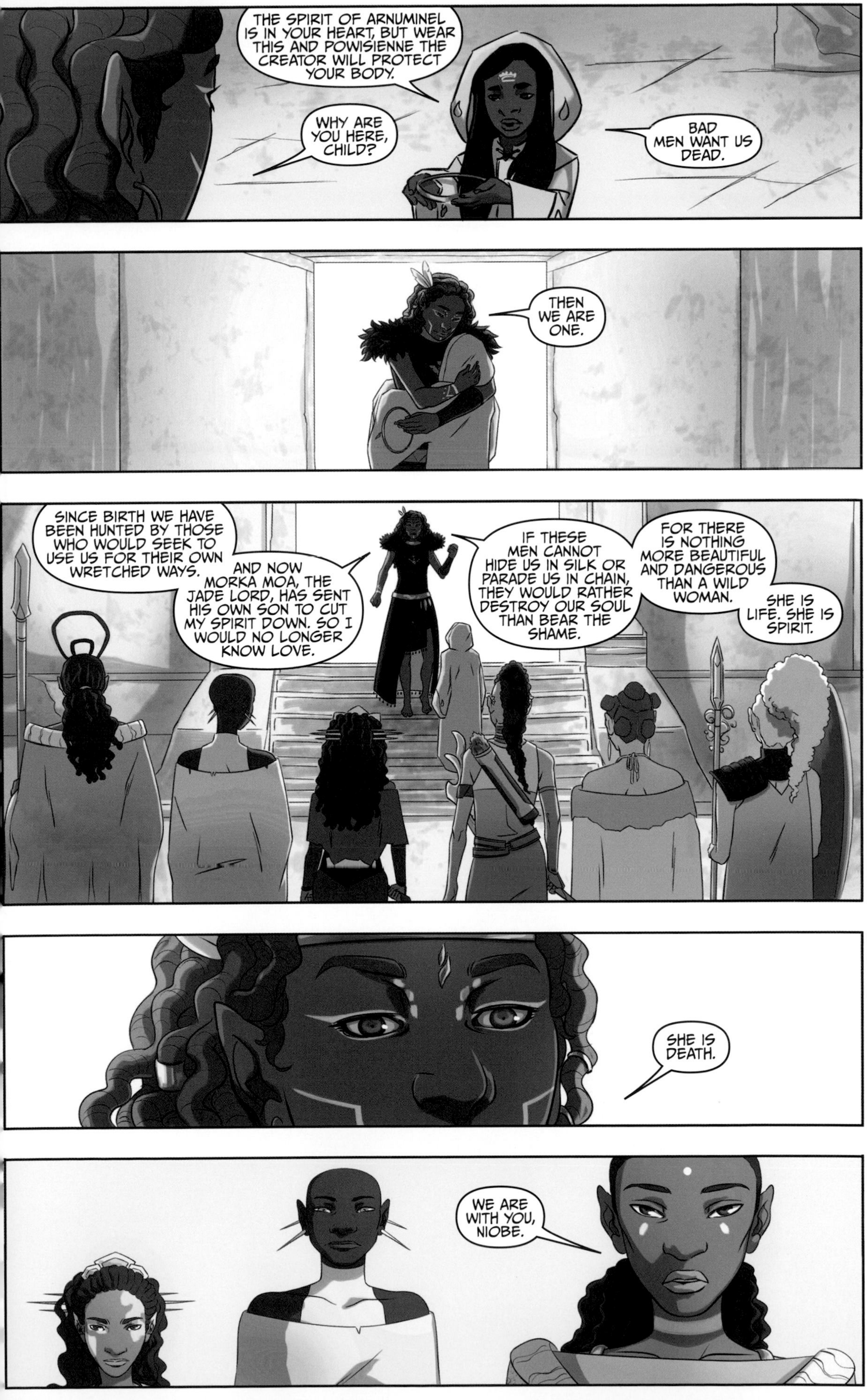
THE SPIRIT OF ARNUMINEL IS IN YOUR HEART, BUT WEAR THIS AND POWISIENNE THE CREATOR WILL PROTECT YOUR BODY.
WHY ARE YOU HERE, CHILD?
BAD MEN WANT US DEAD.
THEN WE ARE ONE.
SINCE BIRTH WE HAVE BEEN HUNTED BY THOSE WHO WOULD SEEK TO USE US FOR THEIR OWN WRETCHED WAYS.
AND NOW MORKA MOA, THE JADE LORD, HAS SENT HIS OWN SON TO CUT MY SPIRIT DOWN. SO I WOULD NO LONGER KNOW LOVE.
IF THESE MEN CANNOT HIDE US IN SILK OR PARADE US IN CHAIN, THEY WOULD RATHER DESTROY OUR SOUL THAN BEAR THE SHAME.
FOR THERE IS NOTHING MORE BEAUTIFUL AND DANGEROUS THAN A WILD WOMAN.
SHE IS LIFE. SHE IS SPIRIT.
SHE IS DEATH.
WE ARE WITH YOU, NIOBE.

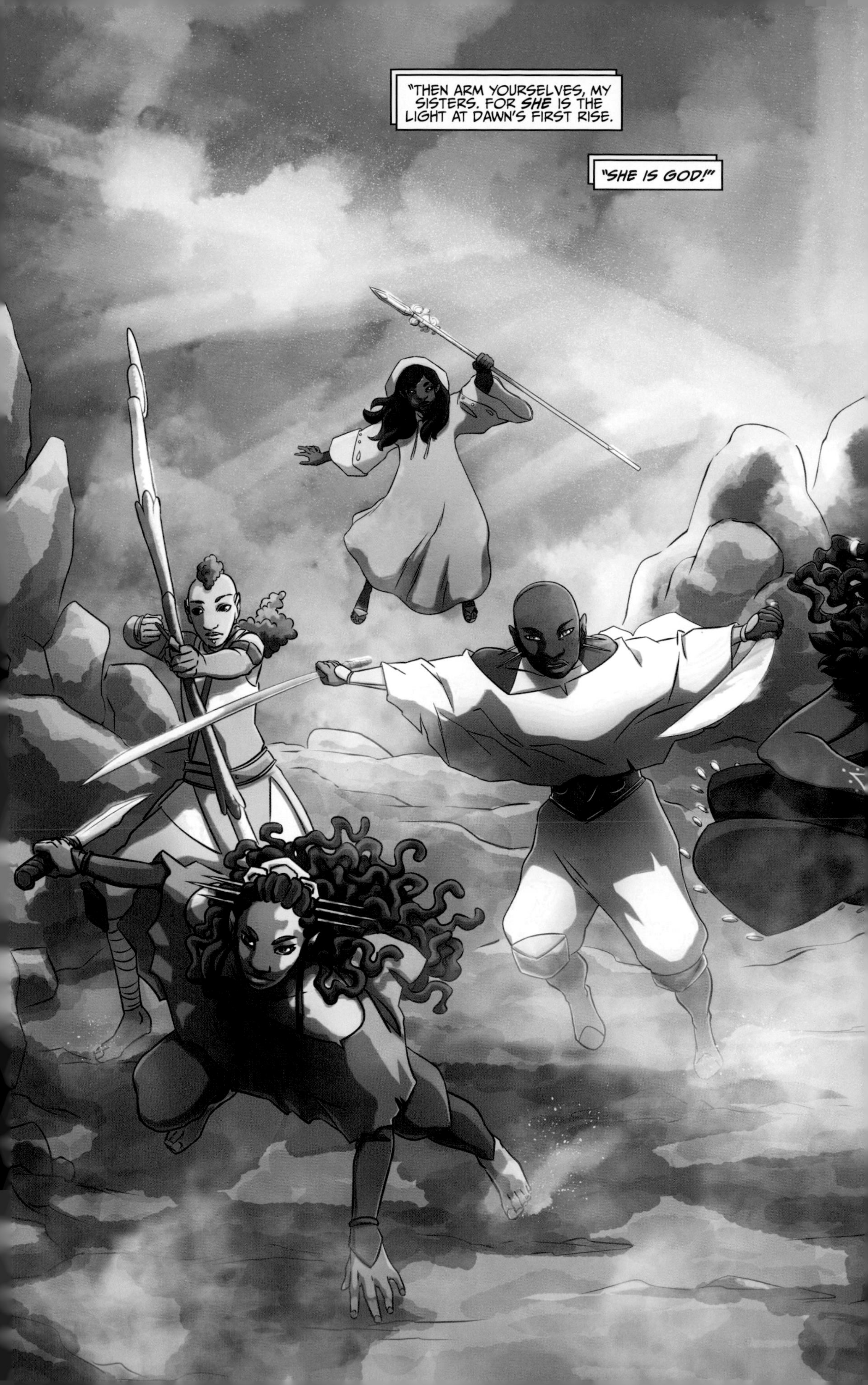
"THEN ARM YOURSELVES, MY SISTERS. FOR *SHE* IS THE LIGHT AT DAWN'S FIRST RISE.
"*SHE IS GOD!*"

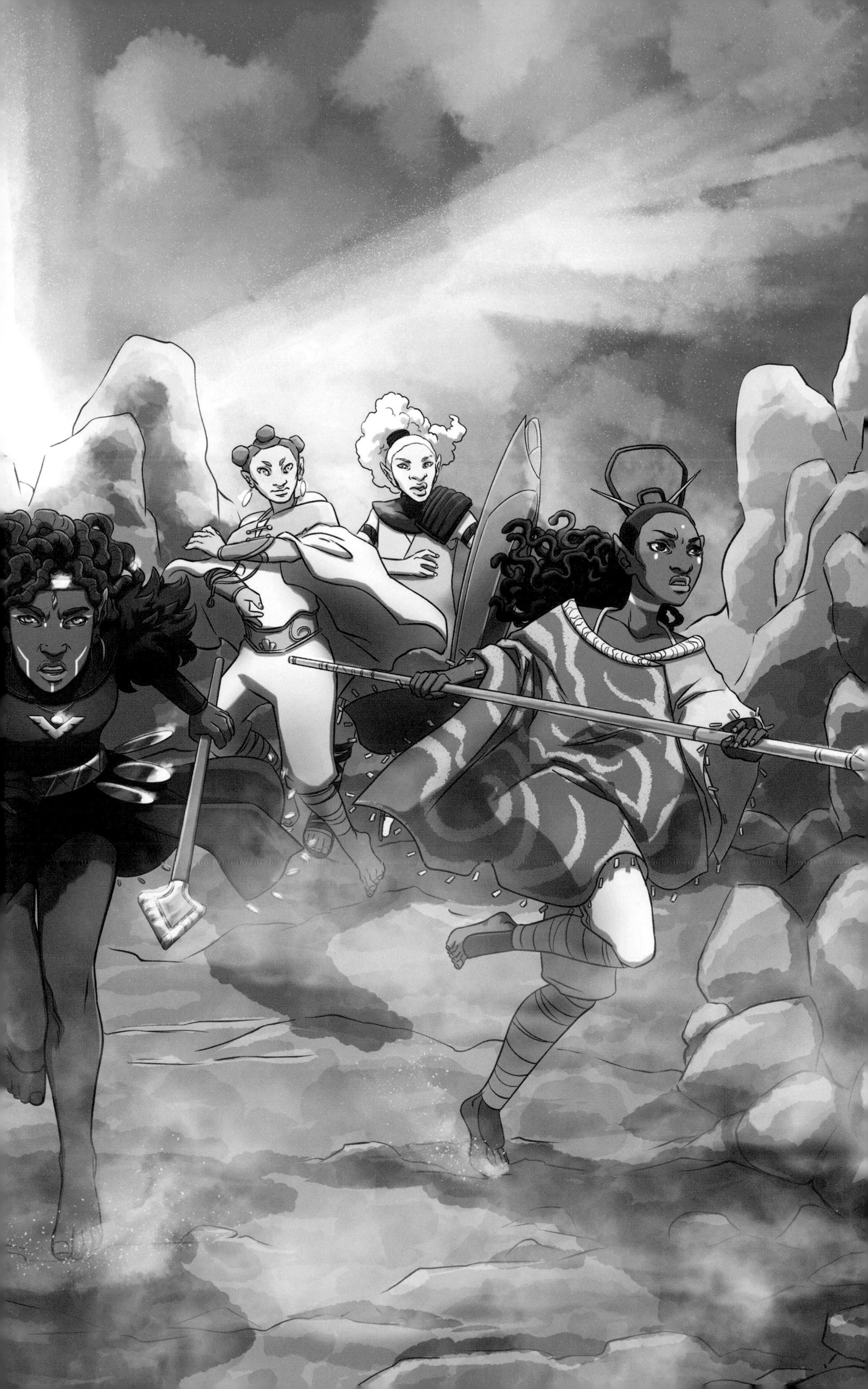

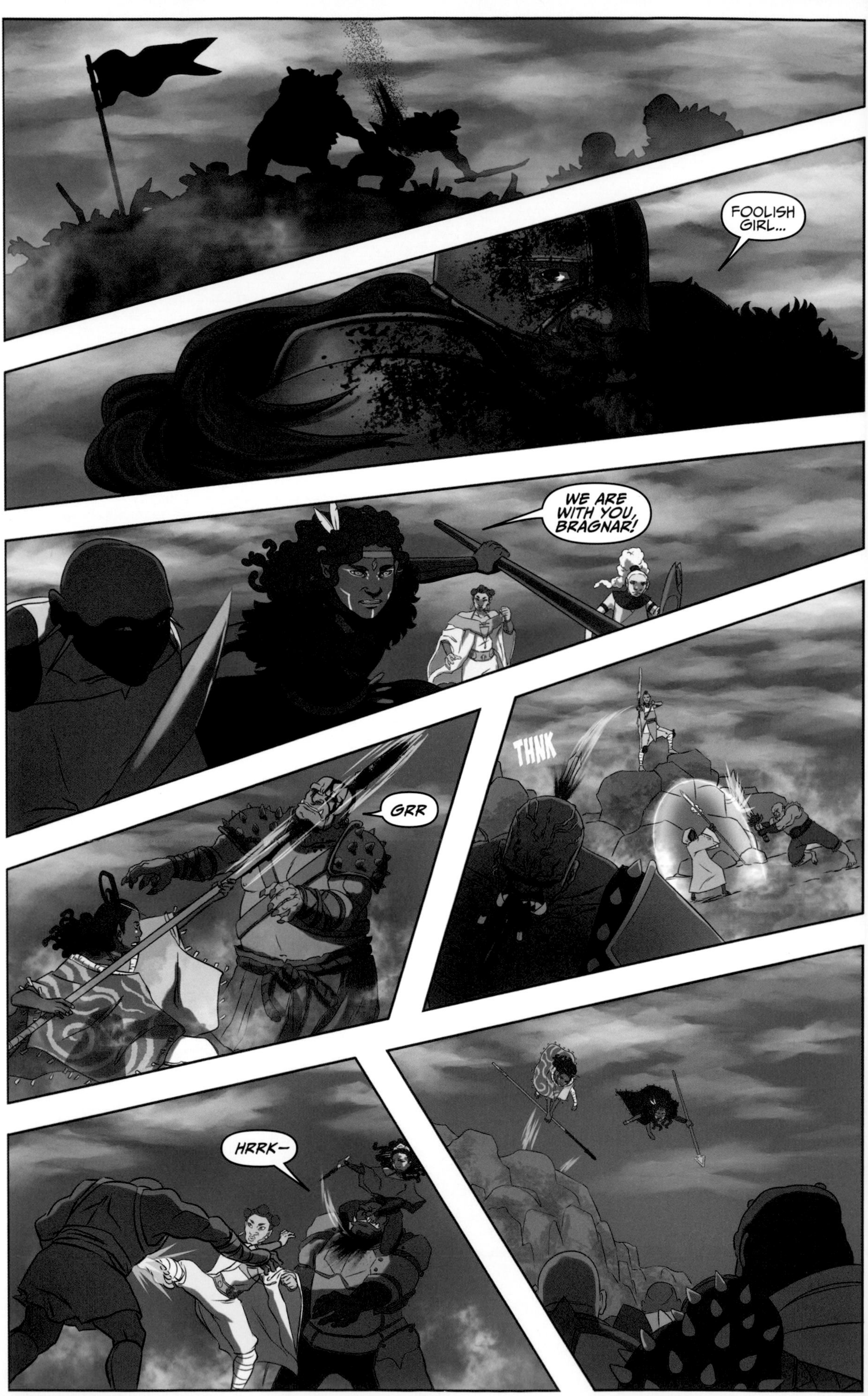
FOOLISH GIRL...
WE ARE WITH YOU, BRAGNAR!
GRR
THNK
HRRK—

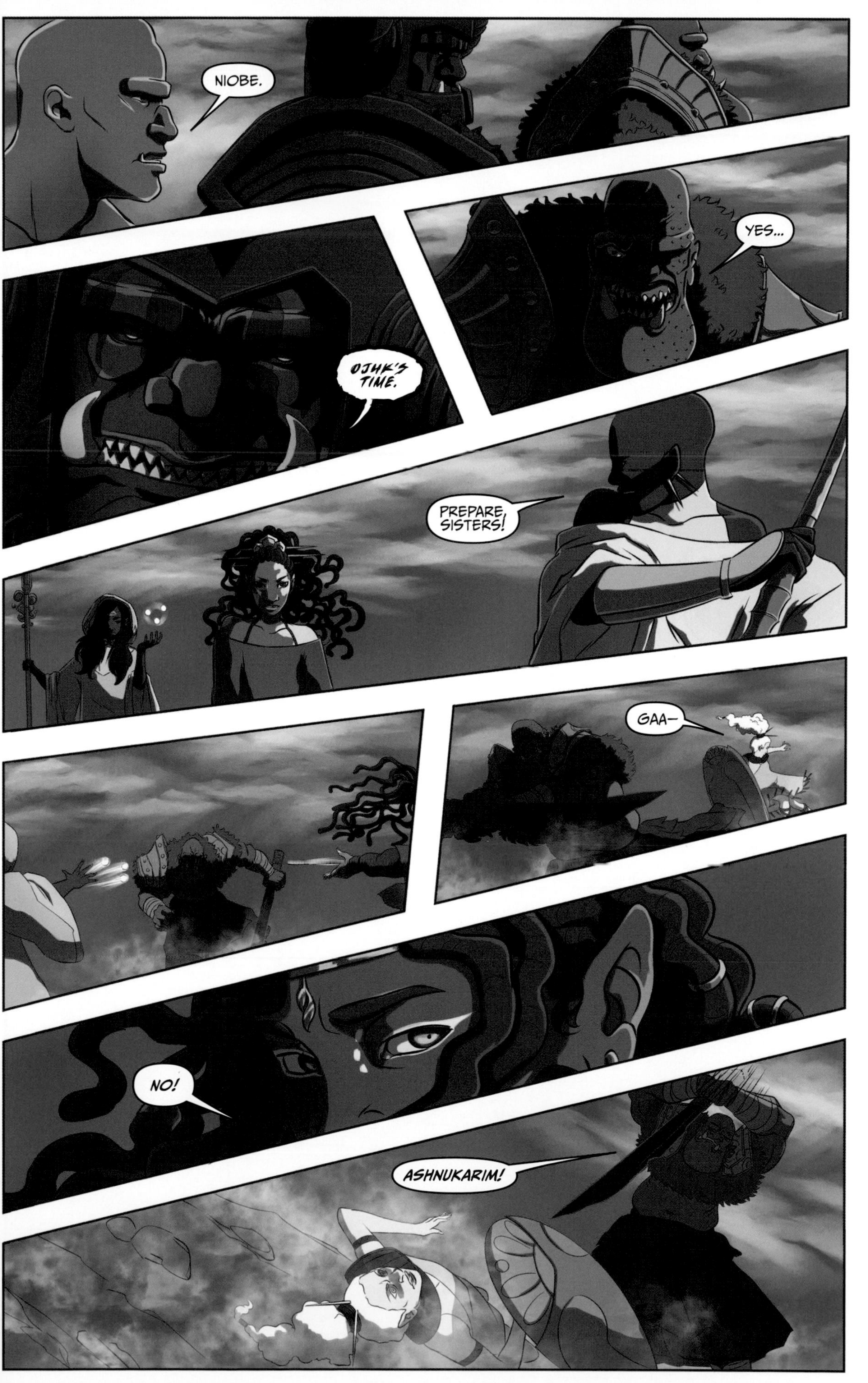
NIOBE.
YES...
OJUK'S TIME.
PREPARE, SISTERS!
GAA—
NO!
ASHNUKARIM!

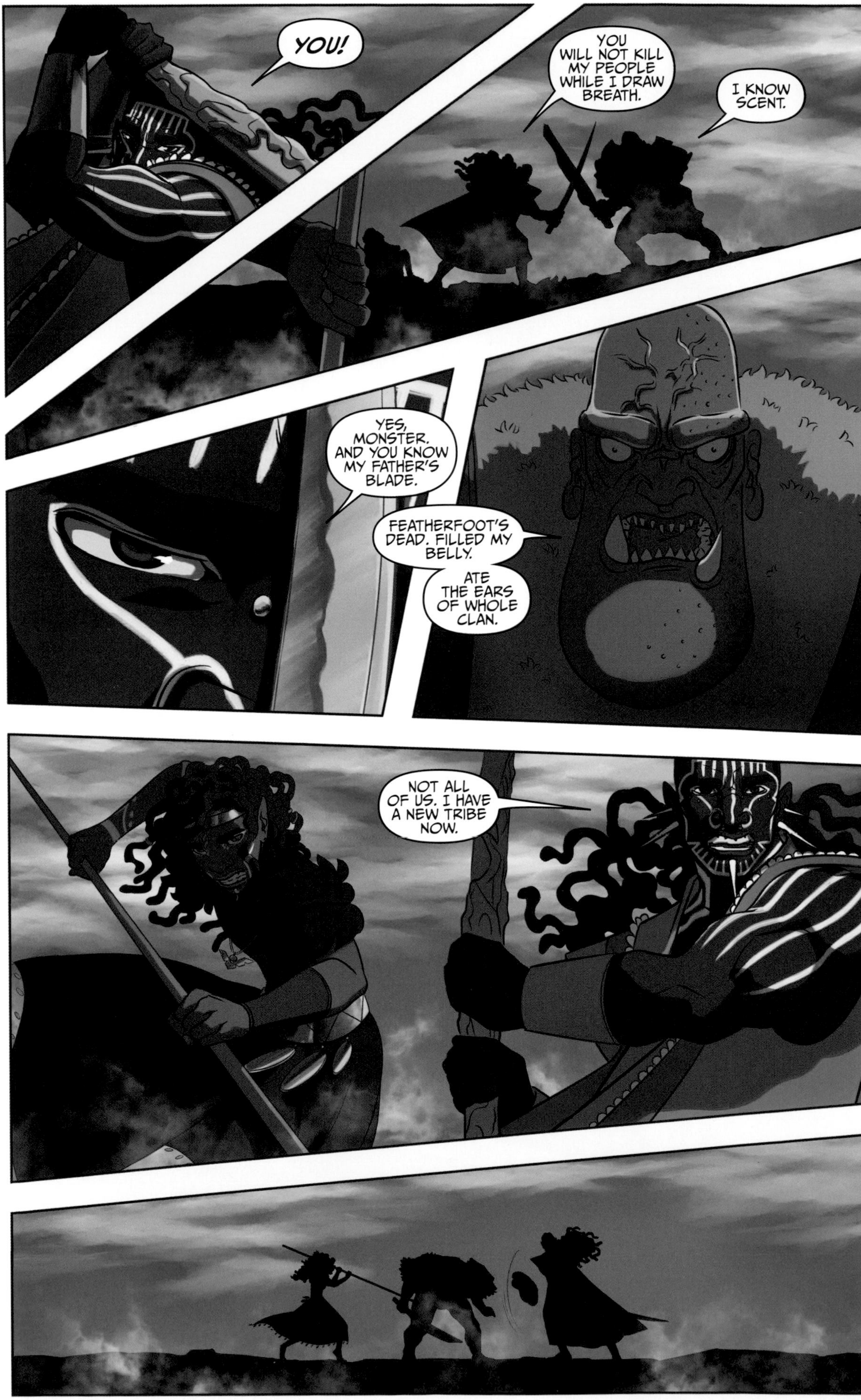
YOU!
YOU WILL NOT KILL MY PEOPLE WHILE I DRAW BREATH.
I KNOW SCENT.
YES, MONSTER. AND YOU KNOW MY FATHER'S BLADE.
FEATHERFOOT'S DEAD. FILLED MY BELLY.
ATE THE EARS OF WHOLE CLAN.
NOT ALL OF US. I HAVE A NEW TRIBE NOW.

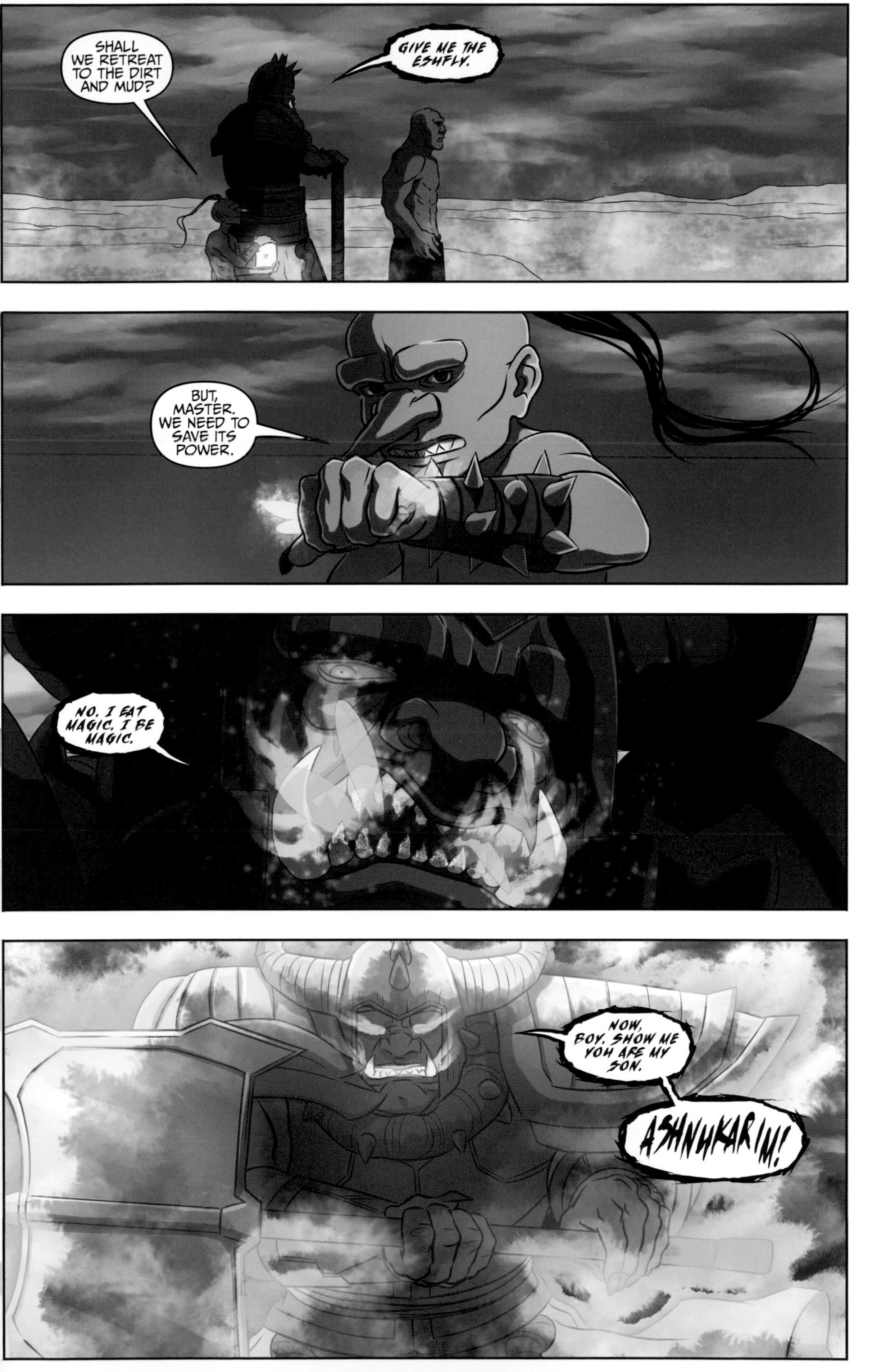
SHALL WE RETREAT TO THE DIRT AND MUD?
GIVE ME THE ESHFLY.
BUT, MASTER. WE NEED TO SAVE ITS POWER.
NO. I EAT MAGIC. I BE MAGIC.
NOW, BOY. SHOW ME YOU ARE MY SON.
ASHNUKARIM!

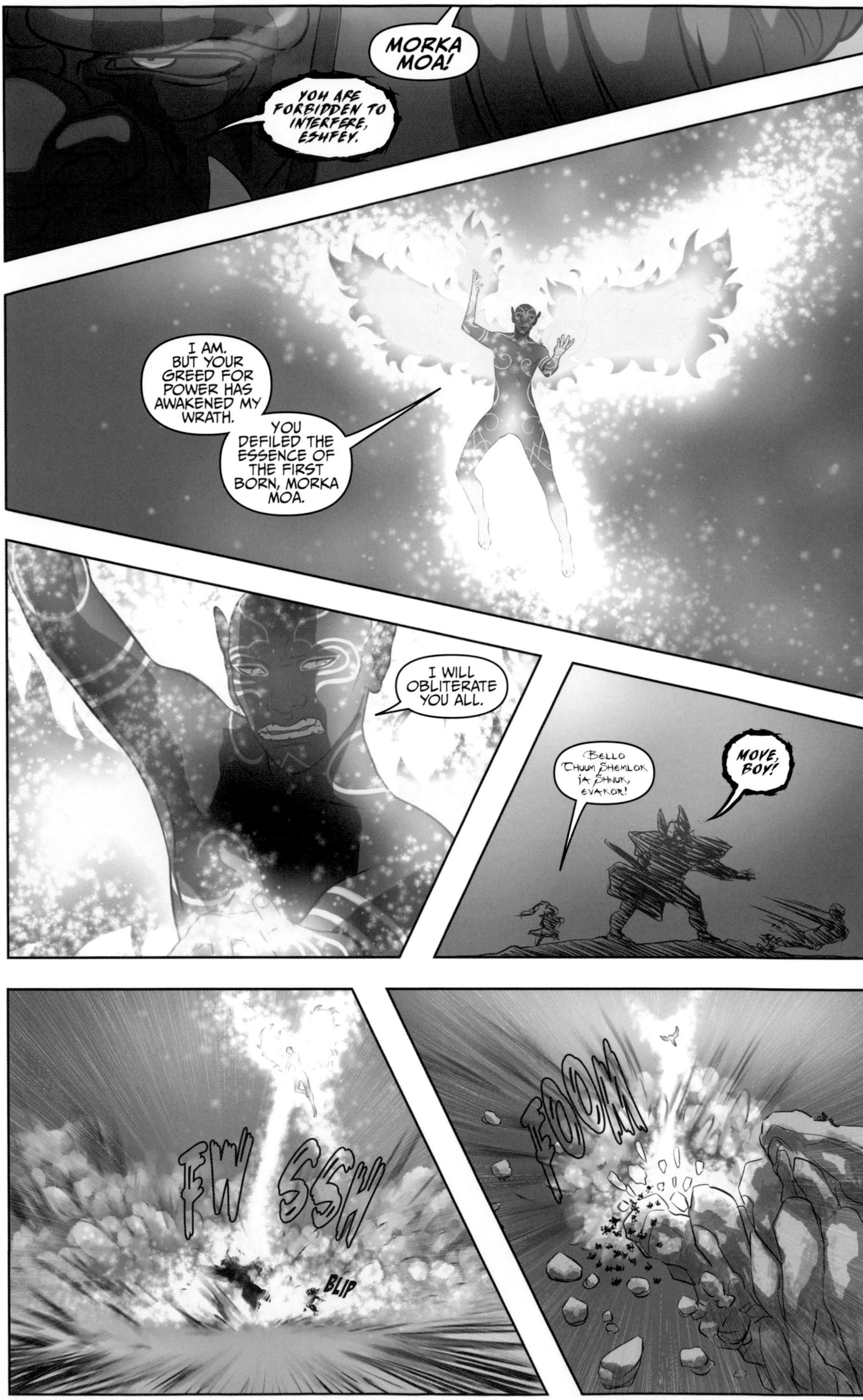
MORKA MOA!
YOU ARE FORBIDDEN TO INTERFERE, ESUFEY.
I AM. BUT YOUR GREED FOR POWER HAS AWAKENED MY WRATH.
YOU DEFILED THE ESSENCE OF THE FIRST BORN, MORKA MOA.
I WILL OBLITERATE YOU ALL.
Bello Thuum Shemlok ia Shnuk, evakor!
MOVE, BOY!
FW SSH
BLIP
FOOM

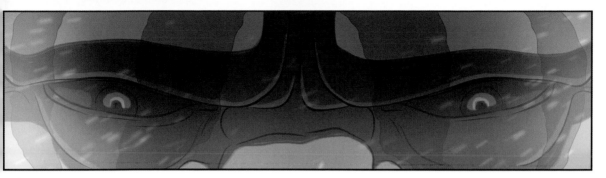

I WEAR THE ARMOR OF XATH AND YOUR ESSENCE COURSES THROUGH MY VEINS.

YOU CANNOT HURT ME, CHARAN.

NOT POSSIBLE.

FWOOSH

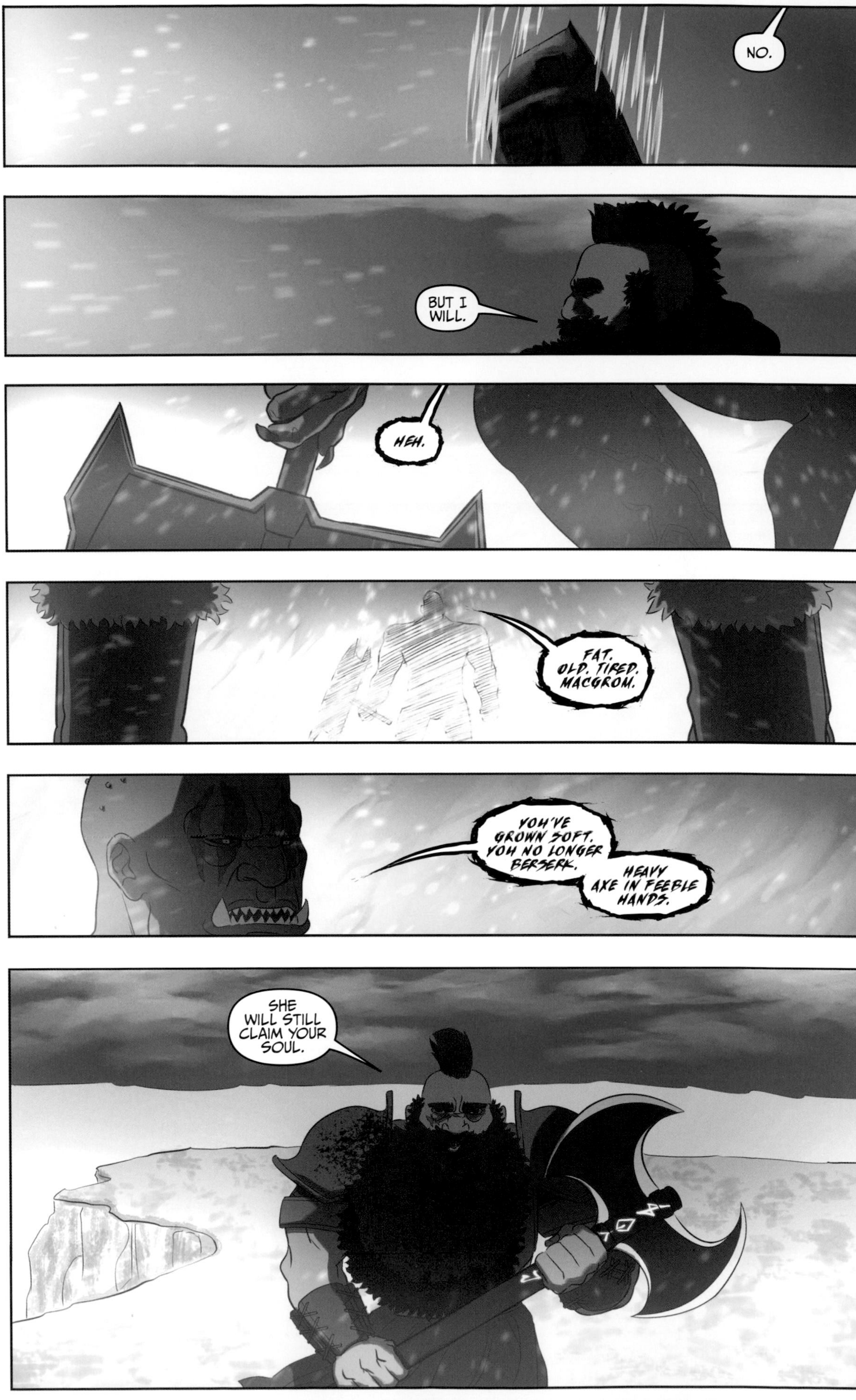
NO.
BUT I WILL.
HEH.
FAT. OLD. TIRED. MACGROM.
YOU'VE GROWN SOFT. YOU NO LONGER BERSERK.
HEAVY AXE IN FEEBLE HANDS.
SHE WILL STILL CLAIM YOUR SOUL.

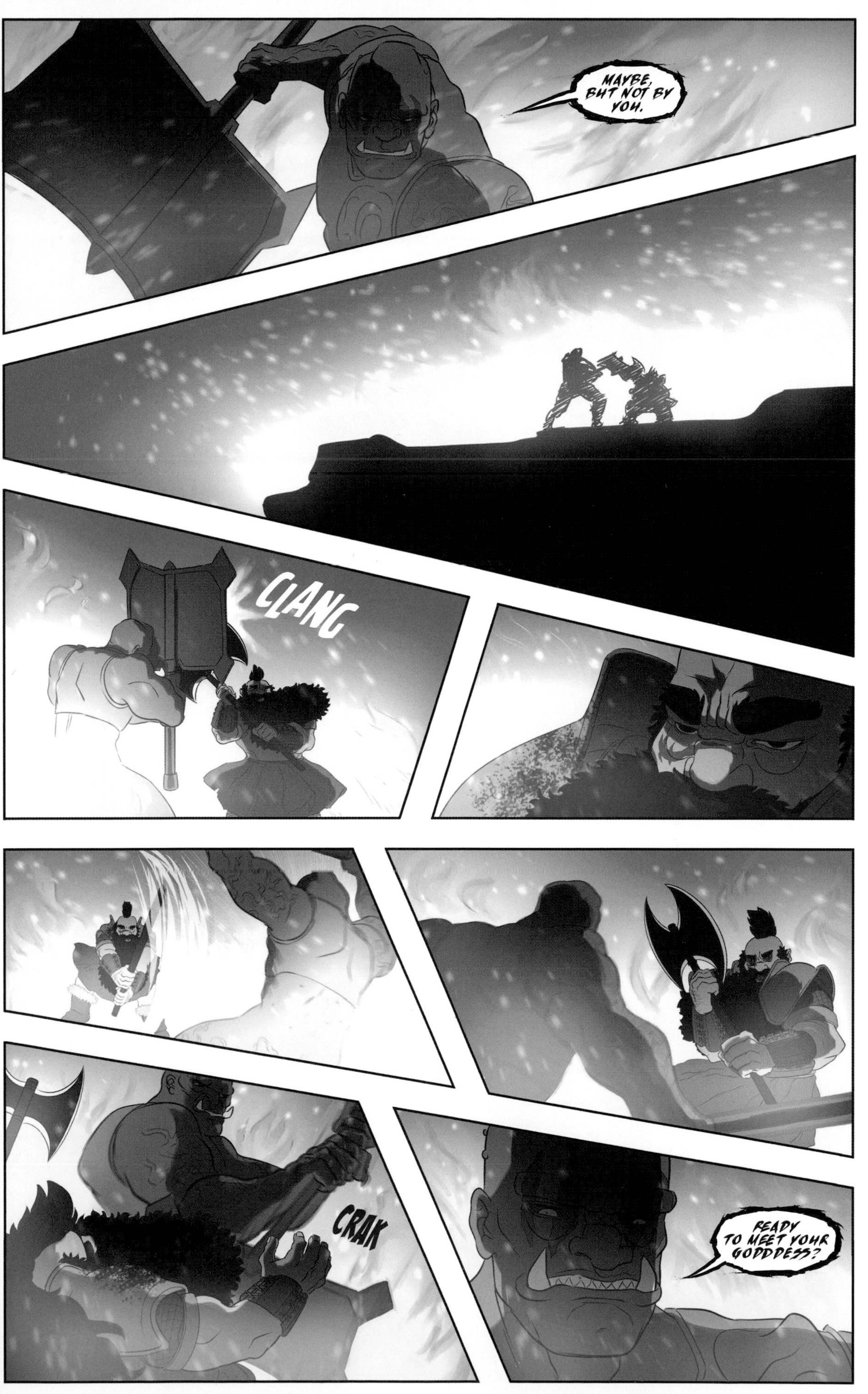
MAYBE, BUT NOT BY YOU.
CLANG
CRAK
READY TO MEET YOUR GODDESS?

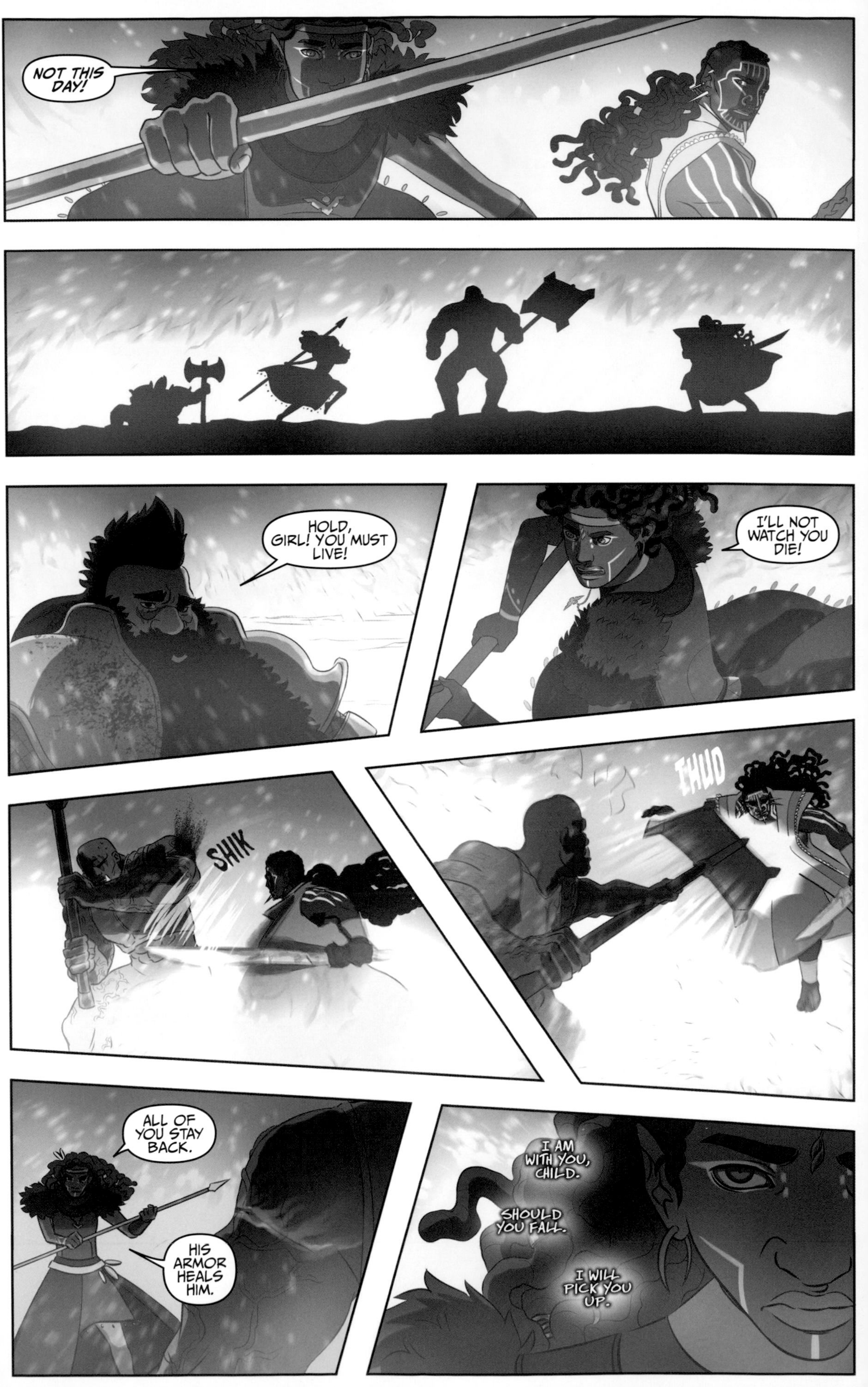
NOT THIS DAY!
HOLD, GIRL! YOU MUST LIVE!
I'LL NOT WATCH YOU DIE!
SHIK
THUD
ALL OF YOU STAY BACK.
HIS ARMOR HEALS HIM.
I AM WITH YOU, CHILD.
SHOULD YOU FALL.
I WILL PICK YOU UP.

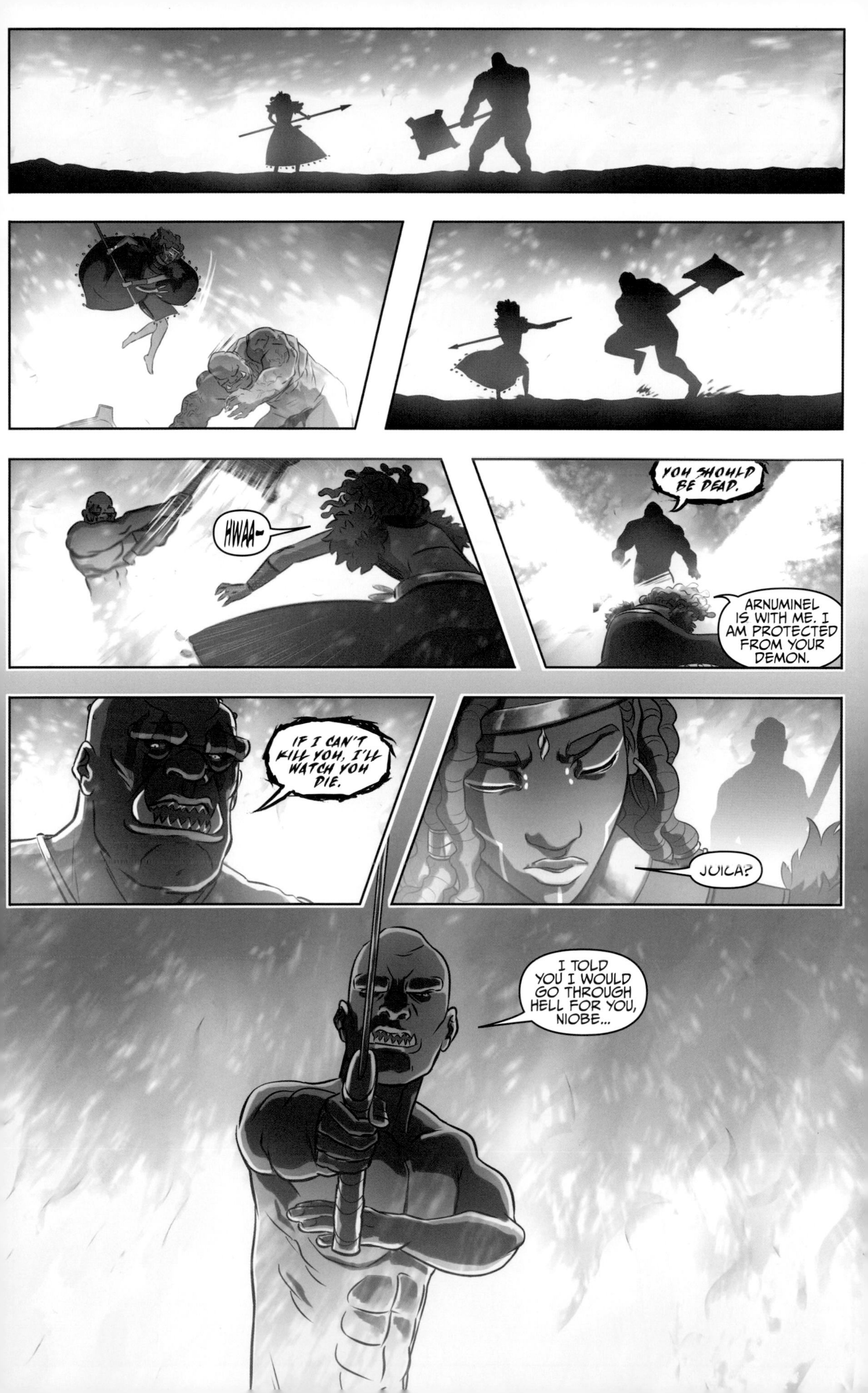
HWAA-
YOU SHOULD BE DEAD.
ARNUMINEL IS WITH ME. I AM PROTECTED FROM YOUR DEMON.
IF I CAN'T KILL YOU, I'LL WATCH YOU DIE.
JUICA?
I TOLD YOU I WOULD GO THROUGH HELL FOR YOU, NIOBE...

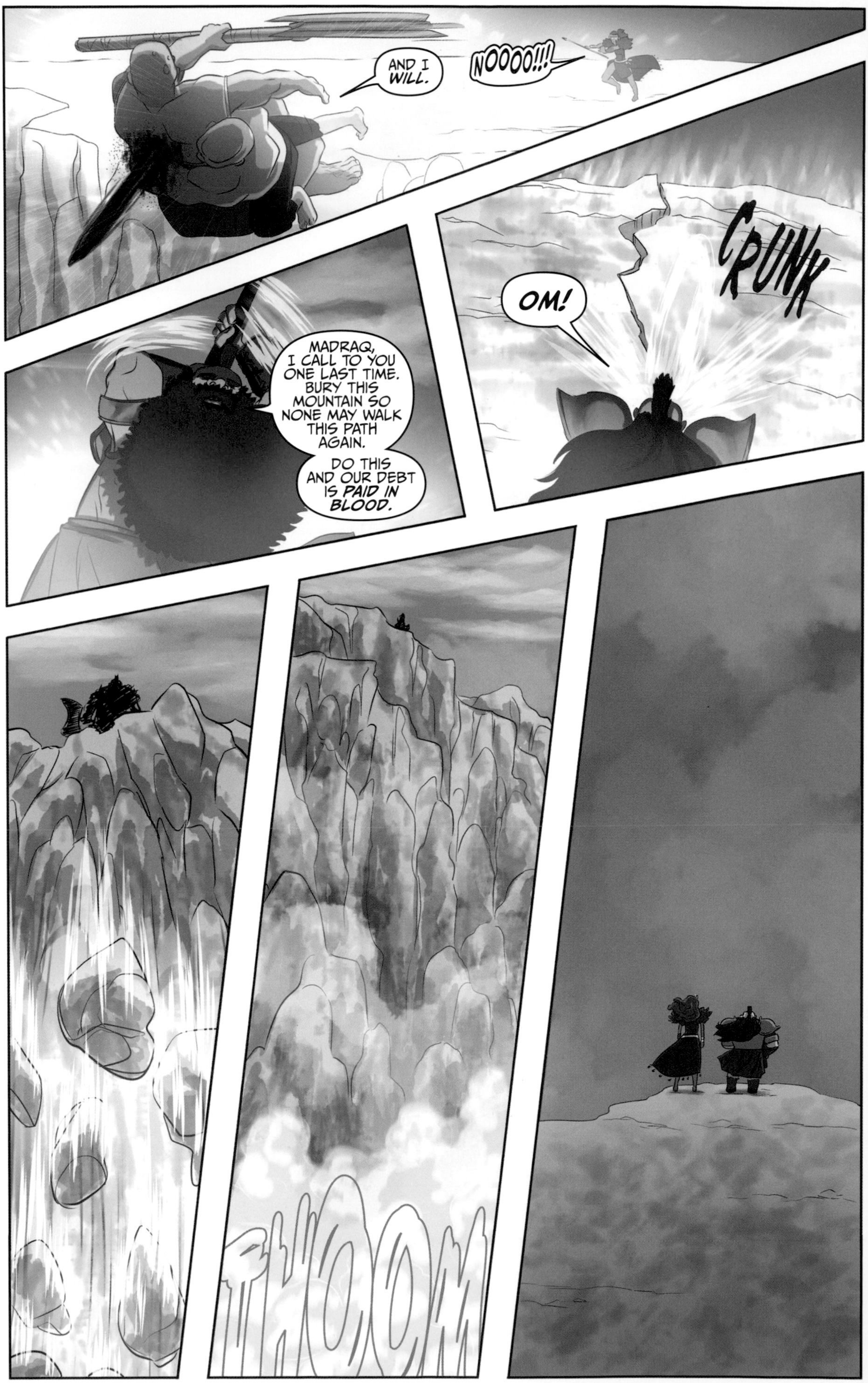
AND I WILL.
NOOOO!!!
OM!
CRUNK
MADRAQ, I CALL TO YOU ONE LAST TIME. BURY THIS MOUNTAIN SO NONE MAY WALK THIS PATH AGAIN.
DO THIS AND OUR DEBT IS PAID IN BLOOD.
THOOM

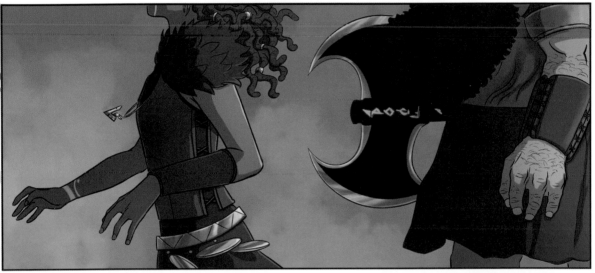

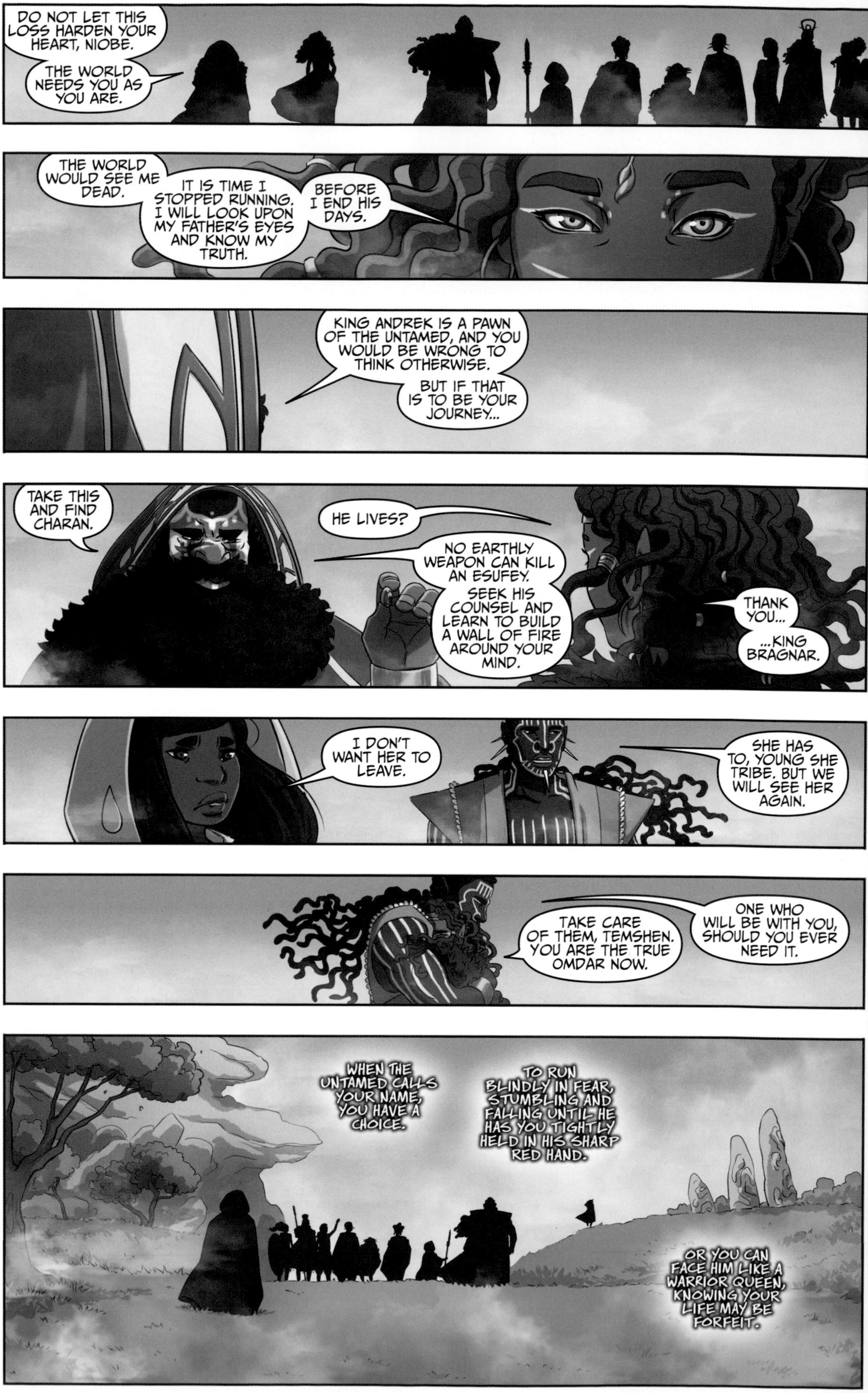
DO NOT LET THIS LOSS HARDEN YOUR HEART, NIOBE.
THE WORLD NEEDS YOU AS YOU ARE.
THE WORLD WOULD SEE ME DEAD.
IT IS TIME I STOPPED RUNNING. I WILL LOOK UPON MY FATHER'S EYES AND KNOW MY TRUTH.
BEFORE I END HIS DAYS.
KING ANDREK IS A PAWN OF THE UNTAMED, AND YOU WOULD BE WRONG TO THINK OTHERWISE.
BUT IF THAT IS TO BE YOUR JOURNEY...
TAKE THIS AND FIND CHARAN.
HE LIVES?
NO EARTHLY WEAPON CAN KILL AN ESUFEY.
SEEK HIS COUNSEL AND LEARN TO BUILD A WALL OF FIRE AROUND YOUR MIND.
THANK YOU...
...KING BRAGNAR.
I DON'T WANT HER TO LEAVE.
SHE HAS TO, YOUNG SHE TRIBE. BUT WE WILL SEE HER AGAIN.
ONE WHO WILL BE WITH YOU, SHOULD YOU EVER NEED IT.
TAKE CARE OF THEM, TEMSHEN. YOU ARE THE TRUE OMDAR NOW.
WHEN THE UNTAMED CALLS YOUR NAME, YOU HAVE A CHOICE.
TO RUN BLINDLY IN FEAR, STUMBLING AND FALLING UNTIL HE HAS YOU TIGHTLY HELD IN HIS SHARP RED HAND.
OR YOU CAN FACE HIM LIKE A WARRIOR QUEEN, KNOWING YOUR LIFE MAY BE FORFEIT.

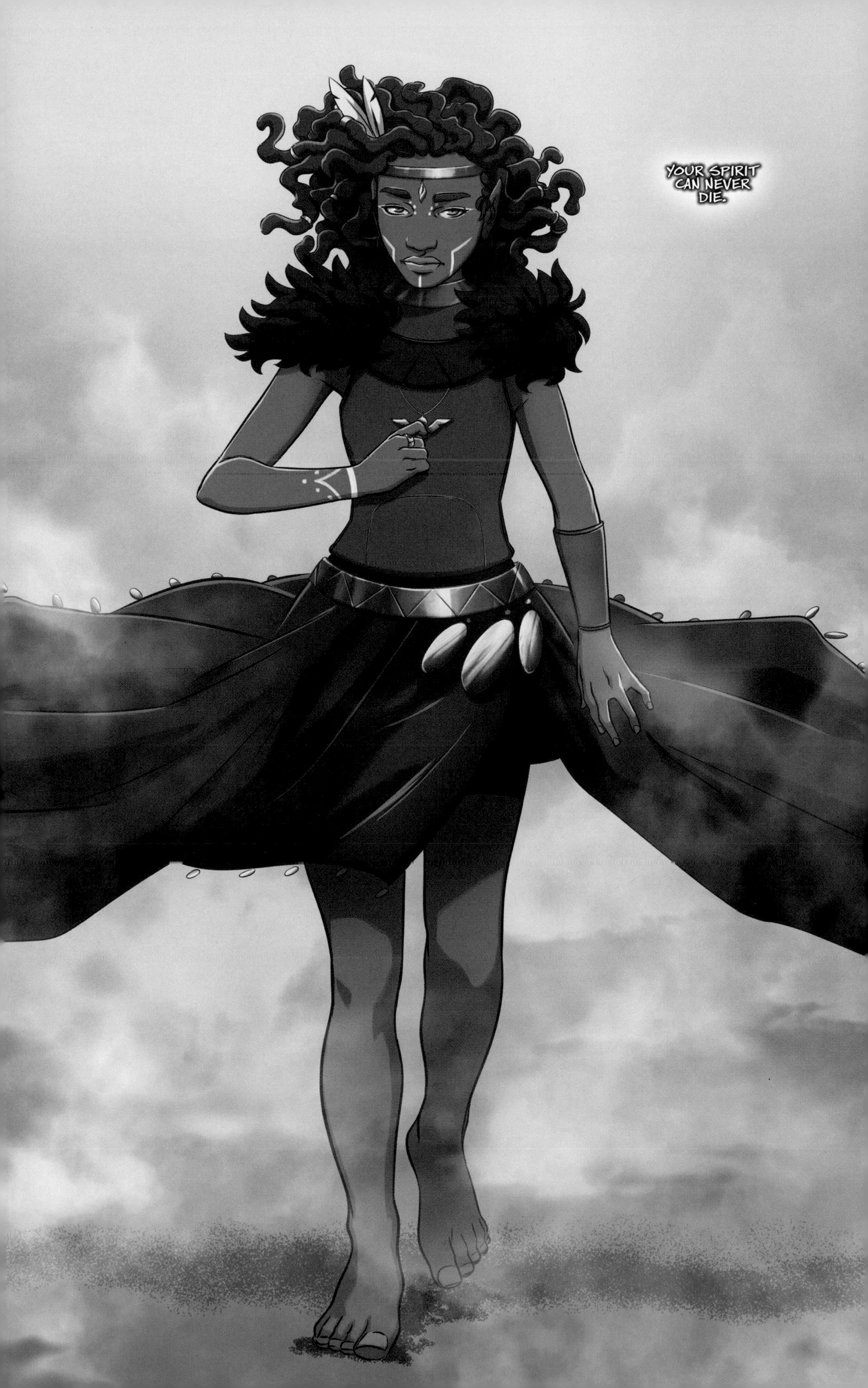
YOUR SPIRIT CAN NEVER DIE.

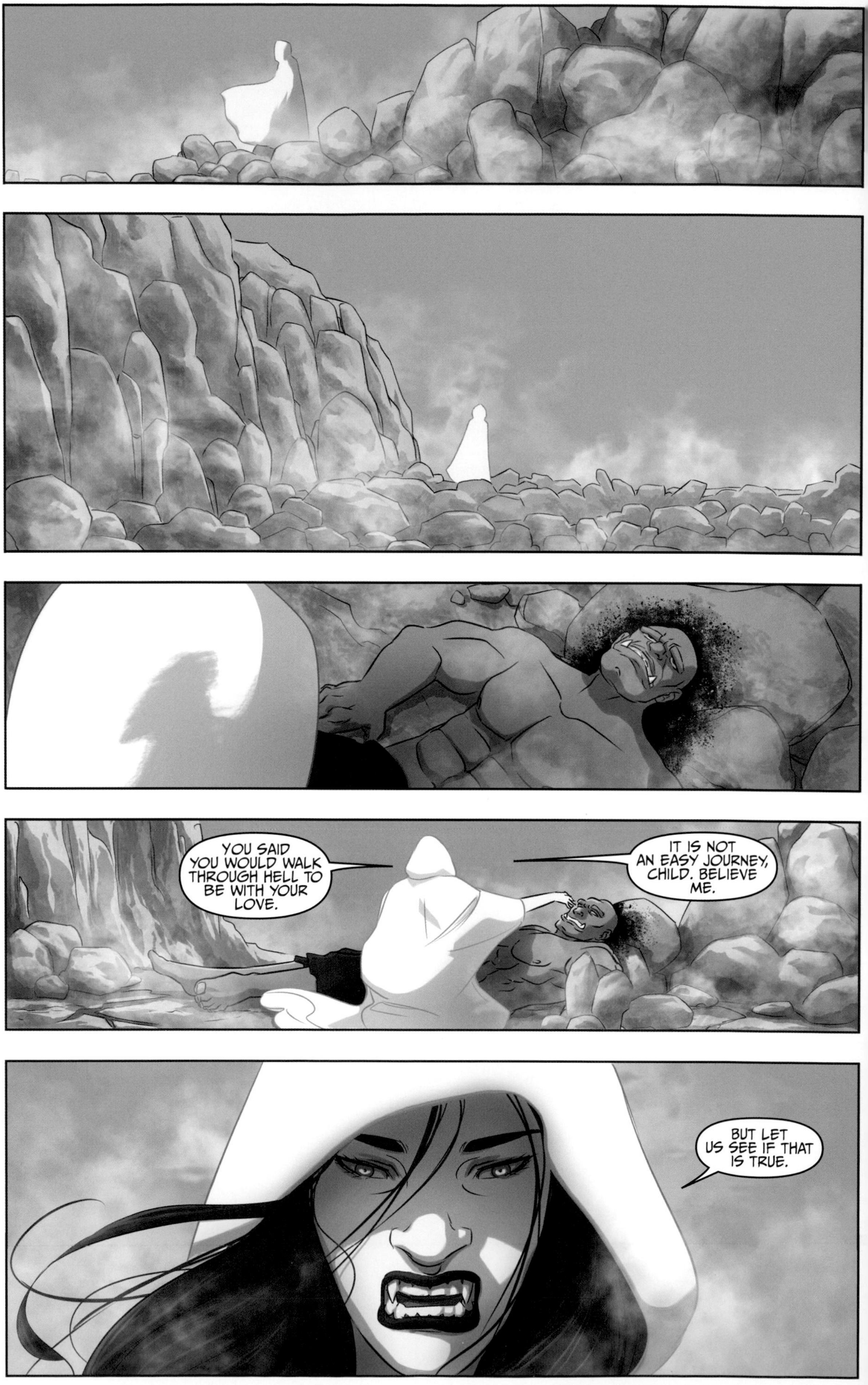
YOU SAID YOU WOULD WALK THROUGH HELL TO BE WITH YOUR LOVE.
IT IS NOT AN EASY JOURNEY, CHILD. BELIEVE ME.
BUT LET US SEE IF THAT IS TRUE.

Hello Stranger

You cannot always run from war. The spirit of conflict will find you and wrench your soul from hiding. He wears many guises, has many faces. He is the friend who smiles too little, the lover who smiles too much, or the man who would seek your ruin just because he can, all to make his own life seem less loathsome. Or it is the face you see in the mirror, challenging you to fight, daring you to fail, and laughing when you fall.

You will not always win against the demon of fear, but if you do not stand, he has already won. So walk tall, even if your back is broken.

She did not want to be a queen; becoming a woman was burden enough. It was not fair. Navigating the rivers of life and death, Niobe had already tasted the blood of those who hunted her and lost the man who had raised her. He was a stranger to all but her, a killer, a father, and a ghost. She missed him. In fact, she felt incomplete without him. She was alone once more.

The earth and trees called to her with whispers of returning to the root of the world. To become a child once more... for the first time. She could run along limbs of sowrie trees and splash in the waters of Ugoma. She could hide in the caves near Turanghem. She could hide. The world was hers to hide. The world was hers. And it rested heavy upon the wings of her back. The land would perish without her she knew. Like a child who needed her mother, she herself had to grow to nurture it. She was one with the world. She is the world.

She is Life. She is Death. She is Spirit. She is God.

But even Gods can die. The Untamed had slain Celebrius, the God of Eternity, and Niobe was an infant. And He was determined to claim her before she blossomed into the angel who would challenge him in heaven and in hell, and all across the vast and volatile world of…

GALLERY

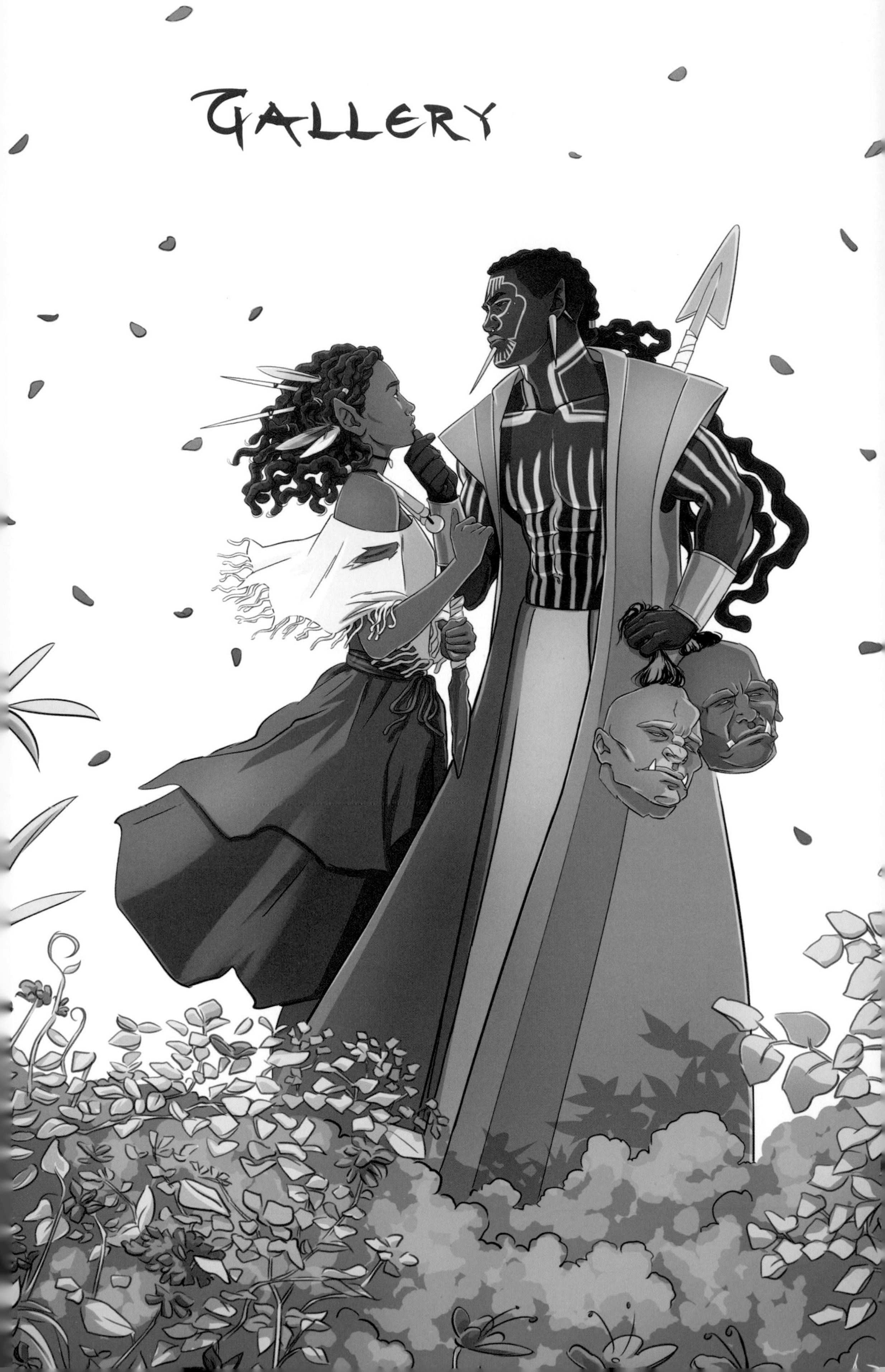

JAMES T. WEBSTER

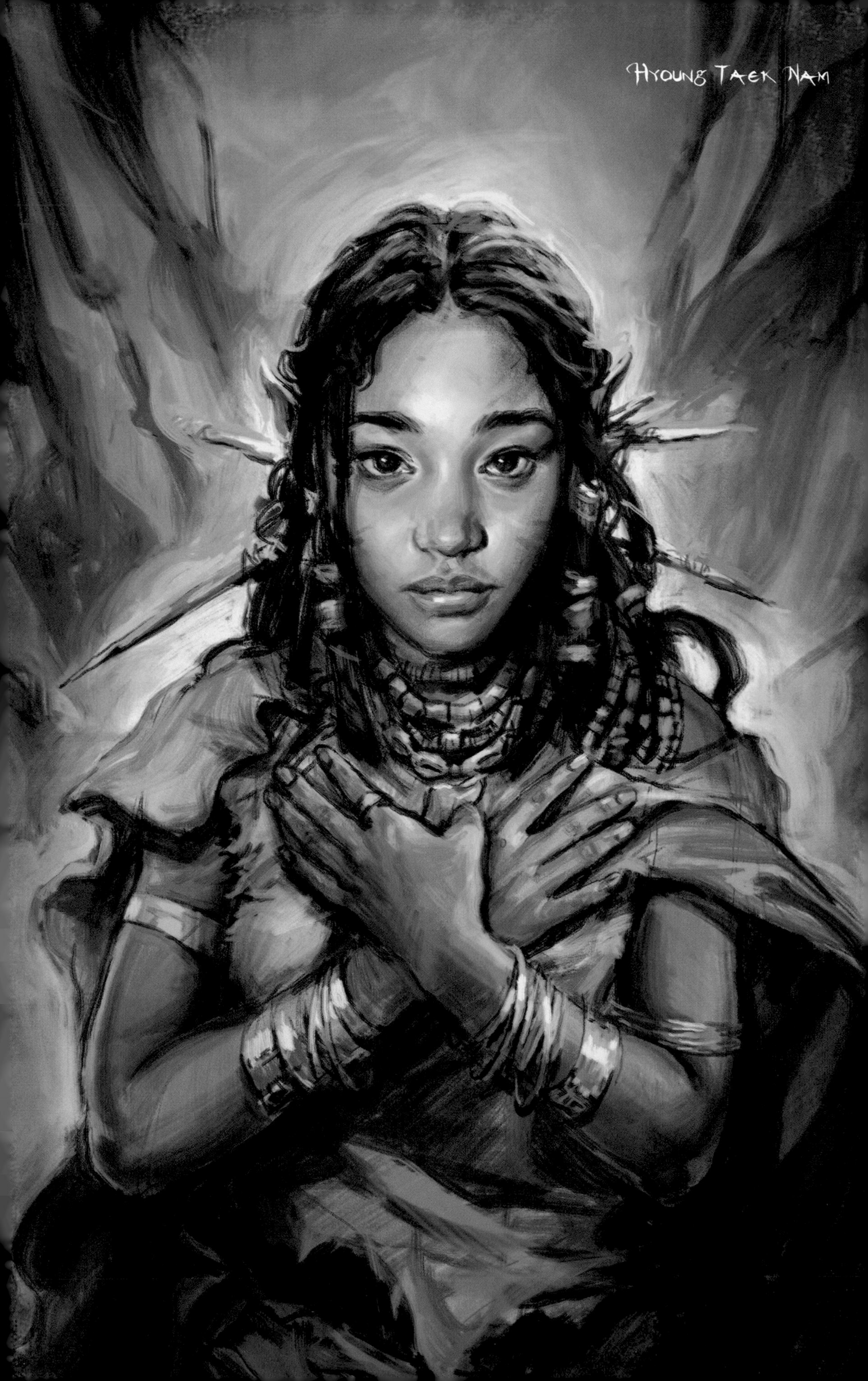
Hyoung Taek Nam

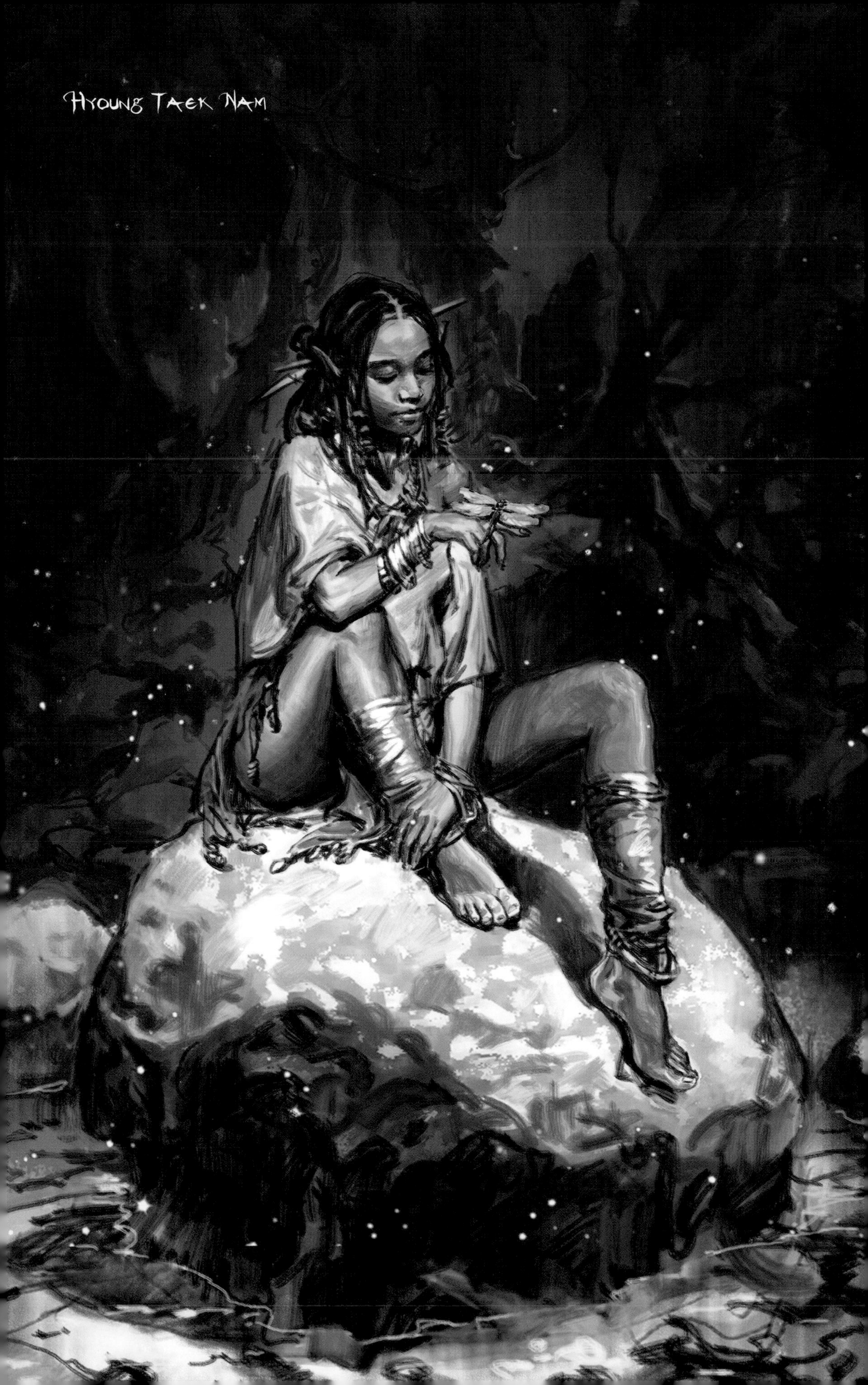
Hyoung Taek Nam

Hyoung Taek Nam

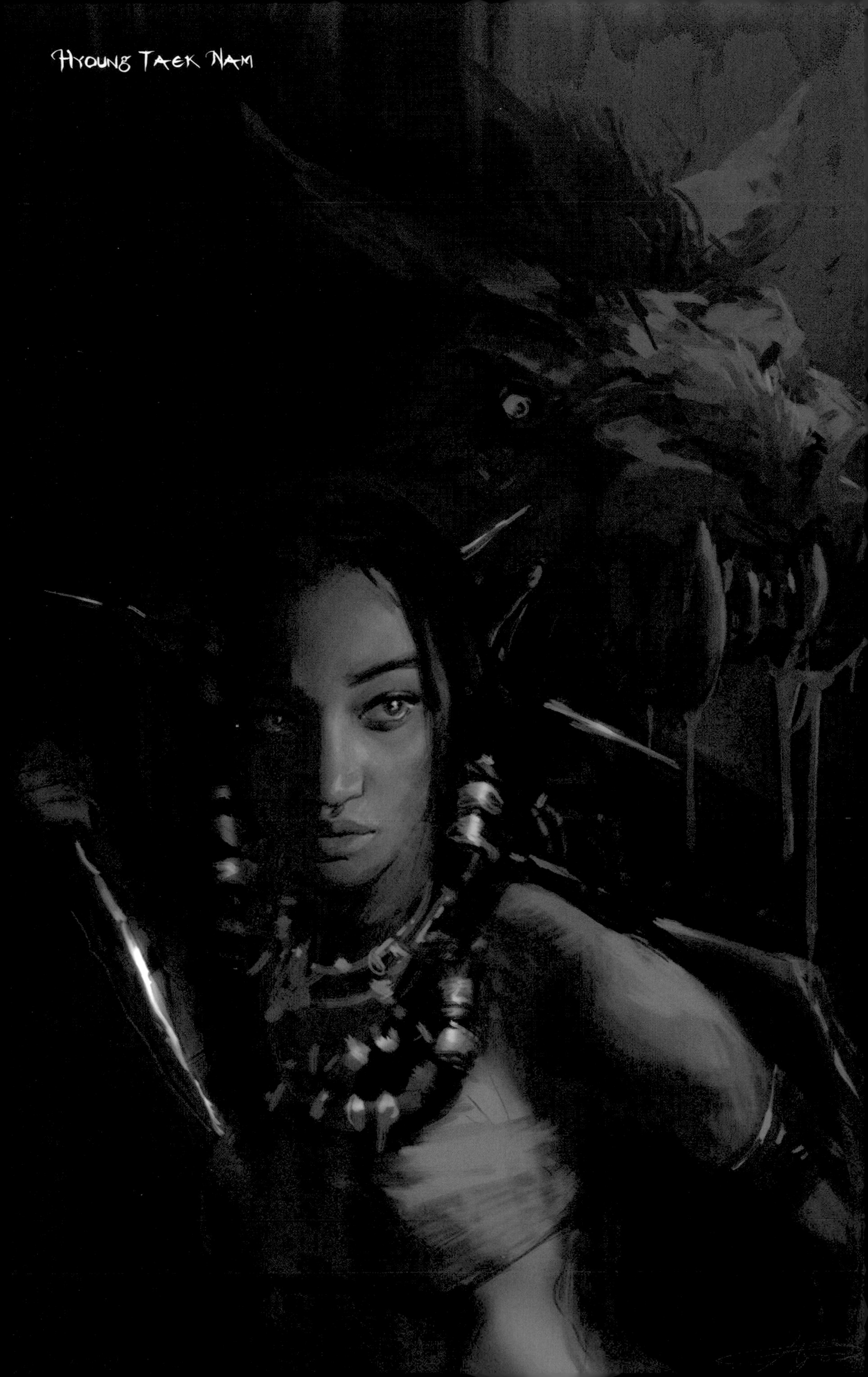

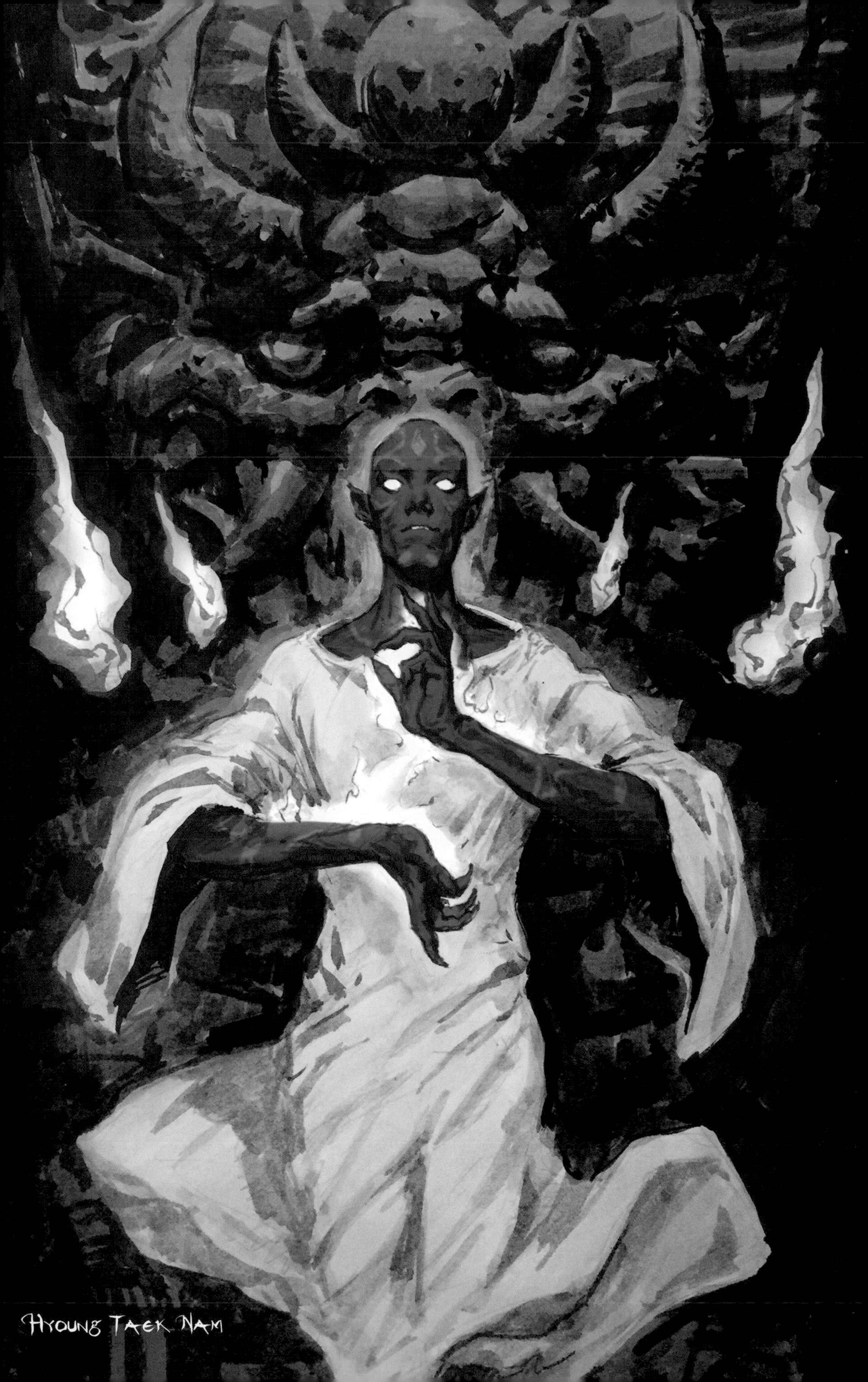
Hyoung Taek Nam

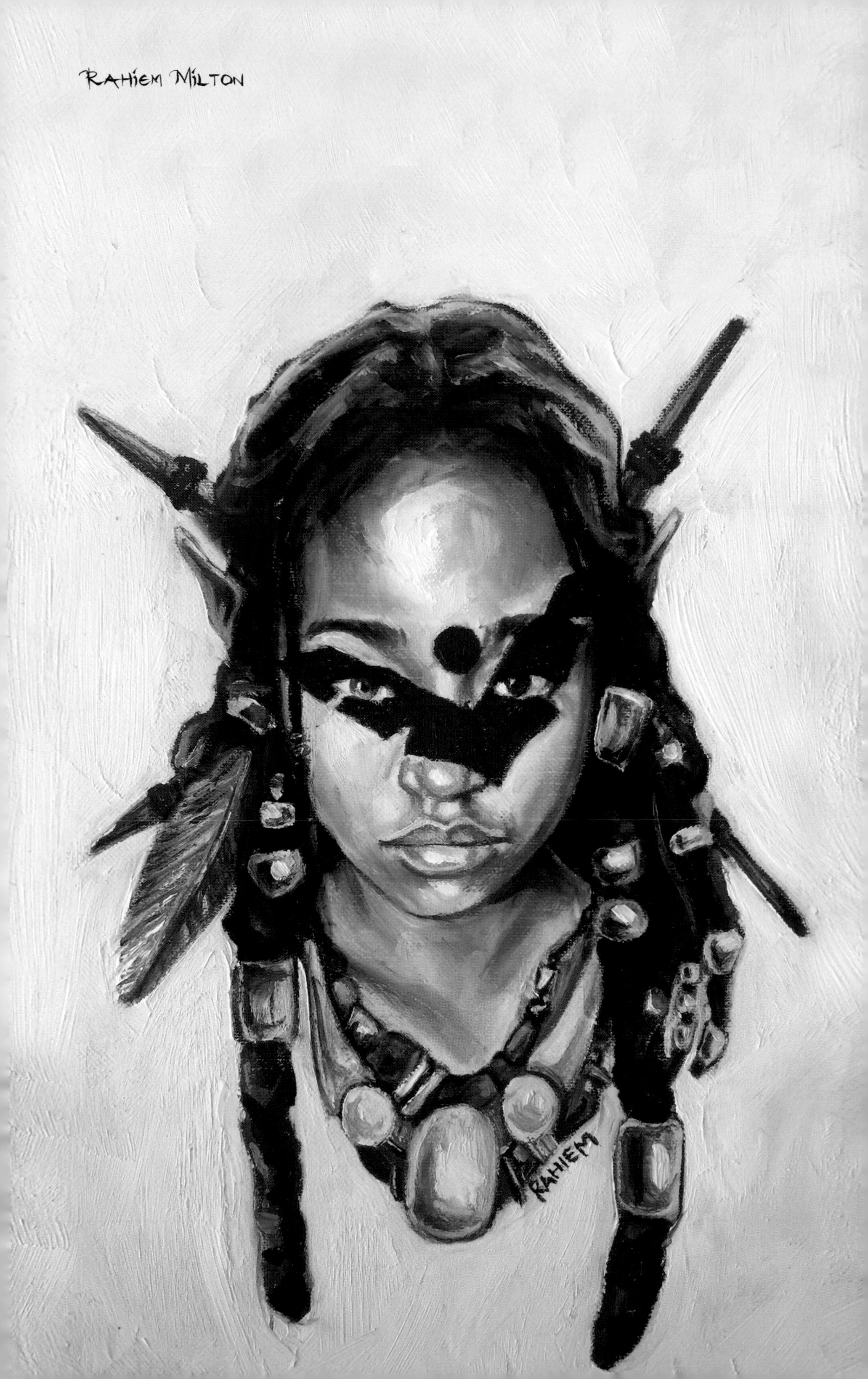
RAHIEM MILTON
RAHIEM

RAHIEM MILTON

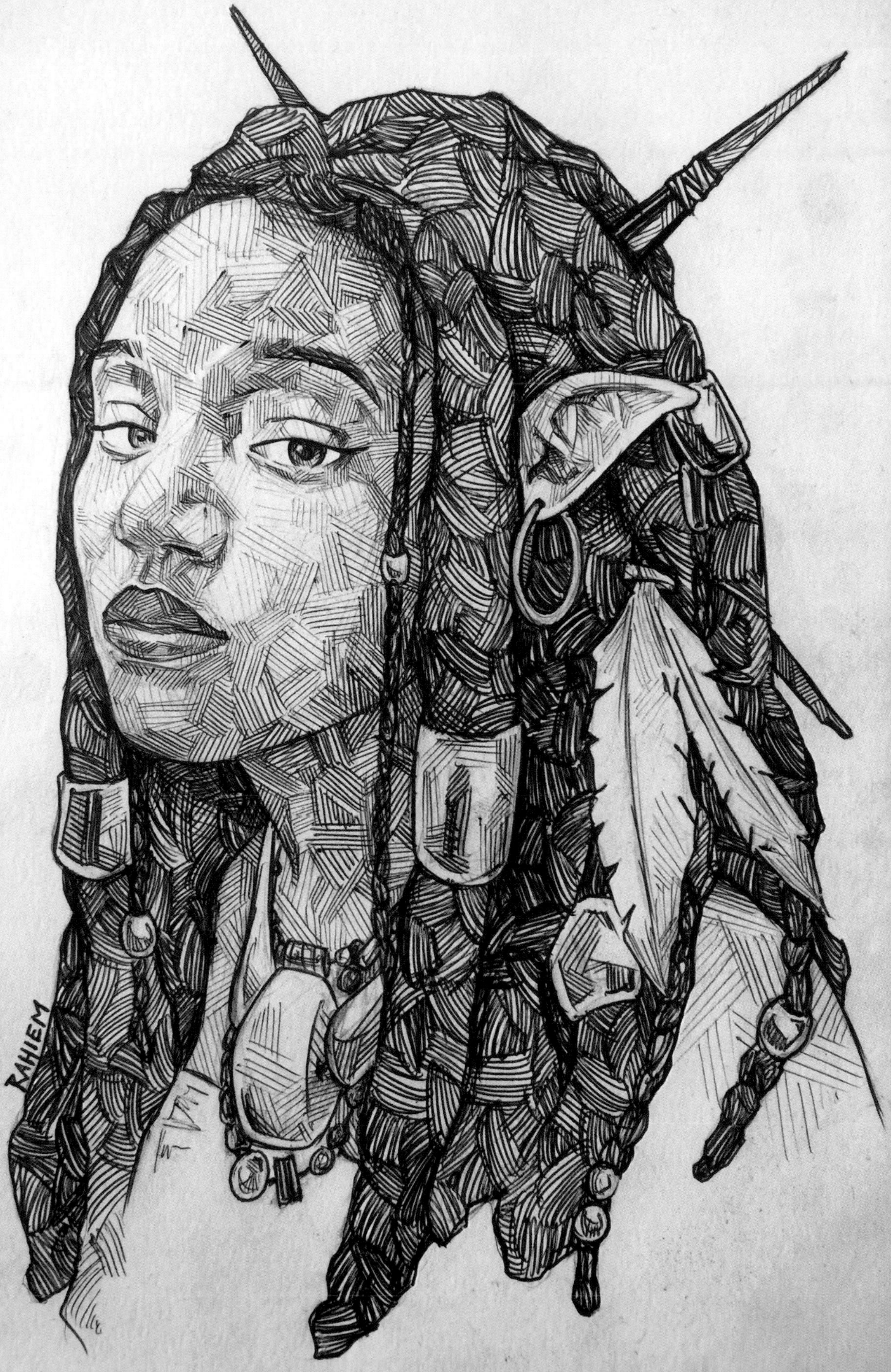
RAHIEM

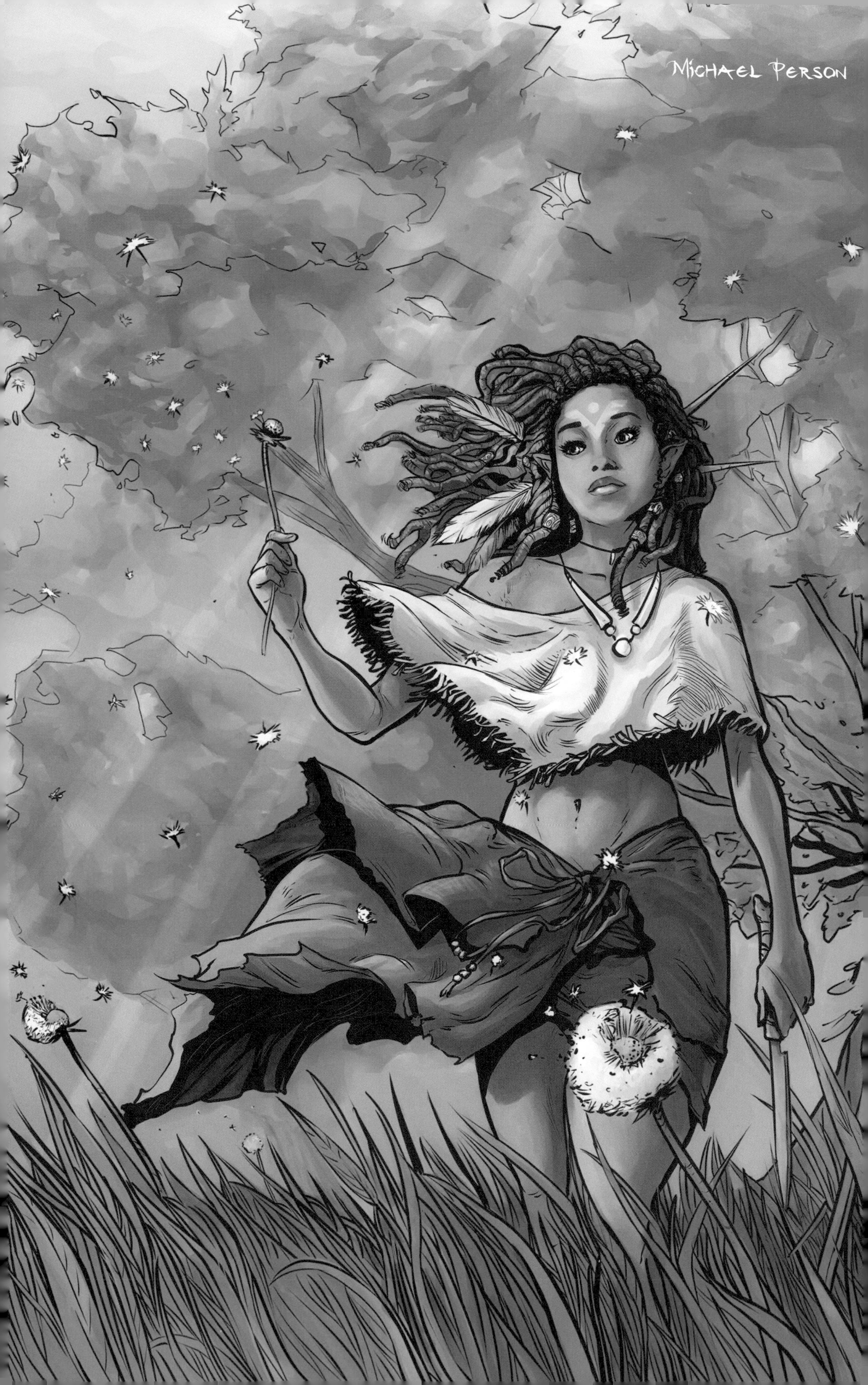
Michael Person

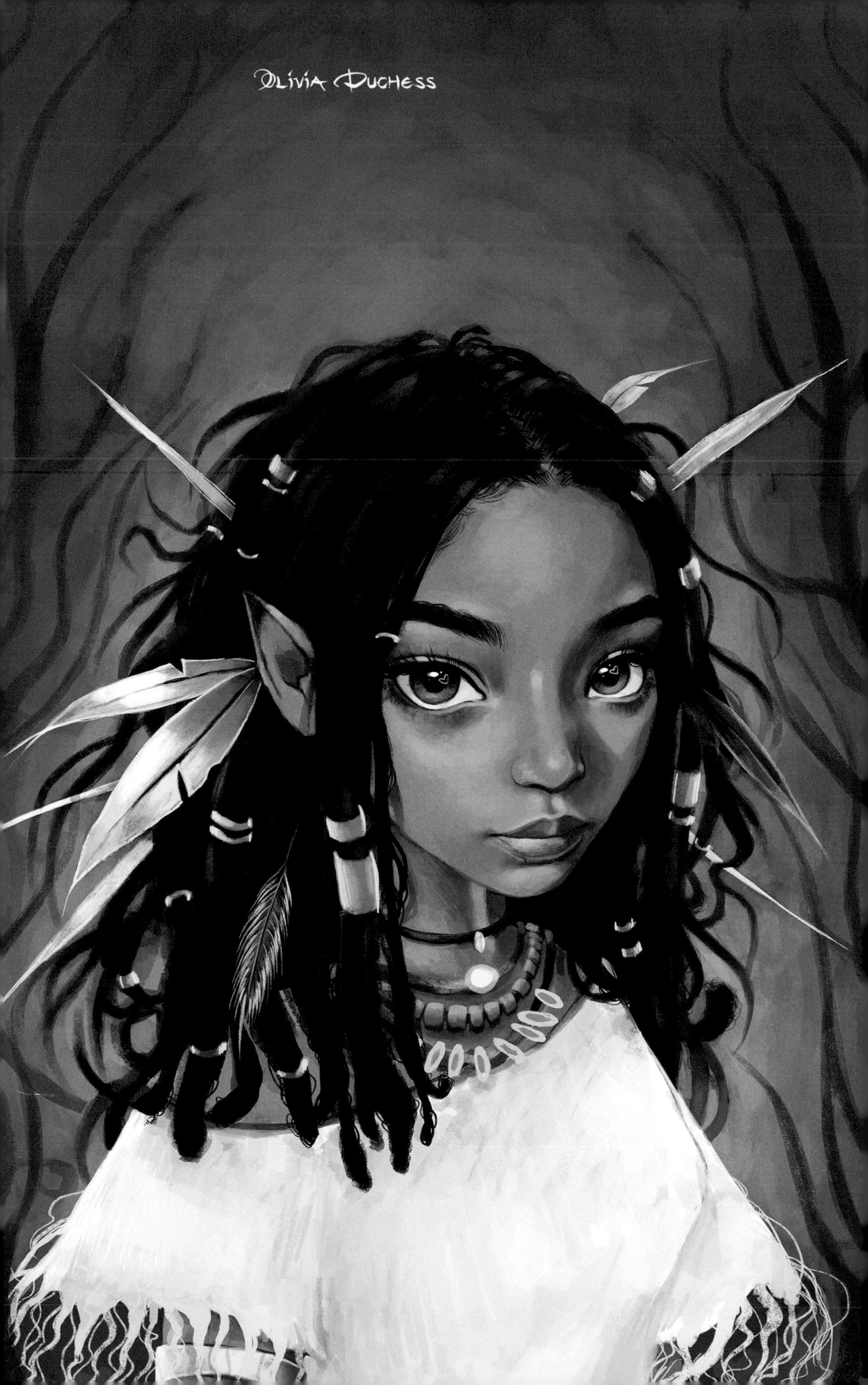
OLIVIA DUCHESS

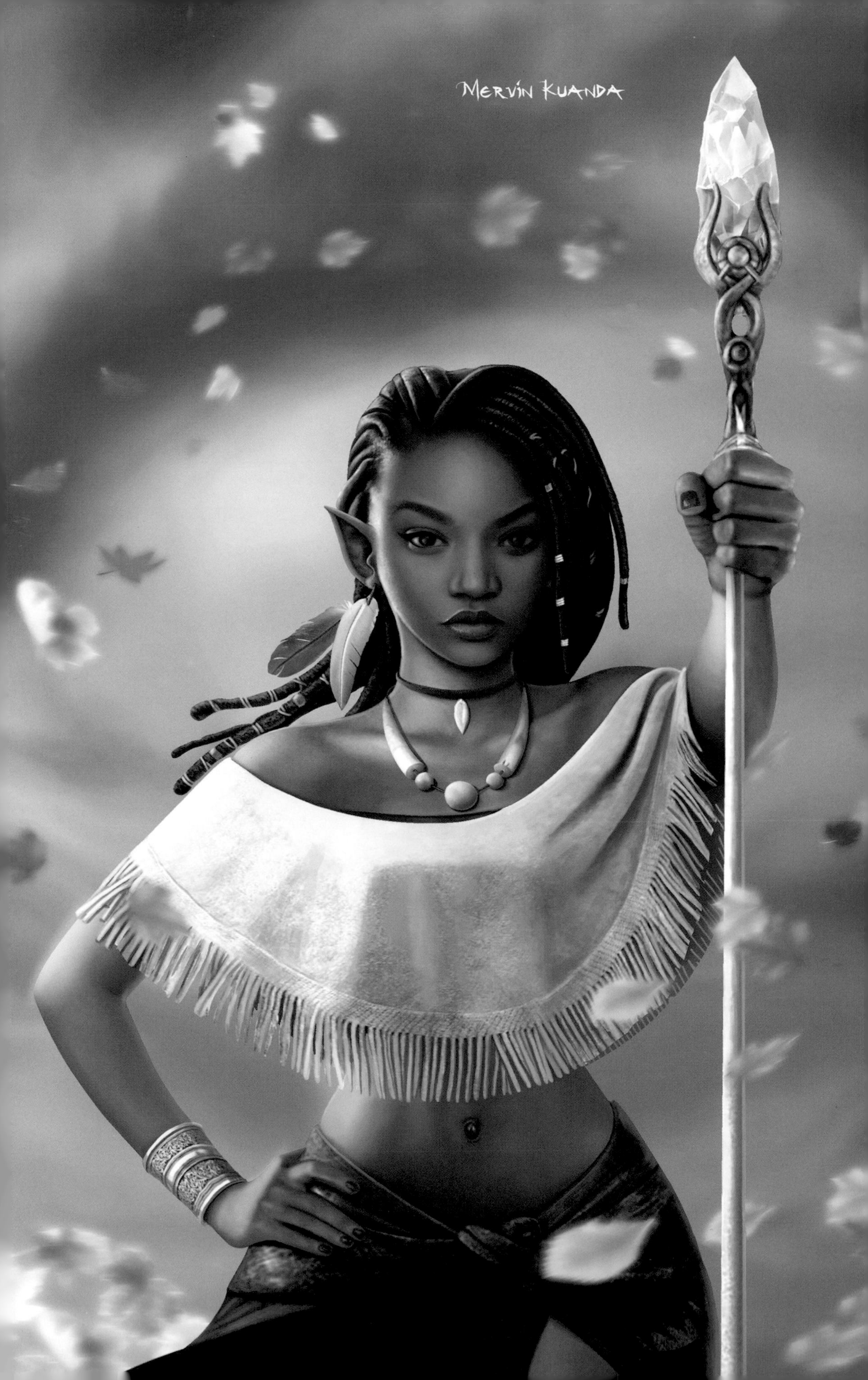
Mervin Kuanda

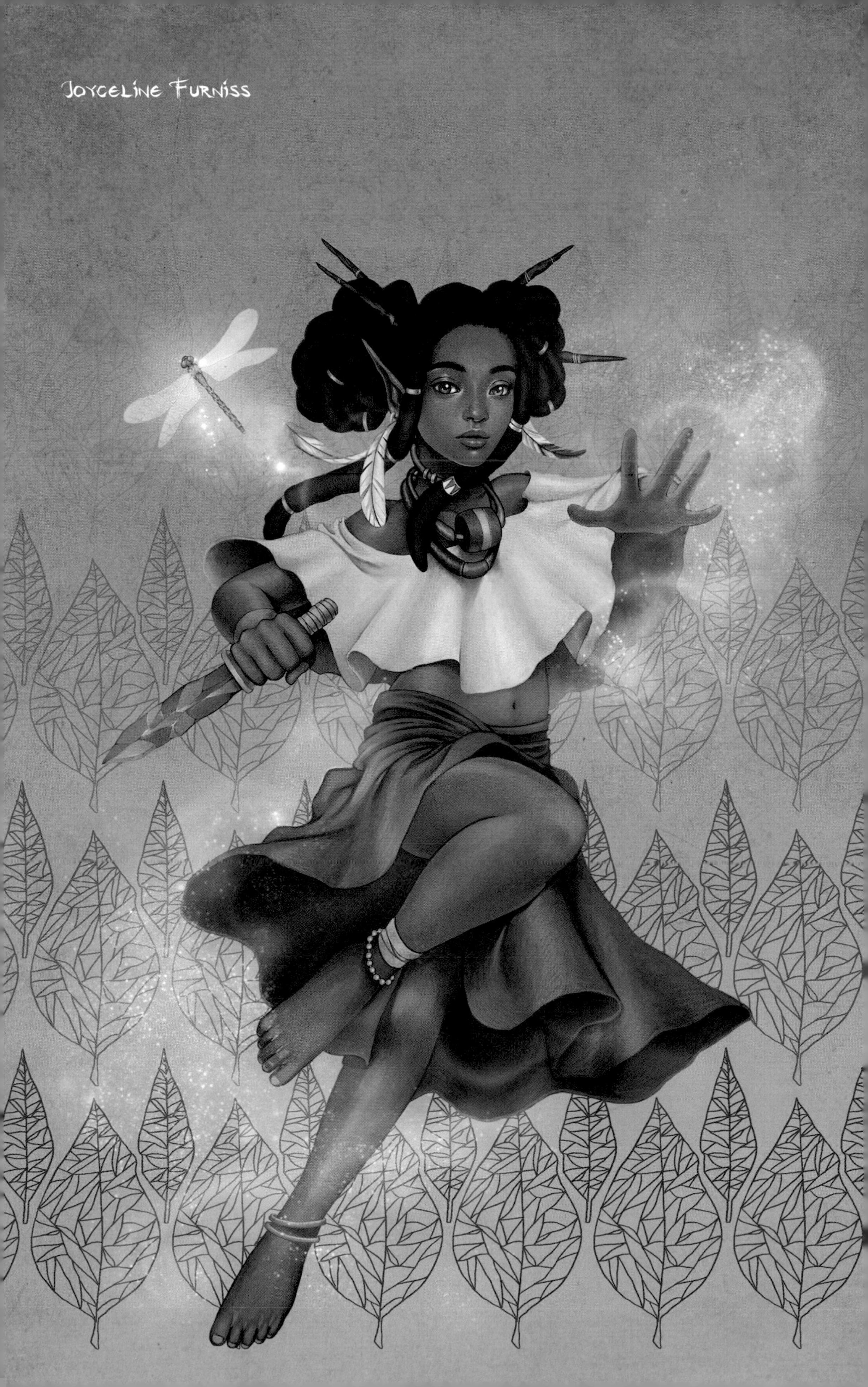
Joyceline Furniss

Markus Prime

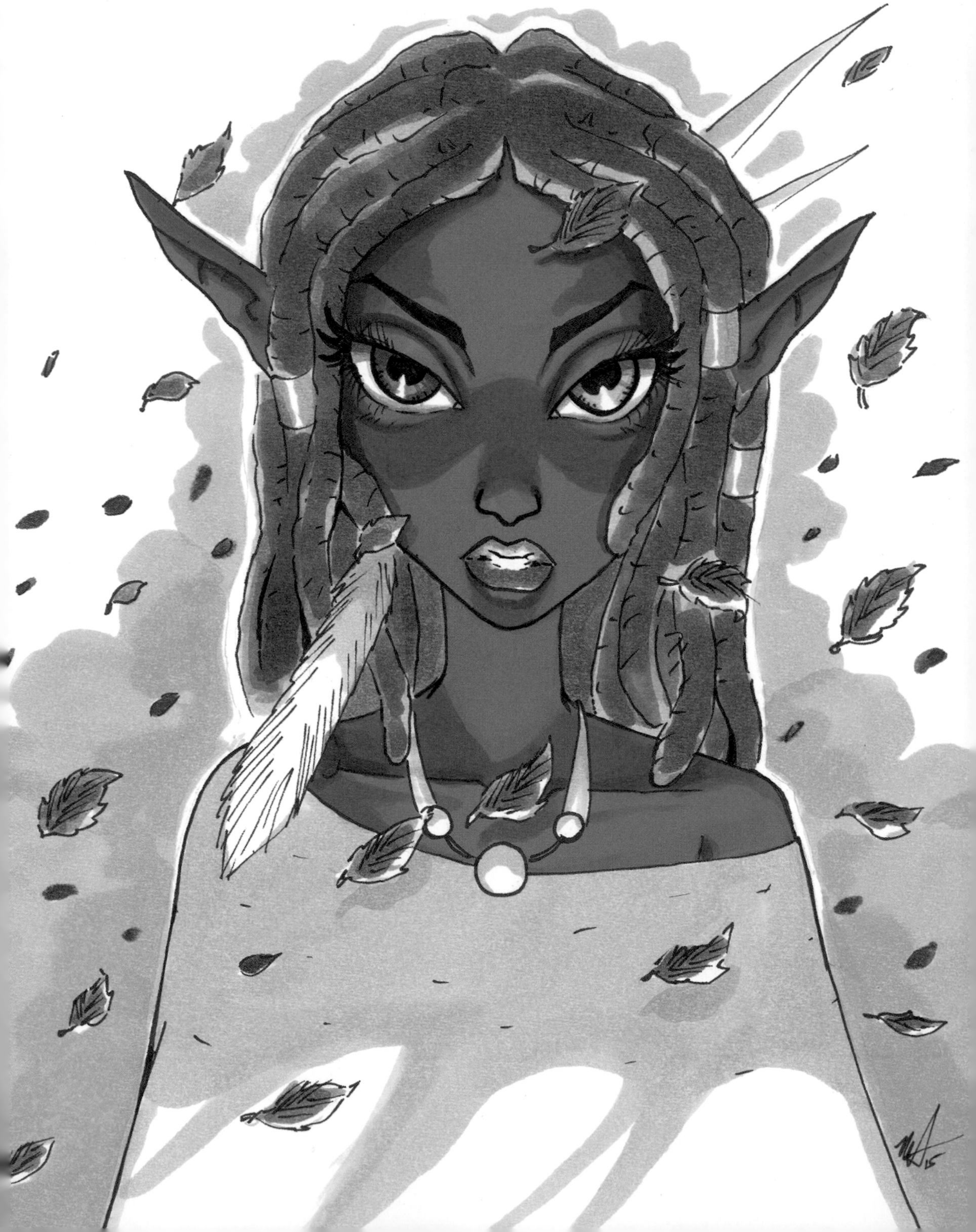

AMANDLA STENBERG

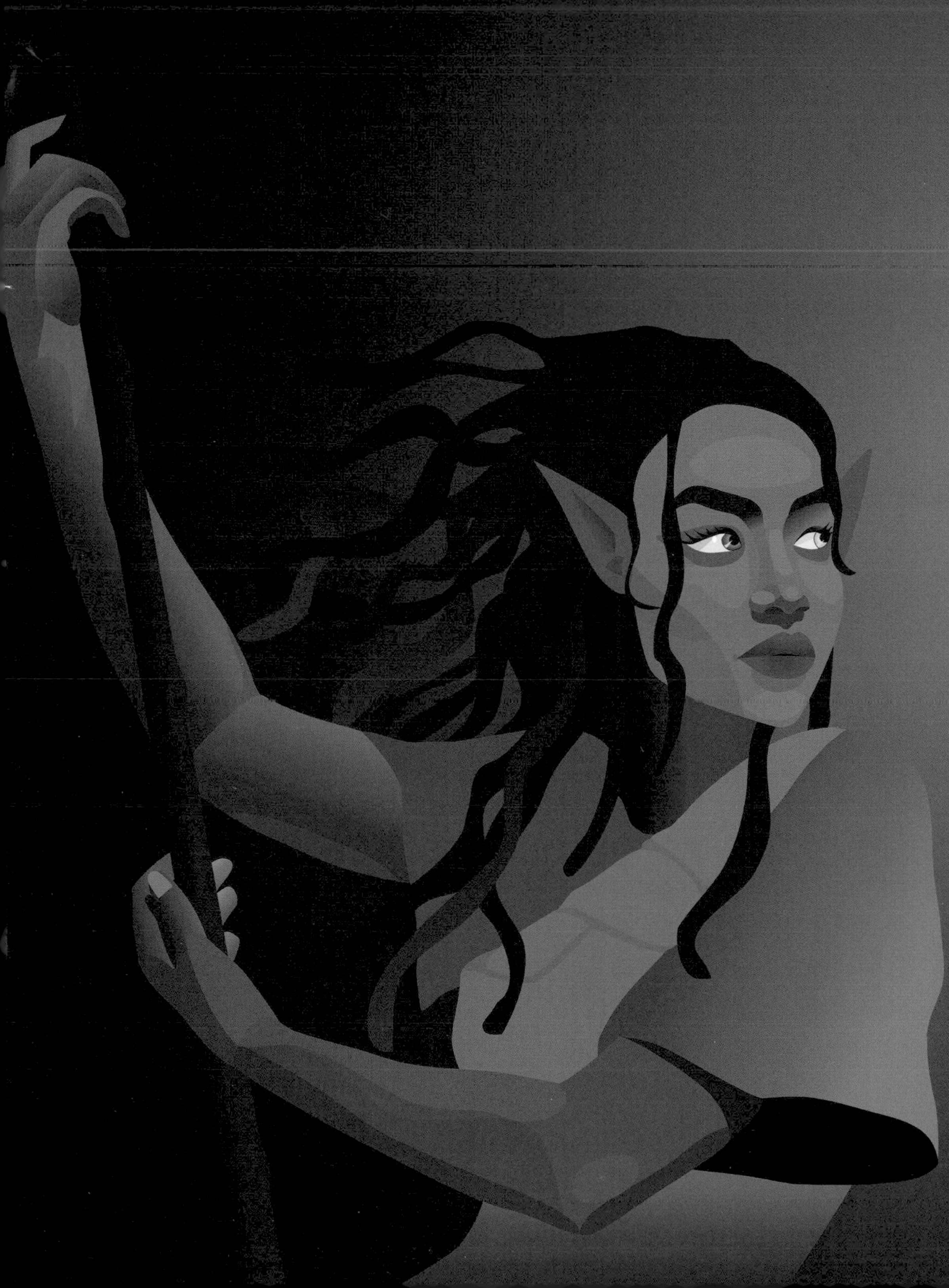

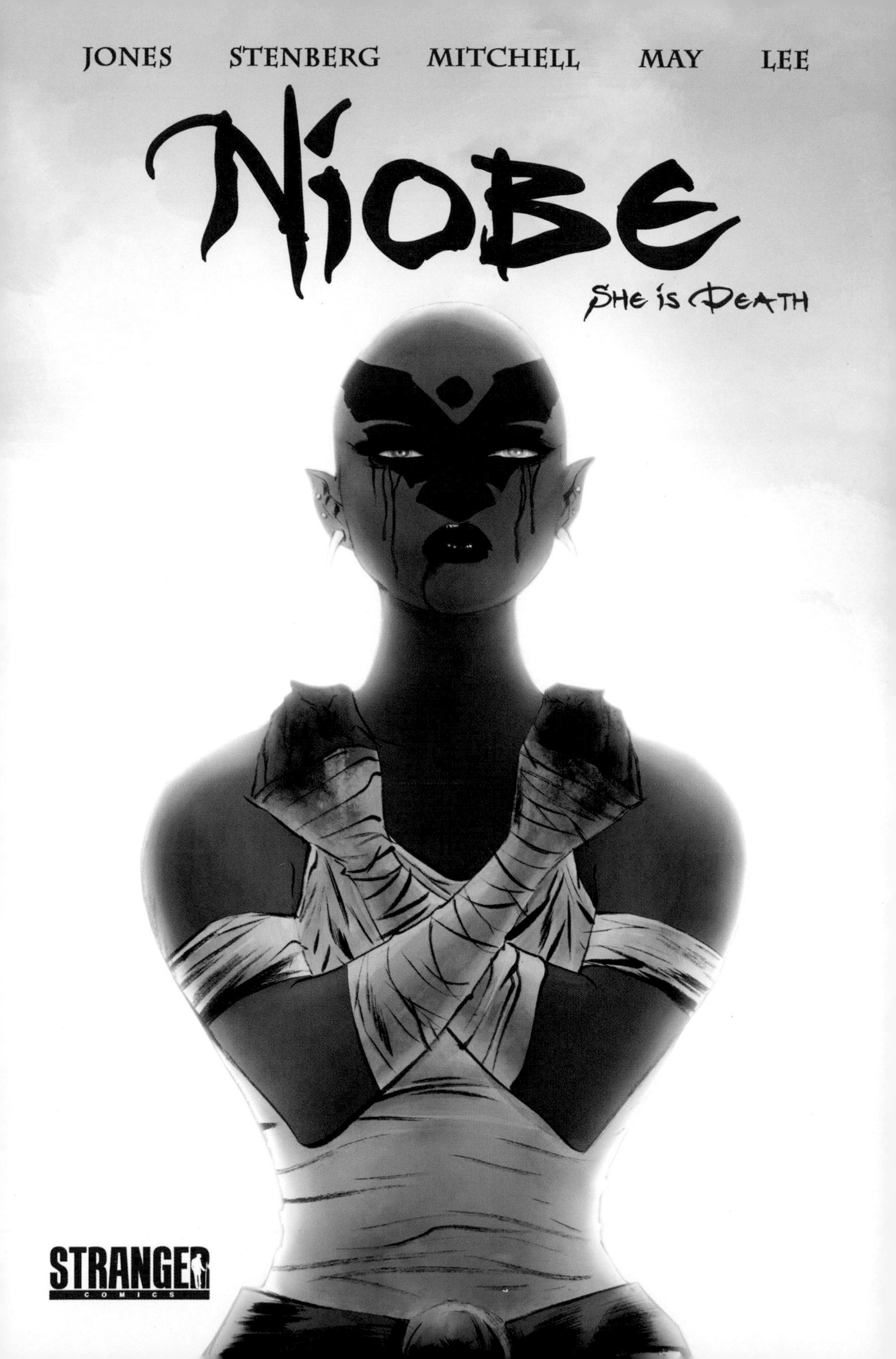
JONES STENBERG MITCHELL MAY LEE
NIOBE
SHE IS DEATH
STRANGER COMICS